MARKETING TODAY

Successes, Failures, and Turnarounds

JOHN B. CLARK

California State University, Sacramento

Prentice-Hall, Inc., Englewood Cliffs, New Jersey 07632

Library of Congress Cataloging-in-Publication Data

Clark, John B. (date)
  Marketing today.

  Bibliography: p.
  1. Marketing—United States—Case studies.
  2. Success in business—United States—Case studies.
  3. Business failures—United States—Case studies.
  I. Title.
  HF5415.1.C54 1987   658.8   86-22555
  ISBN 0-13-557844-2

Editorial/production supervision and
  interior design: Barbara Grasso
Cover design: Ben Santora
Manufacturing buyer: Ed O'Dougherty

Printed in the United States of America

10   9   8   7   6   5   4   3   2   1

ISBN 0-13-557844-2 01

Prentice-Hall International (UK) Limited, *London*
Prentice-Hall of Australia Pty. Limited, *Sydney*
Prentice-Hall Canada Inc., *Toronto*
Prentice-Hall Hispanoamericana, S.A., *Mexico*
Prentice-Hall of India Private Limited, *New Delhi*
Prentice-Hall of Japan, Inc., *Tokyo*
Prentice-Hall of Southeast Asia Pte. Ltd., *Singapore*
Editora Prentice-Hall do Brasil, Ltda., *Rio de Janeiro*

CONTENTS

The Major Divisions of IH
Agricultural Equipment, 1831–1984 / *Trucks, 1923–Present* /
    Construction Equipment, 1928–1982 / *Refrigeration, 1944–1945* /
    Solar Turbines, 1960–1981
Conclusion
Questions

PART THREE
TURNAROUNDS

PREFACE

Success is what it is all about. This is true for individuals, athletic teams, business firms, cooperatives, nonprofit organizations, and a multitude of other institutions that exist and operate in our society. However, the rate of success is often characterized by struggle, and success itself may be achieved at any time in an individual's or organization's life cycle. It may come early or late. For Ray Kroc and Colonel Harlan Sanders, it came late. Kroc founded McDonald's at age 52 and Sanders founded Kentucky Fried Chicken at age 65. For others it came early. Fred Smith was 26 when he incorporated Federal Express in 1971, and Steven Jobs and Stephen Wozniak, two college dropouts, founded Apple Computer at ages 21 and 26.

On the other hand, a number of prominent institutions—among them Penn Central, Braniff International, Woolco, DeLorean Motor Company, W. T. Grant, and the World Football League—have gone bankrupt, and many institutions—including A & P, the United States Football League, and International Harvester—are in trouble.

Other institutions, notably Chrysler, Sears, *USA Today*, and Coca-Cola, have encountered serious problems but have been turned around.

Students and business persons should be informed as to why some institutions succeed and others fail, keeping in mind that many of today's successful firms have had their share of failure and, conversely, that some in trouble today were once the leaders in their respective fields. A corporation can also be on the verge of bankruptcy and make a spectacular recovery as demonstrated by Chrysler Corporation. In this book we present some of the principles and strategies that certain U.S. institutions implemented or failed to implement that led to their success, failure, or turnaround.

This book was developed to supplement the introduction to marketing course at both the undergraduate and the graduate level. It may also be used in a marketing case course. The material is designed to stimulate classroom involvement and discussion, and should evoke creative thinking regarding the particular company and its problems. The book may also be of interest to others outside the classroom.

TO MY COLLEAGUES

Your teaching effectiveness and classroom involvement with students will be enhanced through usage of the Instructor's Manual which contains information that is not in the text. The Instructor's Manual is theoretically, as well as practically, formulated. Marketing principles and concepts are related to questions at the end of each case.

The cases in this book were carefully chosen. It was intentional that the institutions be highly visible ones about which students are already knowledgeable and to which they can relate.

There are three types of questions at the end of the chapters.

Type 1. The student can find the information in the case.
Type 2. Partial information is in the case.
Type 3. Very little information is in the case, but the question is related to the case and forces the student to think.

The major purpose of this text is to stimulate student involvement and participation. I want the students to express their ideas and relate them to marketing.

I encourage you to consider the rather comprehensive Instructor's Manual.

INTRODUCTION

The 16 cases described in this book represent a variety of well-known organizations. Six of these institutions are successes, six are failures, and four are turnarounds. McDonald's is one of the most successful. DeLorean Motors is well recognized as a business and personal failure. Chrysler almost failed but under the leadership of Lee Iacocca was turned around. Not all of the institutions have achieved the same magnitude of success, failure, or turnaround that McDonald's, DeLorean Motors, or Chrysler have, but a variety of institutions are discussed to demonstrate that the marketing principles of success, failure, and turnaround are present in all types of organizations.

The cases chosen demonstrate how certain institutions have reacted to their environment today. The major principles in the functional areas of business, namely, management, marketing, and finance, may be applied to most of the cases; however, marketing principles, concepts, and strategies are emphasized.

PART I: SUCCESSES

The cases in Part 1 have a common theme that binds them together. All of the businesses are successful. McDonald's was a pioneer in the fast-food business and today accounts for 20 percent of all fast-food sales. Its golden arches are America's best-known corporate symbol, and Ronald McDonald, who can be identified by 96 percent of American children, ranks second only to Santa Claus. This business refuses to plateau. It adapts to a changing competitive marketplace with rapid expansion in foreign markets. To date, McDonald's has not diversified into other lines of business.

Federal Express is the industry leader in the overnight delivery of letters and small packages. In 1984, it extended its product line to include large packages. Fred Smith, the founder, is the ultimate entrepreneur. At age 26, he raised $91 million in venture capital and made his idea work. The hub-and-spokes pattern that brought all letters and packages to one central location for redistribution has revolutionized the industry. Federal Express keeps abreast of changing technologies and uses its own satellites to transmit messages. Everyone is familiar with the Federal Express vans that ply our streets.

Anheuser-Busch has always marketed a well-known product. This company fought off a strong challenge by the Miller Brewing Company, which ranked seventh in 1972 and second by 1978. Miller introduced and dominated the market for light beer but Anheuser fought back and pioneered low-alcohol beer. Today these two companies have over 60 percent of the domestic beer market with Anheuser increasing its market share.

Toys "R" Us is the nation's sole national discount toy store chain. The company is highly centralized with almost all decisions made in executive headquarters. The major task of the store managers is to sell toys. Its information retrieval system allows Toys "R" Us executives to accurately predict trends and merchandise that will sell. A new division named Kids "R" Us sells brand-name children's clothing at discount prices.

Apple Computer had its beginnings in the garage of one of its founders. It is interesting to note that the home computer was not the product of an IBM, NCR, GE, or Xerox. Instead the company was founded by two young entrepreneurs named Steven Jobs and Stephen Wozniak. Apple Computer dominated the market for personal computers in its early years. IBM is currently the industry leader. Apple fought back by hiring marketing wizard John Sculley, formerly of Pepsico, went after the office market, and developed new products.

The California Almond Growers Exchange (CAGE) is the most successful cooperative in the United States. CAGE represents approximately 70 percent of the almond growers of California. CAGE developed new uses for almonds and opened up many new markets. It developed markets in countries that had never consumed almonds before, such as Japan. Its Blue Diamond brand is now known throughout the world.

PART II: FAILURES

The cases in Part II are bound together by virtue of their status as failures. However, their failure has varied in degree. The United States Football League (USFL) is a new venture. Its third season concluded in

1985 and the league continued to lose money. The DeLorean Motor Company, Woolco, and Braniff are clear-cut failures. All three had to close their doors, although Braniff has since been reopened in a reorganized, stripped-down form. The last two organizations—namely, the Great Atlantic & Pacific Tea Company (A & P) and International Harvester—are having trouble meeting their goals and objectives. Both organizations have vastly reduced the scope of their operations. Their long-term survival is still questionable.

The USFL has held to a spring schedule for 1983, 1984, and 1985. In 1986, the league planned to move to a fall schedule, placing it in direct competition with the NFL. The USFL has signed a number of superstars at unprecedented salaries, thus pushing up salaries in general. On August 4, 1986, the USFL suspended play for the 1986 season as a result of a hollow victory in its antitrust suit against the National Football League. Play may resume in the fall of 1987.

John DeLorean was successful as a rising young executive at General Motors but failed as an entrepreneur. DeLorean ignored marketing research that showed his car to have a limited market. He insisted on expanding production against the advice of his executives. Some question whether DeLorean was serious about DeLorean Motors or simply using the company as a means of supporting his extravagant lifestyle.

The F. W. Woolworth Company never made a full commitment to its Woolco division. This discount department store chain was started about the same time that S. S. Kresge Company founded its successful K Mart stores. The Woolworth stores and Woolco stores were never successfully integrated. The two divisions were continually at odds with each other. F. W. Woolworth then diversified into specialty retailing. The Woolco stores were not concentrated in geographical markets; they were scattered in numerous markets nationwide. Executives at Woolworth failed to understand the potential of discounting in the 1960s and 1970s.

Braniff International was one of the pioneer passenger airlines in the United States. The company overextended itself in its zeal to become a dominant carrier. Braniff acquired routes that others avoided. Deregulation of the airline industry and a poor economy adversely affected the entire industry but Braniff, with its overcapacity and unfilled seats, was not able to survive. Price wars also contributed to its demise. It still remains questionable whether or not the reorganized Braniff will survive.

International Harvester is one of America's founding industrial corporations. In its early history, it was recognized as an innovator in product development. The company pioneered the development of a modern sales organization and franchised dealership network. Diversifying into trucks, construction equipment, home appliances, and other businesses, the company became unmanageable. Although the company was a behemoth in sales, the profit margins of most divisions lagged behind its competitors. Lack of profits, coupled with a misreading of the market for agricultural equipment, led to the sale of the agricultural equipment division in 1984. International Harvester is no longer international in scope. Today the company only manufactures and assembles trucks.

PART III: TURNAROUNDS

The cases in Part III illustrate various types of turnaround situations. These companies have faltered and have been reoriented towards success.

USA Today is a special kind of turnaround because this national newspaper is a new product. The first day of issue was September 15, 1982. The Gannett Publishing Company planned to sustain substantial losses until 1987. Its goal is to make *USA Today* profitable and the number one paper in circulation. Because losses during the first three years far exceeded projections, the steps taken to reduce these losses can be considered part of a turnaround process. The case illustrates the marketing problems encountered in introducing a new product and sustaining substantial losses, and the strategies employed in obtaining profitability.

Chrysler Corporation is the classic turnaround situation. Teetering on the brink of bankruptcy, the company has made a spectacular recovery. The architect behind this renascence was Lee Iacocca. The new Chrysler Corporation that he created has modernized its plants, controlled its costs, and become a much more efficient producer. Iacocca is a marketing man. He has a keen instinct for new products and is a supersalesman. Iacocca has given Chrysler a new image and returned the company to profitability.

Sears, Roebuck and Company was 100 years old in 1986. In total sales as well as merchandise sales, it is the largest diversified retailer in the United States. During the 1960s and 1970s, the company lost its momentum. The new retailers—discount stores, catalog showrooms, and off-price retailers—cut into Sears' sales and profits. The economic conditions of inflation and recession were not conducive to its type of operation. Sears floundered with a number of different ineffective marketing strategies. In 1980, Sears diversified into financial services and created a new image based on the new "store of the future" that featured fashion, quality, and value. Sears has regained its lost momentum. Today, both its financial and merchanising divisions are prospering.

Coca-Cola made a classic marketing blunder. It deleted a product that a sizable proportion of its customers still wanted, thus causing a consumer revolt. However, it quickly reversed its decision and brought back old Coke while still retaining new Coke. This multiple Coke strategy (megabrand strategy) will impose a complicated marketing strategy for Coca-Cola. It remains to be seen how the various Coke brands will perform against Pepsi and the rest of the soda industry.

1

MCDONALD'S

HISTORY AND GROWTH

McDonald's Corporation is the largest food service organization in the world. Ray A. Kroc, the founder, opened his first restaurant in the McDonald's chain on April 15, 1955. By 1985 the company, its franchises, and affiliates operated more than 8,800 McDonald's restaurants, each serving a limited menu of high-quality, moderately priced food. The restaurants are located in all 50 of the United States, the District of Columbia, and internationally in 41 other countries and territories. In its 31-year history, the company has pioneered food-service technology, marketing techniques, and operational systems that are now the standards of the industry.

The McDonald's motto of Q.S.C.&V. translates into Quality food products; efficient, friendly Service; and restaurants renowned for the Cleanliness and Value they provide. Q.S.C.&V. is McDonald's promise to people around the world.

The sales figures for hamburgers continually rise. It took eight years for McDonald's to sell its first billion hamburgers, but by February 1978, the company had sold 25 billion; by 1980, 30 billion; and, as of 1985, sells a billion more every three months.

The financial statistics of this corporation are amazing. By 1975, after 20 years of operation, its total systemwide sales were $2.5 billion. McDonald's was already a big corporation. Yet it continued its explosive growth. Table 1-1 shows the compounded annual growth rate for selected measures during the 10-year period, 1976-1985.

In 1984, McDonald's announced a three-for-two stock split. This was

1

TABLE 1-1 McDonald's Compounded Annual Growth Rate for Selected Measures, 1976–1985

Total systemwide sales	38%
Total revenues	46%
Net income	34%
Net income per share	32%
Number of restaurants	88%

Source: Calculated from Table 1-2.

the second stock split in two years and the seventh stock split in McDonald's 20-year history as a publicly owned company.

When McDonald's stock was first offered to the public in 1965, 100 shares sold for $2,250. As of April 20, 1985, its twentieth anniversary, those 100 shares had grown to 4,131 shares and were worth $275,000.[1]

McDonald's has not only maintained its commanding position as industry leader, but has continued to increase its share of total franchised-food sales, which by 1977 was just over 20 percent.

The company is continually winning awards as one of America's best-managed corporations. *Fortune, Forbes, Business Week*, and the *Wall Street Journal* have all commented on its outstanding record. In 1977, *Dun's Review* selected McDonald's as one of the five best-managed companies of the year. In 1982, the American Marketing Association's Achievement Award, the marketing profession's highest honor, was presented to McDonald's Corporation for excellence in its marketing programs. Its systemwide sales of more than $11 billion place it among the nation's top 50 companies, and although the company is now considered mature, McDonald's statistics continue to astound financial analysts (see Tables 1-1, 1-2, 1-3, and 1-4).

RAY A. KROC

Ray Kroc (1902–1984) was born in Chicago and at age 15 went overseas during World War I as a member of the Red Cross and Ambulance Corporation. He returned to Chicago after the war and became music director of radio station WGES, playing the piano with Harry Sosnick's well-known band between jobs.

He sold paper cups and milkshake mixes before meeting the McDonald brothers at their restaurant in San Bernardino, California. Kroc was fascinated with their operation that used eight of his machines and had people standing in line for 15-cent hamburgers. He envisioned a chain and tried to convince the McDonald brothers to open more restaurants. Although they weren't interested in running more restaurants themselves, they did agree to franchise their restaurants.

TABLE 1-2 McDonald's Selected Operating Statistics and Per Share Data, 1973–1985

Year	Systemwide Sales (millions)	Total Revenues (millions)	Net Income (millions)	Net Income per Share	Dividend per Share	Number of Restaurants
1985	$11,000	$3,695	$433	$4.99	$0.88	8,901
1984	10,007	3,415	389	4.39	0.76	8,304
1983	8,687	3,063	343	3.83	0.65	7,778
1982	7,809	2,770	301	3.33	0.52	7,259
1981	7,102	2,516	265	2.91	0.41	6,739
1980	6,226	2,215	221	2.44	0.33	6,263
1979	5,385	1,938	189	2.08	0.23	5,747
1978	4,575	1,672	163	1.78	0.14	5,185
1977	3,738	1,406	137	1.50	0.07	4,671
1976	3,063	1,176	109	1.20	0.04	4,178
1975	2,478	973	87	0.96	—	3,706
1974	1,943	785	65	0.51	—	3,232
1973	1,507	624	50	0.43	—	2,717

Source: Annual Reports.

TABLE 1-3 Number of McDonald's Restaurants with Sales over $1 Million, 1973–1984

Year	Number	Year	Number
1984	5,886	1978	1,671
1983	4,869	1977	1,038
1982	4,191	1976	603
1981	3,718	1975	325
1980	2,817	1974	169
1979	2,284	1973	85

Source: Annual Reports.

TABLE 1-4 Number of McDonald's Restaurants with Sales over $2 Million, 1975–1984

Year	Number	Year	Number
1984	306	1979	57
1983	152	1978	35
1982	115	1977	11
1981	109	1976	4
1980	102	1975	0

Source: Annual Reports.

In 1955, Kroc founded the McDonald hamburger chain by opening his first restaurant in Des Plaines, Illinois; by 1960 there were 228 McDonald's. In 1961, Kroc bought the contract along with the name, all trademarks, copyrights, and formulas from the McDonald brothers for $2.7 million.

Kroc recognized early the potential of McDonald's. He was also a keen observer of human behavior and changing lifestyles. He noticed that, "Everyone in this country eats on the run—they run like hell. It's that kind of a country. Speed is the thing."[2]

In reflecting on McDonald's history, he said, "I feel a tremendous amount of pride. We've had principles right from the start. Even in the early days when we were poor, we never scrimped in any area—in quality, cleanliness, service, value, or in opportunities we afforded our employees. We grew up the right way."[3]

Mr. Kroc felt that the last 25 years were the most exciting part of his life. Where did he see the company going the next quarter century?

"I'm a businessman, not a fortuneteller, but what I see in the future is unlimited potential for McDonald's. I see us creating new markets, both at home and abroad, and meeting new consumer foodservice needs around the world."[4]

Ray Kroc received many awards including the Horatio Alger Award, election to the Fortune Hall of Fame, and induction into Babson College's Academy of Distinguished Entrepreneurs.

In his Babson College address in 1978, he said, "I'm just as interested in doing today what I did 23 years ago—whether it's picking up papers off the lot or cleaning the restrooms. I don't care what it is as long as I'm serving the public. There is no way anyone can be in the service business without having humility. When you've lost that, you've lost everything."[5]

His favorite quote regarding individual success stories and McDonald's itself is expressed in the following homily:

> Press on: nothing in the world can take the place of persistence. Talent will not; nothing is more common than unsuccessful men with talent. Genius will not; unrewarded genius is almost a proverb. Education will not; the world is full of educated derelicts. Persistence and determination alone are omnipotent.[6]

In retrospect, his buying out the McDonald brothers for $2.7 million that eventually cost him $14 million with interest payments was an incredible bargain. Kroc's personal stake in McDonald's was worth close to $500 million in 1983,[7] despite the fact that he had already donated millions to charity.

Ray Kroc died Saturday, January 14, 1984, at the age of 81. The employees, franchisees, and associates of McDonald's honored him with a full-page advertisement in all editions of the *Wall Street Journal*.

On behalf of the millions of people around the world whose lives have been touched and brightened by this extraordinary man, we honor the memory of a business pioneer, a humanitarian, and a beloved friend.[8]

THE MARKETING MIX

Customers. Who are McDonald's customers? Current company literature describes them as urban, surburban, and small-town residents; white-collar workers, blue-collar workers, and homemakers; the rich and the poor; the young and the old; the married and the single. McDonald's customers are found in 41 countries and territories around the globe. They order products in at least 15 languages. They are equally divided between men and women. By the end of 1984, more than 18 million customers around the world visited McDonald's every day, or more than 500 million customers a month.

McDonald's customers literally include a cross-section of the public. A recent company research study concluded that the majority of the U.S. population between the ages of 16 and 65 visit McDonald's at least once during an average six-month period.

Most of the people making the visits, both domestically and internationally, are "neighbors," for the typical McDonald's draws about three-quarters of its customers from a three-mile radius surrounding the restaurant.

Approximately one-fifth of the United States customers come alone with the remainder coming in groups. The group most frequently visiting is the family, which accounts for approximately 40 percent of the customers. Friends, fellow workers, and business associates make up the balance of business generated by groups.

Why do these people patronize McDonald's? Their answers vary according to their age. Children say that the restaurants are fun and exciting, that the food is good. Teenagers find that McDonald's is a good place to eat with friends. Adults, who account for about two-thirds of the business, like the restaurants because they are fast and convenient; because the food is high-quality and a good value; and because in today's ever-changing world, McDonald's is reliable—no matter where the customer visits a McDonald's restaurant, he or she can count on a familiar, pleasant experience.

Despite all the billions of McDonald's hamburgers that have been eaten, consumers do not seem to think much of them.[9] This issue has been addressed in its advertising. In an ad that ran during the summer of 1983, John Houseman intoned, "McDonald's has never lowered a single quality standard for the sake of a low price." A recent commercial says, "It's a good time for the great taste of McDonald's."

Product. McDonald's has been responsible for making a hamburger, French fries, and shake one of the world's most popular meals.

TABLE 1-5 McDonald's Major Product Introductions, 1963–1985

	Year	Product
1.	1963	Filet-O-Fish
2.	1968	Big Mac and Hot Apple Pie
3.	1972	Quarter Pounder
4.	1973	Egg McMuffin
5.	1974	McDonaldland Cookies
6.	1977	Complete Breakfast Menu and Sundaes
7.	1983	Chicken McNuggets
8.	1984	Sausage McMuffin
9.	1985	McD.L.T.

Source: Company records.

The company began selling a limited menu that included 15-cent hamburgers, 19-cent cheeseburgers, and 10-cent French fries, as well as shakes and soft drinks.

McDonald's was eight years old before it made its first menu change, the addition of the Filet-O-Fish in 1963. Table 1-5 includes the major product introductions.

The best-selling item on the menu is still the Big Mac. Sales of the Quarter Pounder are lagging. Table 1-6 lists the product deletions.

When it comes to menu expansion, McDonald's is cautious. It will test four or five years before adding a new item to the menu. The McFeast, a big sandwich loaded with lettuce and tomato slices was supposed to complement the Big Mac. Insiders at corporate headquarters nicknamed the McFeast the Whopper Stopper in anticipation of devasting Burger King and its Whopper sales. It was tested in more than 400 stores in 1978 but was finally dropped. In 1985, a similar product, the McD.L.T. was introduced.

McDonald's strives for uniformity in menu and in service. No store is allowed to vary the menu and product consistency is tightly controlled.

Compared to its competitors in the hamburger industry (Burger King, Wendy's, and Jack-In-The-Box), McDonald's has a more restricted menu.

Chicken McNuggets, which was introduced in 1983, currently accounts for about 8 percent of sales. McDonald's likes this product because it does not affect hamburger sales very much and brings additional customers into the store. Within a month of its national introduction, the product made McDonald's the second-largest chicken retailer after Kentucky Fried Chicken.

Fred Turner, chairman of the board and chief executive officer of McDonald's, originated the idea for McNuggets. Although this product came from the top of the company, most of McDonald's other products have originated with franchisees or executives in the field. The Filet-O-

TABLE 1-6 McDonald's Major Product Deletions, 1967–1983

	Year	Product
1.	1967	Triple Ripple ice cream cones
2.	1968	Hulaburgers (pineapple and cheese on a bun)
3.	1969	Double Burgers
4.	1970	Roast Beef Sandwiches
5.	1971	QLTs (quality lettuce and tomato)
6.	1971	Fish and Chips
7.	1980	McFeast (reincarnated QLT)
8.	1981	Beef Steak Sandwich
9.	1982	McChicken Sandwich
10.	1983	McRib

Source: Company records.

Fish sandwich was developed by Lou Growen, a Cincinnati, Ohio, franchisee; the Big Mac was invented by a franchisee in Pittsburgh; and the Egg McMuffin by one in California. Ideas are generated at McDonald's by a bottom-up as well as a top-down approach, especially in the product area.

Price. The original McDonald burger sold for 15 cents, French fries for 10 cents, and a shake for 20 cents. One could have a complete meal for 45 cents in 1955, a bargain by any restaurant standards.

There was no price increase for 12 years—an unusual record for almost any product. In 1967, the suggestion of an increase in the price of hamburgers to 18 cents made newspaper headlines. Some executives wanted to raise the price to 20 cents so people would not be bothered with pennies. But Kroc came to the aid of the consumer saying, "I came down hard on that one—if you look at it strictly from the customer's point of view—which is how I do, because this guy is our real boss—you see the importance of every penny."[10] Sales initially declined due to the price increase, but in a year's time both sales and revenue were higher than ever.

In 1985, with a burger selling for 49 cents, French fries for 50 cents, and a shake for 80 cents, customers could still get a bargain meal for under $2.00. However, if they chose a Big Mac at $1.35, large fries at 70 cents, and a shake at 80 cents, the meal would have cost $2.85. The company policy is to steer customers' attention away from prices and spotlight product and service.

Numerous hamburger wars have existed in the past in the industry. These wars have mainly centered on one advertiser's claims over its competitors. The latest battle is an old-fashioned price war introduced by a new upstart in the industry.

In 1983, Wienerschnitzel International of Newport Beach, California, began serving 39-cent burgers in its new Hamburger Stand chain.

Soon after, Burger King cut its plain-Jane burger from 55 cents to 35 cents and McDonald's followed, reducing its price from 50 cents to 35 cents. In January 1984, Burger King extended its discount program to most parts of the country.

Wendy's International, the third largest burger merchant, has ignored the competition and instead promoted its upscale menu with its "Where's the beef?" campaign.

By April 1984, the big guys brought back the regular price. But in California, the most competitive fast-food market in the country, many franchise owners have extended the offer indefinitely. One Burger King franchise owner said, "If I drop out [of the battle] and the McDonald's down the street continued, I'd lose out."[11]

The industry is also concerned with the explosive growth in the number of new units Hamburger Stand chain has projected.

Stan Spicer, vice-president and general manager of Hamburger Stand, knows that McDonald's and Burger King have been lowering prices in the western United States where Hamburger Stands currently operate. In southern California, where the price wars have been most fierce, some Hamburger Stands have dropped their prices to 25 cents. Spicer said they would continue to be the price leader.

Following is the anatomy of the Hamburger Stand chain's 1984 cheap burger.[12]

Anatomy of a Cheap Burger

Beef	$0.13
Bun	0.06
Onion	0.003
Napkin	0.002
Pickle	0.003
Wrapper	0.004
Mustard	0.0003
Ketchup	0.0008
Salt	0.00009
Total Food Cost	$0.20319
Total Food Cost	21¢
Overhead, franchise fees, labor, miscellaneous	15
Profit	3
Total Cost	39¢

Promotion. In the early days, recognition was gained through neighborhood advertising and newspaper publicity. For example, a columnist in the December 12, 1957, issue of the *Chicago Sun-Times* heralded Ray (McDonald's Drive-Ins) Kroc for serving hot coffee and hamburgers to the Salvation Army Christmas kettle workers.

Local billboard advertising came in 1959, local radio in 1960, network radio in 1962, and home television network advertising in 1967.

The original company symbol, a little hamburger man called "Speedee," was used in the 1950s. In 1962, the company conducted research that revealed that customers more readily identified with the "golden arches" than with Speedee. The results of the survey may have been affected by the widespread local-marketer user of McDonald's first advertising jingle, "Look for the Golden Arches," which had been introduced in 1960. "Speedee" was retired and the golden arches replaced him as the company's new advertising symbol and logo.

The following list is a chronology of the major advertising campaigns, themes, and jingles from 1960 to 1985:

Chronology of McDonald's Advertising Campaigns, Themes, and Jingles

1960	"Look for the Golden Arches"
1961	"All-American menu"—a hamburger, fries, and a shake
1962	"Go for goodness at McDonald's"
1965	"Those who know—go to McDonald's"
1968	"McDonald's is your kind of place"
1970	"You deserve a break today"
1975	"We do it all for you"
1975	"Twoallbeefpattiesspecialsaucelettucecheesepicklesonionsonasesameseedbun"
1976	"You, you're the one"
1979	"Nobody can do it like McDonald's can"
1981	"You deserve a break today"
1982	"McDonald's and you"
1984	"America's meat and potatoes"
1985	"It's a good time for the great taste of McDonald's"

Ray Kroc was always a promotor and had strong feelings about advertising. He commented:

> In our business there are two kinds of attitudes toward advertising and public relations. One is the outlook of the begrudger who treats every cent paid for ad programs or publicity campaigns as if they were strictly expenditures. My own viewpoint is that of the promotor; I never hesitate to spend money in this area, because I can see it coming back to me with interest. Of course, it comes back in different forms, and that may be the reason a begrudger can't appreciate it. He has a narrow vision that allows him to see income only in terms of cash in his register. Income for me can appear in other ways, one of the nicest of them is a satisfied smile on the

face of a customer. That's worth a lot, because it means that he's coming back and he'll probably bring a friend.[13]

It is evident that Ray Kroc took a broad view of advertising and knew that the consumer held the key to his success. The company is heavily involved in all aspects of the promotional mix: advertising, personal selling, sales promotion, publicity, and public relations.

McDonald's sales promotion programs motivate customers to come into a restaurant once, or for a sequence of visits, in order to benefit from an added value such as a premium of a glass piece. A glass promotion gives collectors the incentive to visit McDonald's four different times in order to complete the collection. A game may motivate customers to visit many times in order to fill up the spaces on a game card and win fabulous prizes. Consumer promotions involve innumerable special deals and events.

Public relations and publicity programs put something back into the communities the restaurants serve. Programs such as the Ronald McDonald House, the All-American High School Band, Muscular Dystrophy fund-raisers, and Special Olympics provide opportunities for developing positive community relations with schools, sports organizations, recreational centers, churches, libraries, and business groups. McDonald's sponsored the 1984 Summer Olympics in Los Angeles. The system underwrote the construction of the Olympic Swim Stadium for the games and sponsored a swimming program nationwide for Olympic hopefuls.

McDonald's is increasingly segmenting its advertising and promotions, developing materials aimed at specific segments of the market.

The aging of the Ronald McDonald generation and a declining birth rate have led the company to focus its attention on other market segments—namely, the adult and international markets. In 1979, it renewed its most popular campaign, "You deserve a break today." This campaign is not directed towards a six-year-old child.

McDonald's has established a strong image that has changed over the years. Today the Golden Arches are America's best-known corporate symbol.

Place. The first McDonald's were built in suburban locations, along highly traveled streets, or at busy intersections—places that were easily accessible to the driving public. During the late 1960s, a radical change in building design occurred. Seats were installed and the entire building was redesigned, taking on the more subtle mansard-roof look that is now recognizable throughout the world. More Americans and their families were eating away from home and expecting more restaurant amenities.

After McDonald's had established its reputation in suburban locations, it added smaller towns and finally big cities, concentrating on the central business district.

In the early 1980s, McDonald's expanded into entirely new locations. The emphasis shifted to semicaptive markets or niche markets. These markets have lots of people, but limited eating possibilities. Examples of the latest locations are toll roads, military bases, museums, hospitals, college campuses, airports, and office buildings.

In 1984, an exclusive ten-year contract was signed to operate restaurants at Navy exchange installations worldwide. This encompasses over 300 Navy bases. In 1983, annual sales at the Camp Pendleton Marine Base at Oceanside, California, were over twice the $1.2 million sales in an average unit. Burger King has a similar agreement with the Army and Air Force.

McDonald's has been awarded a number of toll road contracts because its minimum royalty guarantees have far surpassed its rivals. Company estimates showed that a state tollway unit exceeds by one-third the average unit sales.

The company is currently developing McStops, its foray into developing truck stops. This idea evolved from the company's experience with restaurants on interstate highways that became magnets for truckers, long-distance drivers, and local residents. These restaurants were extremely profitable.

Although a whole site will be developed, including a motel, gas station/convenience store, and McDonald's restaurant, the only part of McStop that McDonald's will run is the restaurant.

McDonald's effort to locate in large office buildings has encountered a number of difficulties. Owners of office buildings usually will not consider leasing their retail space to McDonald's or any other fast-food chain. Their lack of interest usually boils down to image. Another problem is the rent. It is not unusual for rents in office buildings to go for $100 a square foot a year, plus a percent of sales. Despite these obstacles, the company is using a 5,300-square-foot space it has leased in a midtown New York office building as a showcase.

Fred Turner says, "McDonald's will keep looking for new markets, new space for its restaurants, and new ways to evolve in the basic business it's already in."[14]

Fred Turner and most of the management team are not receptive to the idea of diversification. They have been able to find growth in fast-food hamburger restaurants long after critics said the market was saturated.

Restaurants. McDonald's restaurant architecture has been represented by two distinctive designs during the company's existence.

The first prototype featured a red-and-white tile, T-shaped building

TABLE 1-7 McDonald's Drive-Thru Restaurants in the United States, 1975–1984

Year	Number of Drive-Thru Restaurants	Percent of Free-Standing Restaurants with Drive-Thrus
1984	6,197	94%
1983	5,621	89%
1982	5,093	85%
1981	4,482	77%
1980	3,738	71%
1979	2,884	59%
1978	1,891	44%
1977	976	24%
1976	393	9%
1975	111	3%

Source: Company records.

with two golden arches. One would order at the counter and take out the meal. There were no chairs or tables.

The first inside seating restaurant opened in 1966. It consisted of a narrow counter with stools and a couple of small tables with chairs. In 1968, a much larger restaurant opened. It featured a brick building with mansard roof, a large expanse of windows, and inside eating for approximately 120 customers. The original candy-stripe model was slowly phased out of the system, and now fewer than 20 of these units remain.

Other architecture developments are the additions of drive-thrus and playland facilities. The drive-thrus were introduced in 1975 so that customers could buy meals without having to leave their cars. At the end of 1984, 94 percent of the free-standing restaurants had drive-thru facilities, which generally account for an average of 40 to 45 percent of a restaurant's sales (see Table 1-7). Many of the drive-thrus were additions to existing restaurants.

McDonald's playlands are play areas for children either inside the restaurant or outdoors, which include many different McDonaldland character play facilities. The playlands were introduced in 1971 (see Table 1-8).

During 1980, the company introduced a new free-standing restaurant building—the series 80 model. This is a small and more standardized model that can serve a lower-volume operation. It has resulted in lower average construction costs and shorter construction periods as compared with previous models.

The latest architectural development is the McSnack, a scaled-down McDonald's offering a less complete menu and carryout service only. The restaurant is being tried where the standard McDonald's will not fit. This

TABLE 1-8 Number of McDonald's Playland Facilities, Selected Years, 1971–1984

Year	Number
1984	2,287
1983	2,018
1982	1,533
1981	979
1980	581
1979	353
1978	204
1971	43

Source: Company records.

is part of the company's effort to find new types of locations for its restaurants. As of October 1985, only a few McSnacks were open, but they obtained immediate profitability.

Another interesting fact concerning the restaurants is that the average number of days it takes to construct a new U.S. free-standing restaurant building from real estate release to opening has steadily declined (see Table 1-9).

MARKETING AND SOCIETY

McDonald's has built a tradition of contributing to its communities through both national and local programs. Each program is designed to fill a need, whether it is raising funds for the local charity or saluting the achievements of young people.

The involvement is tailored to the strengths, resources, people, and problems of each community. Many of the local store activities are designed to address important community concerns such as litter, crime prevention, safety, childhood health, and sports events.

The company stresses community service. Each licensee is expected to spend a portion of earnings on it, and there is some latitude in selecting promotions or community service.

Ray Kroc personally gave millions of dollars to many worthwhile causes and in 1976 McDonald's set aside $440,000 for its national contributions program. This program has been continually expanded. Kroc believed in the business philosophy of "putting something back into the communities where we do business."

HAMBURGER UNIVERSITY

McDonald's is known worldwide for the excellent training it provides its franchisees, managers, and crewpeople. The company prefers to promote from within—to develop its own management people—and Hamburger University, McDonald's management training center, does exactly that.

TABLE 1-9   Average Days to Construct a New U.S. Free-Standing McDonald's Restaurant, 1978–1984

Year	Days
1984	105
1983	107
1982	110
1981	115
1980	138
1979	169
1978	171

Source: Company records.

In the early days, the Hamburger University curriculum centered on the technical expertise that franchisees and restaurant managers needed to operate a restaurant. In recent years, however, the curriculum, which is built on a college-type format, has expanded to courses in personnel and management services so that graduates will have people and capital management skills.

In 1983, a new campus-style Hamburger University, complete with multilingual capabilities for its international student body, opened in Oak Brook, Illinois.

The program is accredited by the American Council of Education who recommends that 18 McDonald's courses and programs qualify for a total of 40 hours of college credit. In 1982, the State of Illinois granted McDonald's Management Institute, a part of Hamburger University, approval to operate a two-year college. This work-study program, unique to the fast-food service industry, is designed for career-oriented operations employees.

In 1984, more than 13,000 people attended restaurant operations and management courses at U.S. regional offices. In addition, there are Hamburger Universities operating in England, Germany, and Japan.

Also in 1984, more than 2,200 people attended classes at Hamburger University, while more than 28,000 have been graduated from Hamburger University since its first classes in 1961.

McDONALD'S INTERNATIONAL DIVISION

McDonald's International Division was formed in 1969 to meet the needs of its world customers. Since then, the division has begun McDonald's operations in international markets around the globe.

Expansion outside the United States is accomplished through the development of restaurants operated by (1) the company, through wholly owned subsidiaries; (2) franchisees, individuals who are granted franchises by the company, a wholly owned subsidiary, or an affiliate; and (3) affiliates companies in which McDonald's equity is generally 50 percent or less and the remaining equity is generally owned by a resident national.

The following series of tables presents statistical data on the International Division.

Table 1-10 lists the number of international restaurants by country and by geographic region. Table 1-11 shows the percent of international restaurants and international sales by geographic region for 1984 and 1979. Table 1-12 shows the International Division's restaurants, total revenues, and operating income as a percent of the systemwide total from 1972 through 1984.

CONCLUSION

In 1984, McDonald's celebrated its thirtieth birthday. It is one of this country's most successful companies. It has been built into a billion-dollar giant, and it will soon become a huge international corporation. Not one company-owned outlet has ever failed. Although others have said that McDonald's market has been saturated for years, management has continually found new markets. The current leadership is against diversification and desires to remain in the hamburger business.

QUESTIONS

1. What do you see as McDonald's formula for success?
2. In 1982, McDonald's received the American Marketing Association Achievement Award, the marketing profession's highest honor for excellence in marketing programs. Construct your criteria for this award.
3. Discuss Ray Kroc's philosophy toward customers, work, promotion, education, and the community.
4. Give examples of how McDonald's has implemented the following: market penetration, market development, product development, and diversification.

	Existing Products	New Products
Existing Markets	Market Penetration	Product Development
New Markets	Market Development	Diversification

TABLE 1-10 Number of McDonald's International Restaurants by Country and by Geographic Region, 1980–1984

Country	Year				
	1984	1983	1982	1981	1980
Australia	152	147	137	123	116
Guam	2	2	2	2	2
Hong Kong	26	24	22	18	15
Japan	455	395	346	302	268
Malaysia	6	5	2	0	0
New Zealand	19	17	17	16	10
Philippines	8	5	3	2	0
Singapore	13	9	7	4	3
Taiwan	5	0	0	0	0
Total Pacific	686	604	536	467	414
Andorra	1	0	0	0	0
Austria	12	12	12	12	7
Belgium	9	9	8	6	4
Denmark	7	7	4	2	0
England	165	133	96	68	51
Finland	1	0	0	0	0
France	18	15	8	19	17
Germany	208	190	169	155	133
Ireland	5	5	3	3	3
Netherlands	33	27	24	18	17
Norway	1	1	0	0	0
Spain	11	10	6	1	0
Sweden	18	15	12	10	9
Switzerland	9	8	6	6	4
Total Western Europe	498	432	348	300	245
Canada	465	442	417	389	366
Bahamas	3	2	2	2	2
Brazil	29	21	14	6	3
Costa Rica	3	3	3	3	3
El Salvador	3	3	3	3	3
Guatemala	3	3	2	2	2
Netherlands Antilles	3	2	2	2	2
Nicaragua	1	1	1	1	1
Panama	6	6	6	5	5
Puerto Rico	6	5	4	2	1
Virgin Islands	3	3	3	3	3
Total Latin America	60	49	40	29	25
	1,709	1,527	1,341	1,185	1,050
As a percent of Systemwide restaurants	21	20	18	18	17

Note: Reprinted from 1984 Annual Report, p. 20.

TABLE 1-11   McDonald's International Restaurants and Sales by Geographic Region, 1984 and 1979 (Percent)

	1984		1979	
	Restaurants	*Sales*	*Restaurants*	*Sales*
Canada	27.2	35.1	37.7	40.2
Pacific	40.2	37.1	38.5	30.9
Western Europe	29.1	24.6	21.2	27.1
Latin America	3.5	3.2	2.6	1.8
Total	100.0	100.0	100.0	100.0

Note: Adapted from 1984 Annual Report, p. 20.

TABLE 1-12   Restaurants Revenues, and Operating Income from McDonald's International Division as a Percent of Systemwide Totals, 1972–1984

	Percent of Total Restaurants	*Percent of Total Revenues*	*Percent of Total Operating Income*[a]
1984	21	23	18
1983	20	22	17
1982	18	19	14
1981	18	20	15
1980	17	20	15
1979	16	20	14
1978	13	19	13
1977	13	17	12
1976	11	15	10
1975	10	13	9
1974	9	11	7
1973	8	8	5
1972	6	5	3

[a] Before general, administrative, selling expense, interest expense, and income tax.
Source: Annual Reports.

5.   Discuss the relationship between products and markets.

6.   Has McDonald's managed its product line well?

7.   It was stated in the case that consumers do not think highly of McDonald's hamburgers. If this is true, how does McDonald's remain number one?

8.   What should McDonald's strategy be towards Hamburger Stand discount hamburgers? How could this upstart competitor affect McDonald's and the mature hamburger industry?

9.   How has McDonald's location strategy changed over time?

10. Suggest some markets (locations) that may still be feasible for McDonald's. Suggest some locations for McSnack.

11. Why has the architecture of McDonald's buildings changed?

12. Discuss Ronald McDonald, his mission, and his fellow colleagues. Does Ronald have a competitor?

13. Discuss McDonald's civic activities in your community. Discuss reasons why some residents may not want a McDonald's restaurant as a neighbor.

14. Should McDonald's emphasize expansion in foreign markets?

15. What factors should McDonald's be aware of as it enters the foreign market? Should any changes be made in its marketing strategy?

16. McDonald's was founded in 1954. Why didn't a company like this emerge earlier in our business history?

17. Has McDonald's responded successfully to its competitors?

18. Is it time for this company to diversify?

NOTES

1. McDonald's Corporation 1985 Second Quarter Report, p. 1.
2. *McDonald's 20th Anniversary Journal*, 1975, p. 28.
3. *McDonald's 25th Anniversary Journal*, 1980, p. 1.
4. Ibid.
5. Ray Kroc's Acceptance Speech, *Babson Bulletin*, Summer 1978.
6. Ray Kroc with Robert Anderson, *Grinding It Out* (Chicago: Henry Regnery Company, 1977), p. 189.
7. Arthur M. Louis II, "The Hall of Fame For U.S. Business Leadership," *Fortune*, April 4, 1983, p. 144.
8. *Wall Street Journal*, January 18, 1984, p. 37.
9. Monci Jo Williams, "McDonald's Refuses to Plateau," *Fortune*, November 12, 1984, pp. 36 and 38.
10. Kroc and Anderson, *Grinding It Out*, p. 151.
11. "Fast Food Lovers Gobble Up Bargain Buyers," *Sacramento Bee*, March 19, 1984, p. A1.
12. "Fast Food Lovers Gobble Up Bargain Buyers," *Sacramento Bee*, March 19, 1984, p. A12. Reprinted with permission from Wienerschnitzel International, Inc.
13. Kroc and Anderson, *Grinding It Out*, pp. 106–107.
14. Williams, "McDonald's Refuses to Plateau," p. 40.

2

FEDERAL EXPRESS

INTRODUCTION

The main concepts examined in this case are the marketing of a service and the importance of innovation in marketing. Federal Express excels in the implementation of both of these concepts. Federal Express revolutionized the package delivery system with its "hub-and-spokes" pattern of doing business. It diversified into the delivery of letters, messages, data, and other kinds of information. Its telecommunication network is fully integrated and Federal has become involved with the electronic transmission of information. In 1984, its eclectic use of technologies and equipment offered customers a satellite-based, high-speed, image transmission service. Documents and graphic material are picked up, scanned, and delivered on the same day.

Innovation is an important marketing concept. This company continues to change and rapidly adapts itself to new technologies and ways of doing business to better serve its customers.

DESCRIPTION OF BUSINESS

The range and types of services offered by Federal Express were described in its 1984 Annual Report as follows:

> Federal Express Corporation provides overnight, door-to-door delivery of business goods (150 pounds or less per package) and documents throughout the United States, using its integrated, air-ground transportation system. Other services include ZapMail, a one-to-two-hour electronic document transmission service; Standard Air, a one-to-two-day package and docu-

TABLE 2-1   Key Statistics for the First Day of Federal Express Operations, April
1973

Employees	150
Aircraft	10
Cities served	22
Packages per night	15

Source: Company records.

ment delivery service; and special handling of restricted articles. In addition, Federal Express provides high-priority, customs-cleared service between the United States and Canada, and operations have been initiated outside North America. The company operates 57 aircraft, almost 10,000 radio-dispatched delivery vans and a central sorting facility. Local offices are maintained in 300 cities served from 145 airports.

Monday through Saturday, couriers across the country pick up shipments addressed to recipients in any of some 40,200 communities in the United States. A small percentage are segregated at regional sorting centers and trucked overnight to nearby cities. Most shipments are loaded on Federal Express aircraft. Following a hub-and-spokes pattern, the aircraft fly to the central sorting facility in Memphis, most arriving between midnight and 1:00 A.M. The packages are unloaded, sorted by destination and reloaded. The aircraft return to their points of origin, carrying only shipments destined for those areas. Couriers then make deliveries of priority shipments by 10:30 A.M., to most communities, completing the overnight, door-to-door cycle.[1]

HISTORY OF FEDERAL EXPRESS

Federal Express was incorporated in Delaware in June 1971. Air freight service began in April 1973 with the delivery of 15 packages the first night (see Table 2-1). During the first 26 consecutive months of business, the company sustained a loss of $29 million (see Table 2-2).

The first few years of business were agony and there were major financial problems. During 1973, things got so bad that its 150 employees were asked not to cash their paychecks right away. Later during the year, the company was able to raise additional funds through venture capital and bank loans. The first profitable month was July 1975.

On December 28, 1978, Federal Express Corporation common stock commenced trading on the New York Stock Exchange. Previously the stock had been traded on the over-the-counter market.

When the company first started, the original investors paid $1 to $3 a share of stock. The stock has split two-for-one in 1978, 1980, and 1983. As of October 1985, the stock was selling for $45 a share. Investors have enjoyed a tremendous appreciation on their stock.

Tables 2-2, 2-3, and 2-4 illustrate this impressive growth in finan-

TABLE 2-2   Federal Express Corporation Selected Operating Statistics and Per Share Data, 1974–1985

Year[a]	Gross Revenue (millions)	Net Income (millions)	Earnings per Share	Dividends per Share	Common Stock Price Range (rounded)[b]
1985	$2,013.0	$ 76.0	$1.61	Nil	61–31
1984	1,436.3	115.4	2.52	Nil	47–27
1983	1,008.1	88.9	2.04	Nil	49–32
1982	803.9	78.4	1.85	Nil	40–20
1981	589.5	58.1	1.42	Nil	36–20
1980	415.4	37.7	1.00	Nil	25–9
1979	258.5	20.3	0.62	Nil	13–5
1978	160.3	13.6	0.45	Nil	9–3
1977	100.2	4.0	0.13	Nil	NA
1976	75.1	1.6	0.05	Nil	NA
1975	43.5	(11.5)	Deficit	Nil	NA
1974	17.3	(13.4)	Deficit	Nil	NA

[a] Year ends May 31 of that year.

[b] For calendar year.

Sources: Annual Reports; *Standard & Poor's NYSE Stock Report,* Vol. 53, No. 28, Sec. 6, Feb. 10, 1986, p. 865m.

TABLE 2-3   The Growth of Federal Express in Number of Packages and Full-Time Employees, 1977–1984

Year	Total Packages and Documents (millions)	Average Daily Package Volume	Full-Time Employees	Packages Processed per Full-Time Employee
1984	67.0	243,385	18,368	3,647
1983	43.0	100,420	12,507	3,438
1982	32.1	125,881	10,092	3,181
1981	22.1	87,191	8,080	2,741
1980	17.2	68,002	6,806	2,528
1979	11.7	45,833	4,883	2,393
1978	7.5	29,516	3,224	2,335
1977	5.6	20,840	2,444	2,287

Source: Annual Reports.

cial and nonfinancial areas of the company. In almost every category, each year surpassed the previous year's performance, in some cases by a considerable amount. Not only is Federal a growth company, it is growing in efficiency (productivity) as illustrated by the packages processed per full-time employee (see Table 2-3).

Table 2-2 illustrates a dramatic decline in earnings for fiscal 1985. The reason for this decline was the large capital expenditures necessary to implement ZapMail and the doubling of the Business Service Centers.

TABLE 2-4 The Growth of Federal Express in Number of Aircraft, City Stations, and Calls Received, 1977–1984

Year	Aircraft Operated	City Stations	Calls Received by Customer Service Centers on June 1
1984	57	300	NA
1983	76	215	78,228
1982	67	180	64,228
1981	62	166	41,320
1980	56	139	20,137
1979	44	119	11,080
1978	36	84	5,120
1977	32	NA	NA

Source: Annual Reports.

Estimated earnings per share were $3.25 for fiscal 1986 (ending May 31, 1986).

By 1979, the number of customer service calls involving information, tracing, and pickup requests had increased dramatically (see Table 2-4). One-third of these calls were handled in Memphis by COSMOS I at the new computerized center. Because centralized telephone service was the most efficient way to handle such a large volume of calls, regional customer service centers were established in the following areas:

Somerset, New Jersey	1979
Sacramento, California	1980
Chicago, Illinois	1983
Dallas, Texas	1984
Phoenix, Arizona	1984
Boston, Massachusetts	1985
Orange County, California	1986

To augment its pickup service, staffed customer convenience centers and overnight delivery counters, which are drop-box facilities in high-density areas, were established. These facilities allow shippers to drop packages at their convenience and allow Federal to accept packages later than permitted by customer requested pickups (see Table 2-5).

In 1979, a sophisticated computer-based system named COSMOS (Customer Oriented Service and Management Systems) was established. It was implemented in three stages:

In 1981, a complementary system named DADS (Digitally Assisted Dispatcher System) was implemented. This system uses small terminals in delivery vans where messages may be displayed on a screen. It allows Federal to dispatch a greater number of orders and helps the couriers to better structure their pickup schedules. In 1984, a hand-held DADS

TABLE 2-5 Customer Convenience Centers and Overnight Delivery Counters, 1979–1984

Year	Customer Convenience Centers	Overnight (Self-Service) Delivery Centers
1984	115	5,000
1983	80	4,500
1982	60	3,000
1981	15	1,500
1980	32	500
1979	15	None

Source: Annual Reports.

1979 COSMOS I	Reduces pickup time and handles service calls.
1980 COSMOS II	Scans and records each step in the handling process as packages move through the system—an automatic package tracking system.
1981 COSMOS III	Enhances the functions of COSMOS I and II, provides for automatic parcel sorting in the super hub. Makes possible business service centers and allows direct communications between the computer and terminals in courier vans.

microprocessor was introduced, which enables a foot courier to obtain dispatch information while making stops in buildings and away from the van.

In 1982, the three customer service centers (Memphis, Somerset, Sacramento) were connected to a satellite earth station network. As the other customer service centers came on line, they were also connected to the satellite earth station network.

In 1983, an enhancement of the convenience network was announced with the establishment of Business Service Centers. These staffed, storefront facilities are located in high-traffic, high-density areas. They permit face-to-face contact with many small or medium-sized customers who may prefer to bring in their packages or documents. All contain electronic transmitting and receiving equipment and offer other business services, such as high-quality copying. These centers play a large role in providing ZapMail service by reducing the delivery time and cost for customers who bring documents to Federal.

In July 1985, ZapMail was implemented, providing a two-hour delivery of documents and graphics through combined land and satellite transmission. The operating losses for ZapMail in fiscal 1985 were $125 million, but outside orders for ZapMail equipment had risen to 10,000 units, far exceeding the 3,000-unit forecast.

Federal has not been primarily engaged in the international market. However, a U.S. Customs clearance is established at the Memphis Superhub and the international customer service department is multilingual and trained to meet the needs of customers.

In 1984, Gelco Express International was acquired. This worldwide, onboard courier service has offices in London, Amsterdam, Paris, Brussels, Hong Kong, Tokyo, and Singapore. Its acquisition gave Federal an instant presence in 84 countries. During 1984 and 1985, the Gelco operation was absorbed into the system with the Federal Express name and identity.

Another major development was the announcement of regional sorting centers. Because of the sharp increase in volume, it was more efficient for Federal to move a portion of their volume point-to-point rather than through the Memphis Superhub. When feasible, packages and documents move by truck between points close enough to meet service commitments.

In 1985, the first of several regional sorting centers opened in Newark, New Jersey. Other centers are planned for Boston, Chicago, Oakland, Los Angeles, and Orlando. By the end of fiscal 1985, approximately 25 percent of total volume was routed directly, resulting in significant cost savings.

Highlights in the history of Federal Express are summarized in Table 2-6.

FREDERICK W. SMITH

In 1966, Frederick W. Smith turned in his senior thesis at Yale University. Its premise was, "There is no way airlines can compete effectively with either truckers or railroads in the transportation of bulk freight."[2] His reason was that passenger route patterns were wrong for freight and cost would not come down with volume. The only way to make air freight service sufficient and effective was to design a new system. Smith's idea was to bring the packages to one central location along routes that resemble the spokes of a wheel. The hub of the wheel, Memphis, Tennessee, would sort the packages, then reload them on aircraft. The aircraft would then return to its point of origin by reversing their spokes pattern. For this effort, Frederick's professor gave him a low grade of C on his thesis.

Fred Smith was 26 years old when he incorporated Federal Express in 1971. It took him a number of years to acquire the amount of money necessary to start the business. This was not a $1 or $2 million venture capital start-up. In the end, Smith raised $91 million, said at that time to be the largest amount of venture capital ever amassed. This is astounding

TABLE 2-6 Federal Express Corporation Highlights, 1979–1985

Year	Highlights
1979	Courier Pack overnight box introduced. Courier Pack overnight tube introduced. COSMOS I implemented. Customer Service Center opened in Somerset, New Jersey. Customer Convenience Centers opened.
1980	COSMOS II implemented. Customer Service Center opened in Sacramento, California. 100,000 packages processed on a single night, November 15, 1980.
1981	COSMOS III implemented. DADS (Digital Assisted Dispatch System) test marketed in Memphis and Chicago. Overnight Letter introduced, June 1, 1981.
1982	Three customer service centers connected to satellite network using earth stations. 10:30 A.M. delivery in most areas.
1983	Weight limitation increased from 70 pounds or less to 125 pounds or less. 208,000 packages processed on a single night, December 1983. 100 new Business Service Centers to be established. DADS in 2,500 delivery vans in 18 major cities.
1984	ZapMail implemented—two-hour cross-country delivery of messages. 351,000 packages processed on a single night, May 1984. Weight limitation increased to 150 pounds or less. Gelco Express International acquired.
1985	First Regional Sorting Center opened in Newark, New Jersey.

Source: Annual Reports.

considering he was a young man with little business experience. All he had to offer was a blueprint for his air freight system, backed by market research that showed a strong need for such a service. There was no proof that his theory would work.

Fred Smith considers himself both an entrepreneur and a professional manager. He disagrees with those who believe that entrepreneurs do not make good managers. He believes they are two very different traits but not necessarily mutually exclusive. He said, "I view myself primarily as a professional manager. I've always felt that way. The fact that I am also someone who saw an opportunity was coincidental to that, not the other way around."[3]

Federal Express is one of America's most decorated corporations and Fred Smith has received many awards. Following are some of these citations.

Financial World in its March 15, 1979, issue named Fred Smith as one of America's ten most outstanding chief executive officers. *Fortune Magazine* in its December 31, 1979, article, "Business Triumphs of the Seventies," chose Federal Express as one of the ten triumphs. *Dun's Business Month,* in its December 1981 issue, named Federal Express as one of the five best-managed companies in 1981. In 1983, Fred Smith received the Parlin Award from the Philadelphia Chapter of the American Marketing Association recognizing individuals who have made outstanding contributions to the field of marketing. In 1983, Babson College elected Fred Smith to its famous roster of the Academy of Distinguished Entrepreneurs.

FEDERAL EXPRESS AND ITS COMPETITION

The major competitors of Federal Express are the U.S. Postal Service, Airborne, Emery, Purolator, and other air freight forwarders. In electronic mail, its major competitor is MCI Communications, the long distance telephone company.

In the 1970s, Emery Air Freight was the leader of the overnight delivery business. This freight forwarder used scheduled airlines to move goods between cities. They specialized in packages weighing over 70 pounds. As the reliability of scheduled air freight service declined, so did Emery's reliability and profits. Federal concentrated on the light end of the market with letters and parcels weighing 70 pounds or less.

In the early 1980s, Emery went heavily into debt and completely restructured its operation. They purchased 24 Boeing 727 freighters and leased 40 other aircraft. A new superhub for sorting packages was opened in Dayton, Ohio. Previously as many as four sorting centers around the country had been used. Basically, Emery became a copycat of Federal's system.

Emery's market share shrank in the 1981–1983 recession, but after the recession it boomed. The recovery of the economy and just-in-time inventory systems generated a large number of overnight deliveries which benefited Emery. In 1982, Emery diversified into handling small packages, pouches, and letters. Some freight forwarders question the practice of handling both large and small packages. They believe that this can result in inefficiencies.

Federal countered Emery's move into the small package market by increasing its weight limitations from 70 pounds to 125 pounds in 1983, and to 150 pounds in 1984.

Despite its strong turnaround, Emery has not been able to hold its number two position. In 1983, Airborne Freight Corporation, a long-time freight forwarder, surpassed Emery in the number of packages delivered overnight. Airborne's television commercials show a youthful runner in an Airborne uniform passing other joggers in competitor's uniforms. The commercial says, "So it's good-bye, Emery. Watch out, Federal. Here comes Airborne."[4] In contrast to Federal's centralized customer service operation, Airborne will keep its operation localized.

Another formidable competitor is the U.S. Postal Service. It currently handles over 200 million pieces of certified, registered, special delivery, and Express Mail per year. By 1984, Express Mail, which handles everything from a few ounces to a package of up to 70 pounds, was averaging 95,000 deliveries per day. Federal introduced its Overnight Letter in June 1981. In its first year, this service contributed $56 million to revenues and obtained an average daily volume of 27,000. During the following year, 1983, its average daily volume was 35,000.

In 1982, the largest shipper was Purolator with overnight shipments of 53 million versus 32 million for Federal. Purolator, however, specializes in the short-haul, small-package market. It uses ground transportation primarily and specializes in local markets rarely exceeding 300 miles. Because it uses ground transportation and ships direct, it is a low-cost operator for short distances.

In the race for overnight express package delivery, Federal Express is the undisputed industry leader. As of March 1984, Federal Express handled 230,000 packages a day compared to 46,000 for its nearest competitor, Airborne. A study done during the summer of 1983 by Alfred H. Norling, analyst at Kidder, Peabody & Co., Inc., New York, showed Federal Express with 53 percent of the market, the U.S. Postal Service with 17.8 percent, Airborne with 9.3 percent, Emery with 7.1 percent, and Purolator with 6.7 percent.

Federal Express has built up a reputation for reliability of on-time delivery that is almost impossible to beat. Its "absolutely, positively overnight" theme is entrenched in the mind of its customer as well as the general public. The competition has also established excellent reliability but customers perceive Federal as having the best on-time record.

Federal has continuously expanded its market coverage. In 1982, it served 74 percent of the population; in 1983, 82 percent of the population; and in 1984, 90 percent of the population, which encompassed 311 of the 323 Standard Metropolitan Areas. Its goal is to expand coverage to 95 percent of the population by 1987. The U.S. Postal Service services more customers with its normal postal service and now offers Express Mail service at most locations.

The competition in electronic mail is very new. MCI began in September 1983 and Federal Express introduced its ZapMail in July 1984. The two companies have different strategies and different technologies. ZapMail makes minimal demands on sender and recipient. A courier picks up the sender's document and takes it to a Federal Express office, where it is faxed to an office near the recipient. A courier at that end hand delivers it. Federal Express promises delivery within two hours. With MCI Mail, a more complex system, the sender keys the message into an electronic machine, and MCI's network can then transmit it instantaneously to the recipient's machine or MCI can retransmit it to a processing center for delivery through the U.S. mail or by Purolator courier. Hand delivery at its fastest occurs within four hours of transmission.

Both systems have their strengths and weaknesses. Anyone can use the Federal system, because neither the sender nor the recipient needs electronic equipment. Moreover, Federal's facsimile system will transmit virtually anything that can be printed on paper, including charts, blueprints, and graphics.

In the MCI system, users must originate messages on their own electronic machines: computers, word processors, telex machines, or electronic typewriters with memories. MCI is restricted to alphanumerics and company logos and signatures that have been registered with MCI.

MCI will cost less whatever the length of the message but ZapMail has the edge in speed and convenience.

PROMOTION

The promotional mix of Federal Express consists of advertising, personal selling, and publicity, with advertising receiving the greatest emphasis. Advertisements can be found in numerous magazines, newspapers, and journals. A full two-page ad was used in the *Wall Street Journal* and *Business Week* (color) to introduce the new ZapMail service. Television commercials are also used. Federal has always had outstanding advertising.

In 1979, the Gallagher Report poll rated the company's advertising as the best in the country, while the American Marketing Association gave Federal its second "Effie" award for advertising effectiveness, and the company won top awards in virtually every significant national advertising awards competition.

The advertising agency for Federal Express is Ally & Gargano, Inc., of New York City. In 1983, the agency created two of Federal's best-known commercials, "Fast Paced World" and "Ambidextrous." These commercials emphasize speed and reliability of delivery through the use of a fast-talking individual, John Moschitta, who can talk at an incredible pace of 534 words per minute. "Ambidextrous" emphasized how much work could be done in the hour and a half gained by using Federal's new 10:30 A.M. delivery. It won the top award in the broadcast category for the best business advertising in a poll conducted by *Nation's Business* magazine. Thomas A. Oliver, senior vice-president of marketing, said, "We figure just about every bright brain in every ad agency in America with an express account is trying to figure out how to beat Ally & Gargano in the express advertising business."[5]

In addition to national advertising, Federal Express maintains a field force of 200 salespeople and 60 telephone sales representatives who call on major business accounts.

Federal Express is also entering major events. In 1982, they participated in the World's Fair in Knoxville. The company's pavilion was well received with an estimated 2 million people visiting their exhibit.

The company receives considerable publicity. In August 1984, many newspapers carried a picture and article on the last 727 aircraft built by the Boeing Aircraft Company, which was delivered to Federal Express. This aircraft was the most popular jetliner ever built.

Federal Express has achieved strong brand-name recognition. Its name has become generically identified with the solution to high-priority logistic problems.

CONCLUSION

Federal Express stated in its 1983 Annual Report that the foundation of its success is, "The system of networks we have built on the ground, in the air, and electronically. Interacting smoothly at critical points, these networks make possible the fulfillment of our primary mission: to provide responsive, dependable service to our customers."[6]

Fred Smith is a visionary. He is also a good manager. The application of his future-oriented conceptions and people philosophy has created a unique blend of creativity and spirit in this company to accept challenges.

In effect Federal Express created the industry. It found a need and satisfied it. It has priced its product according to the service rendered, taking into consideration its competitors. Federal has placed this service so that it is available to 90 percent of the U.S. population and the company continues to expand its market coverage. It has effectively used several promotional activities to communicate this service to the public. Federal Express has defined its marketing mix and produced the response desired from its target market.

QUESTIONS

1. Every product or service has attributes. What are the attributes of Federal Express?
2. What marketing management philosophy best describes Federal Express?
3. Is Memphis, Tennessee, a good location for a superhub?
4. Should Federal Express open another superhub? Where?
5. Should Federal Express challenge Purolator, who is predominately a local delivery service?
6. You must ship a 20-pound package overnight from New York City to Washington, D.C., a distance of 300 miles. Would you use Purolator or Federal Express?
7. Federal has entered Emery's specialty—the big package market and Emery has entered Federal's specialty—small packages and messages. Are these companies making a mistake?
8. Is price an important variable in this industry?
9. Should Federal add passenger service during the day when most of their aircraft are idle?
10. The promotional mix has emphasized advertising. What other promotional areas could be emphasized?
11. Why can the overnight letter that was introduced June 1, 1981, compete with the U.S. Postal Service Express Mail?
12. ZapMail may cannibalize some of Federal's overnight delivery. Was the introduction of ZapMail a wise decision?
13. Is there a market for express mail and packages in foreign countries. What countries?
14. How has Federal Express employed technology to improve its marketing?
15. Discuss the services that Federal offers.

NOTES

1. Federal Express Corporation 1984 Annual Report, p. 1.
2. Dan Dorfman, "Overnight Highflyer," *Esquire,* August 15, 1978, p. 10.
3. Katie Hafner, "Interview, Fred Smith: The Entrepreneur Redux," *Inc.,* June 1984, p. 40.
4. Joani Nelson-Horchler, "The Overnight Race: Airborne's Flying Right at Federal Express," *Industry Week,* March 19, 1984, p. 67.
5. Kathy Root, "Kudos for a Tramp and a Motor Mouth," *Nation's Business,* April 1984, p. 47.
6. Federal Express Corporation 1983 Annual Report, p. 5.

3

ANHEUSER-BUSCH

BACKGROUND ON THE BEER INDUSTRY

The brewery industry began in the United States in the first half of the nineteenth century. The early U.S. brewers were usually of German ancestry and the breweries were located primarily in the eastern and central cities of the United States. Among the brewers still in business today, Anheuser-Busch began operations in 1852 in St. Louis, Miller began in 1855 in Milwaukee, and Coors began in 1873 in Golden, Colorado, a short distance from Denver.

Cities such as New York, Philadelphia, Milwaukee, St. Louis, Detroit, Albany, Pittsburgh, and Cincinnati became well known for their beer. In fact, just about every city with a population of 50,000 had its own local brewer and in some cases two or three. Patronage at the local level was strong, and citizens identified with their local brewers and tavern owners.

Prior to 1870, all markets were local, but by 1900 a few brewers had developed small regional markets. The completion of the rail system, the introduction of refrigerated freight cars, and a new pasteurization process fostered this development. By 1920, it is estimated that 1,500 breweries existed in the United States (see Table 3-1).

Following a peak of 1,500 breweries, the industry went through three major periods of consolidation.[1] The first consolidation was a result of Prohibition, which became effective nationwide in 1920 and ended 13 years later in December 1933. Brewers during this period diversified their businesses or closed their doors. The industry was devastated and only 750 breweries opened after Prohibition.

A second period of consolidation followed World War II. When

TABLE 3-1 Number of U.S. Brewers, Selected Years, 1900–1990

Year	Number of Brewers
1990ᵃ	10
1983	46
1975	54
1970	93
1945	457
1933	750
1920	1,500
1900	1,500

ᵃ Industry estimates.

Source: United States Brewer's Association.

servicemen who had formerly patronized local brands were sent overseas, they were exposed to the regional and national brands that were shipped to them at the front. Americans were being exposed to new places, new products, and new ideas. Following the war, the United States went through a major demographic, cultural, social, and economic transformation and the number of brewers declined from 457 in 1945 to 93 in 1970.

A third period of consolidation resulted from the ongoing war between the industry leaders, Miller Brewing Company and Anheuser-Busch. Between 1970 and 1983, the number of brewers declined from 93 to 43. Industry experts predict that the continued shakeout will result in 10 or fewer brewers by 1990.

The beer war actually began in 1969 when Philip Morris, a marketing oriented company, purchased Miller. Marketing strategists at Miller were the first practitioners to truly segment the beer market.[2] Their research revealed that 20 percent of all beer drinkers consumed 80 percent of the beer. This target market of heavy beer drinkers was thoroughly studied and Miller High Life, "The Champagne of Bottled Beers," was repositioned to appeal to the real beer drinkers who would consume five or six beers a day. Promotional expenditures were doubled and targeted to the heavy beer drinker.

In June 1972, Miller acquired several of the brands of Meister Brau Company of Chicago. One of these brands was Lite, a reduced-calorie beer. Research revealed that the concept of a reduced-calorie beer had high consumer interest, even among heavy beer drinkers. During 1973 and 1974, Miller Lite was perfected.

The product was introduced in 1975, giving it a two-to-four-year lead over its major competitors. "In 1976 Miller Lite sold 5 million barrels, the company's total annual sales when it was purchased by Philip Morris. In 1977 Lite sales reached about 9 million barrels, two-thirds of the total reduced-calorie beer market."[3] By 1983, Miller Lite outsold Miller High Life 17.9 million barrels to 17.3 million barrels.

TABLE 3-2 Top Ten Beer Brands, 1983

Rank	Brand	1983 Market Share (%)	1983 Volume (million bbls.)	1982 Volume (million bbls.)	1983 Brand Growth (%)
1.	Budweiser[a]	22.8	42.0	40.0	+ 5.0
2.	Miller Lite	9.7	17.9	17.2	+ 4.1
3.	Miller High Life	9.5	17.6	20.0	−12.0
4.	Coors	5.2	9.6	8.4	+14.3
5.	Pabst	4.3	7.9	8.1	− 2.5
6.	Michelob[a]	3.9	7.2	8.3	−13.3
7.	Old Milwaukee	3.7	6.9	5.9	+16.9
8.	Stroh's	3.1	5.7	5.6	+ 1.8
9.	Old Style	3.0	5.6	5.5	+ 1.8
10.	Bud Light[a]	2.1	3.8	3.3	+15.2
	Top Ten Total	67.3	124.2	122.3	+ 1.6
	Other brands	32.7	60.3	59.5	+ 1.3
	Industry Total	100.0	184.5	181.8	+ 1.5

[a] Anheuser-Busch brand.

Note: Reprinted from *Beverage World*, March 1984, p. 36, with permission of Keller International Publishing Corp.

Miller Lite was the second leading brand (see Table 3-2). It was also the most successful new beer introduced since 1900.

Miller expanded very rapidly during the 1970s. The seventh largest brewery in 1972, it had become the second largest by 1977.

Industry analysts have concluded that the innovator in this industry during the 1970s was the Miller Brewing Company.

Anheuser-Busch reacted to this threat by dramatically increasing its market share. August A. Busch III said, "Miller brought marketing powers to the industry, and we sure are using it, God bless 'em."[4] Together these two brewers captured over 60 percent of the market by 1986.

Miller and Busch have economies of scale and enormous funds for advertising and marketing. They are truly national in scope, and both have well-developed distributorships and multiple modern breweries that are geographically dispersed.

As a result of the battle between Miller and Anheuser, many companies failed or were absorbed by others. As larger size appeared to be the only way to compete, mergers and acquisitions became commonplace.

G. Heileman Brewing Company grew to national strength by acquiring regional breweries across the country. Stroh Brewing Company acquired F & M Schaefer Brewing Company in 1981 and Joseph Schlitz in 1982. Pabst acquired Olympia in 1983.

The maverick was Coors, whose traditional stronghold was its regional market in the West. By 1979, Coors was losing market share in

TABLE 3-3 Anheuser-Busch Beer Brands

Brand	Year of Introduction	Description
Budweiser	1876	Company's principal product Largest selling beer in the world Premium beer
Michelob	1896	Superpremium beer
Busch	1955	Regular-priced beer, slightly sweeter and lighter
Natural Light	1977	Light beer, popular price range
Michelob Light	1978	Superpremium lite beer
Bud Light	1982	Premium lite beer
Michelob Classic Dark	1983	Superpremium dark beer
LA Beer	1984 (April)	Reduced-alcohol beer with traditional beer taste

Source: Anheuser-Busch 1985 Fact Book, p. 3.

its home market so it decided to expand nationally. In 1983, Coors entered the Southeast and captured 11 percent. In 1985, Coors entered the Northeast and captured 10 percent. It plans to enter the mid-Atlantic in 1987.

The third period of consolidation created a two-tier beer industry. The first tier consists of Anheuser and Miller, who dominate the national market and have grown at the expense of the smaller regional brewers. The second tier are "the others"—the survivors who have adopted acquisition and expansion strategies to counter the national brewers.

HISTORY OF ANHEUSER-BUSCH

Anheuser-Busch Companies, Inc., is a diverse corporation consisting of several subsidiaries. Its principal subsidiary is Anheuser-Busch, Inc., a brewery. Other subsidiaries include Cambell Taggart, Inc., the second largest producer of baked goods; Family Entertainment (Busch Gardens, Adventure Island, and Sesame Place); Busch Properties; Anheuser-Busch Wines, Inc.; and the St. Louis Cardinals, to name a few.

Anheuser-Busch, Inc., began operations in 1852. It ranks as the world's largest brewer and has held the position of industry leader in the United States since 1957.[5] Its well-known family of quality beers include eight naturally brewed products (see Table 3-3). Except for Busch and Michelob Classic Dark, all Anheuser brands are nationally distributed. There are 11 breweries located across the nation from California to Florida to New York. There is also an international division, which has the goal of exploring and developing market opportunities abroad.

TABLE 3-4 Anheuser-Busch Selected Operating Statistics and Per Share Data, 1973–1983

Year	Barrels Sold (millions)	Net Sales (millions)	Net Income (millions)	Earnings per Share	Dividends Common Stock	Dividends Preferred Stock
1983	60.5	$6,034.2	$348.0	$6.50	$1.62	$3.60
1982	59.1	4,576.6	287.3	5.97	1.38	—
1981	54.5	3,847.2	217.4	4.79	1.13	—
1980	50.2	3,295.4	171.8	3.80	0.99	—
1979	46.2	2,775.9	196.4	4.34	0.90	—
1978	41.6	2,259.6	111.0	2.46	0.82	—
1977	36.6	1,838.0	91.9	2.04	0.71	—
1976	29.1	1,441.1	55.4	1.23	0.68	—
1975	35.2	1,645.0	84.7	1.88	0.64	—
1974	34.1	1,413.1	64.0	1.42	0.60	—
1973	29.9	1,109.7	65.6	1.46	0.60	—

Source. 1983 Annual Report, pp. 50, 51.

Anheuser's financial, brand ranking, and market share data is impressive. Net sales increased from $1.1 billion in 1973 to $6.0 billion in 1983, and net income increased from $65.6 million in 1973 to $348 million in 1983. The company enjoyed a particularly good year in 1983 with an increase of 31.8 percent in net sales and 27.0 percent in net income over 1982 (see Table 3-4).[6]

In brand ranking data, Anheuser had three of the top ten brands in 1983. Budweiser was the number one brand with a commanding 22.8 percent of the market (see Table 3-2).

Market share data shows that Anheuser now has nearly a one-third share of the total market. It has increased its market share from 20.7 percent in 1973 to 32.5 percent in 1983 (see Table 3-5). Anheuser is clearly the undisputed leader of the industry.

OUTSTANDING INDIVIDUALS

Anheuser-Busch has been fortunate in having many family members who have been outstanding leaders and administrators. Two have been selected for their contributions.

Adolphus Busch (1839–1913), recognized as the legendary founder, was the son-in-law of Eberhard Anheuser. Busch was an innovator, promoter, and visionary. His contributions ranged from the use of railside ice houses and refrigerated freight cars to the introduction of a pasteurization process to ensure freshness. The creation of Budweiser, using time-consuming traditional methods and only the finest barley malt, hops, and rice with a beechwood aging process, was ingenious. Busch developed a draught beer for connoisseurs and coined the name *Michelob*.

TABLE 3-5 Market Share Data for the U.S. Brewing Industry, 1973, 1978, and 1983 (Percent)

Brand	1983	1978	1973
Anheuser-Busch	32.5	25.1	20.7
Miller	20.1	18.9	5.0
Stroh's	13.0	3.8	—
G. Heilman	9.4	4.3	—
Coors	7.4	7.6	7.1
Pabst	6.9	9.3	12.8
Schlitz[a]	—	11.9	14.2
Olympia[b]	—	4.1	—
All others[c]	10.7	15.0	40.2
Total	100.0	100.0	100.0

[a] Acquired by Stroh's in 1982.

[b] Acquired by Pabst in 1983.

[c] Remaining companies in 1973 and 1978 have less than 5 percent market share per company. All remaining companies in 1983 have less than 2 percent market share per company.

Sources: Anheuser-Busch 1984 Fact Book, p. 1; U.S. Brewer's Association.

Busch also excelled at promotion. Pocket knives were used as calling cards and one of the company's most successful promotions of all time was the distribution of a large painting of "Custer's Last Fight" for display in taverns across the country.[7]

As a visionary, Busch saw the possibilities of a national market as the new pasteurization process ensured the beer's freshness in transit over long distances.

August A. Busch III (1937–   ) is the current president and chief executive officer. He became president in 1974 after 17 years experience in every aspect of the business. In 1975, he became chief executive officer. He is the fourth generation of the Busch family to run the company, which was 122 years old when he assumed its presidency.[8] He is credited "with transforming Anheuser-Busch from a lumbering giant into a modern and efficient corporation, from a mere brewery into an aggressive marketing force, and from an authoritarian family business into a corporation dedicated to participatory management."[9]

Busch's weakest year as president was 1976 when a horrible strike resulted in a loss of market share. Miller also began to excel with Miller Lite. Eventually these difficulties were overcome and August A. Busch III implemented the following changes.

A totally new marketing strategy was developed and the company's advertising was increased and refocused. The company opened its tenth brewery, acquired its eleventh, and launched the largest brewery expansion projects in company history. Five new brands of beer were introduced and the beer business increased its vertical integration capabilities. Anheuser also diversified into other new lines of business.

TABLE 3-6   U.S. Consumption of Beer, Liquor, and Wine, 1970–1984 (Gallons per Person)

Year	Beer	Liquor	Wine
1984[a]	24.3	1.55	2.30
1983	24.7	1.60	2.20
1982	24.5	1.65	2.15
1981	25.0	1.70	2.10
1980	24.0	1.75	2.00
1979	23.5	1.80	1.80
1978	23.0	1.85	1.75
1977	22.0	1.90	1.70
1976	21.8	1.80	1.65
1975	21.4	1.85	1.60
1974	21.0	1.80	1.50
1973	20.0	1.75	1.60
1972	18.8	1.70	1.50
1971	18.5	1.65	1.45
1970	18.2	1.60	1.40

[a] Estimated as of September 1984.

Sources: U.S. Brewer's Association; Distilled Spirits Council of the U.S.; Wine Institute.

THE BEER ENVIRONMENT TODAY

The demographic, cultural, social, and political environments for the beer industry have undergone rapid changes since 1980. These changes have affected the per capita consumption of beer.

Historically the beer industry has continually increased its sales irrespective of the various changes that took place in its environment. It was assumed that beer consumption would continue to grow during the 1980s at the same 3 to 4 percent annual growth rate experienced in the 1970s. This has not happened. Sales peaked in 1981. In 1982, beer consumption dropped considerably (see Table 3-6). In 1983, sales rebounded just 0.5 percent to 177.5 million barrels. In 1984, sales dropped 1.1 percent during the first five months.

Long-term sales may have leveled off and, if the flat sales trend continues, the smaller producers will be forced to reexamine their marketing strategies. The big producers, Anheuser and Miller, will then grow exclusively at the expense of the smaller producers. This will accelerate the trend of mergers, acquisitions, and eliminations in the industry.

ANHEUSER'S MARKETING STRATEGY

Anheuser became the industry leader in 1957 when it took over this position from Schlitz. During the 1960s, these two companies were formidable contenders for the number one position but Anheuser-Busch was in an enviable position—it was running out of beer every summer.[10] Management did not take the Schlitz challenge seriously and Anheuser became somewhat complacent. Schlitz eventually made a series of marketing blunders in the 1970s and was acquired by Strohs in 1982.

In the 1970s Anheuser's major competitor was Miller Brewing Company. Miller initiated the following steps. In 1972 Miller High Life, "The Champagne of Bottled Beers," was repositioned in the market and given a more macho image in order to compete against Budweiser, "The King of Beers." Also in 1972 Miller introduced the 7-ounce "pony" bottle. In 1974 Miller introduced Lowenbrau, a super premium beer to compete against Budweiser's Michelob. In 1975 Miller introduced Miller Lite, a reduced calorie beer that was marketed two years earlier than other light beers.

Anheuser reacted to the Miller challenge by expanding its number of brands from three in 1976 (Budweiser, Michelob, and Busch) to eight in 1984. Natural Light was introduced in 1977, Michelob Light in 1978, and Bud Light in 1982. In 1984 Michelob Classic Dark and LA, the first reduced alcohol beer, were introduced.

Anheuser also increased its advertising budgets, improved its packaging, and gained better support from its wholesalers.

The organizational structure was also altered. Brand management teams staffed by recruits from consumer packaged-goods companies and a marketing services department to unite such functions as promotions and point-of-sale displays were created. The national market was divided into six regions and 20 target states.

August A. Busch III had installed his brand of leadership and participative management. Competitors did not like this aggressive marketing strategy. August Busch replied by saying, "We are working very hard to be humble."[11]

Anheuser is also being challenged by the second tier group: Strohs, G. Heileman, Coors, and Pabst. The weaker brewers are gone and the second tier group can only increase their market share at the expense of Anheuser and Miller. They are basically engaged in short-term promotional and price attacks in their strong regional markets. They do not have the advertising budgets, national brand name recognition, or distribution strengths of Anheuser or Miller.

In April 1984 Anheuser launched a major attack against Miller and the second tier group. A new low alcohol beer named LA was introduced. This beer has approximately half the alcohol content of regular beer. Anheuser spent $20 million promoting LA in 1984. Advertising copy in the September 14, 1984, issue of *USA Today* newspaper read as follows:

Say 'LA'
For all the unique taste and drinkability of a premium pilsner beer with

only half the alcohol of our regular beer—Say 'LA'! For the way you live today, LA[12]

The campaign theme, "For the way you live today LA," was extensively repeated over television commercials during the Summer Olympics in Los Angeles in 1984.

It is doubtful that other brewers will allow Anheuser to develop the two-to-four-year lead that Miller had with Lite. In May 1984, G. Heileman introduced Blatz LA and Black Label LA. The company planned to spend $2 million to promote these brands in 1984. Heileman is preparing low-alcohol extensions of its more than 30 regional brands and others are expected to follow suit.

CONCLUSION

Dun's Business Month named Anheuser-Busch as one of the five best-managed companies of 1982.[13] Anheuser has met many challenges in the long history since its founding in 1852. Miller was the marketing innovator of the 1970s but Anheuser learned from Miller's successes and implemented its own successful marketing strategy.

The beer war of the 1970s was fought nationally between Miller and Anheuser. The beer war of the 1980s will probably be fought on a regional basis with the smaller brewers taking the offensive.

Anheuser-Busch is well organized, structured, and positioned. It has an aggressive competitor-marketing strategy and is expected to capture 40 percent of the U.S. beer market by the end of the decade.[14] Miller, although vulnerable, will hold its number two position. The remaining producers will battle for what is left. Some may retrench to serve smaller regional markets and others will merge to survive. By 1990, there will be fewer than 10 brewers remaining in the United States, a considerable drop from the 1,500 that existed in 1920.

QUESTIONS

1. During Prohibition (1920–1933), the number of brewers declined. The number of brewers also declined during the Great Depression (1929–1935). Did the Depression affect beer consumption?
2. Discuss the factors that have caused the per capita consumption of beer to level off in the early 1980s.
3. What strategy should Anheuser implement to deal with declining beer consumption?
4. Table 3-6 shows consumption data on beer, liquor, and wine. How are these products related and what trends are emerging?

5. Should Miller have repositioned Miller High Life in 1972 to compete against Budweiser?

6. Anheuser countered the Miller Lite strategy by offering three brands of light beer. Was this a good strategy?

7. Was it a good strategy for Miller to introduce Lowenbrau to compete against Michelob?

8. List five critical questions that should have been asked about LA beer.

9. G. Heileman grew by acquiring regional brewers. It currently has about 30 brands with Old Style accounting for about 38 percent of its beer volume. Does Heileman have a sound strategy?

10. The beer industry can practice four strategies: product, sales, customer, and competitor. Which strategy do you prefer?

11. In 1983, Miller Lite surpassed Miller High Life, its long-time leader in market share (see Table 3-2). Is this good or bad?

12. The current antidrinking sentiments of the public have affected beer sales. How should Anheuser deal with this movement?

13. Why is price competition conducted on a selective or regional basis?

14. Summarize Anheuser's marketing strategy in less than 40 words.

NOTES

1. *Inc.*, January 1983, p. 36.
2. John B. Clark, *Businesses Today: Successes & Failures* (New York: Random House, 1979), pp. 32–43.
3. Ibid., p. 37.
4. "Anheuser-Busch The King of Beers Still Rules," *Business Week*, July 12, 1982, p. 53.
5. Anheuser-Busch 1984 Fact Book, p. 3.
6. Anheuser-Busch 1983 Annual Report, p. 1.
7. Anheuser-Busch 1984 Fact Book, p. 18.
8. Ibid., p. 19.
9. "Anheuser-Busch: The Once and Future King," *Dun's Business Month*, December 1982, p. 48.
10. "Anheuser-Busch The King of Beers Still Rules," p. 52.
11. Ibid., p. 52.
12. *USA Today*, September 14, 1984, p. 16C.
13. "Anheuser-Busch: The Once and Future King," p. 47.
14. Ibid., p. 49.

4

TOYS "R" US

INTRODUCTION

Toys "R" Us is the world's largest and fastest growing toy specialty retail chain in terms of market share, sales, and earnings. As of January 1986, the company operated 246 toy stores, 233 domestically (serviced through 14 warehouse/distribution centers) and 13 abroad; 4 conventional department stores; and 23 children's clothing stores.

Under the leadership of Charles Lazarus and a top-notch management team, this company emerged from bankruptcy in 1977 to dominate the toy industry. In 1978, one year after bankruptcy, sales were $349 million. In five years, sales surpassed $1 billion; in another three years, they topped $2 billion (see Table 4-1). In 1979, the stock was listed on the New York Stock Exchange. Since then, it has split three-for-two in 1980, 1981, 1982, 1983, and 1984. Earnings per share and the price of the common stock have soared. The company pays no cash dividends because it is reinvesting for future growth.

Currently the company is diversifying. In 1983, Kids "R" Us, a discount clothing chain, began operations with the opening of two stores. A director of international operations was also appointed.

Toys "R" Us seeks to perpetuate its phenomenal growth and profit performance by perfecting its current operations and becoming the premier discount toy retailer worldwide.

TABLE 4-1 Toys "R" Us Selected Operating Statistics and Per Share Data, 1975–1985

Year [a]	Revenue (millions)	Net Income (millions)	Earnings per Share	Dividends per Share	Common Stock Price Range [b]
1985	$1,976	$120	$1.39	Nil	42–25
1984	1,702	111	1.30	Nil	35–21
1983	1,320	92	1.08	Nil	32–17
1982	1,042	64	0.78	Nil	25–8
1981	783	49	0.63	Nil	10–4
1980	597	29	0.38	Nil	7–2
1979	480	27	0.36	Nil	4–1 5/8
1978	349	17	0.24	Nil	1 7/8–1
1977	274	10	0.13	Nil	1 1/8–1/2
1976	242	10	NA	Nil	7/8–1/4
1975	219	10	NA	Nil	3/8–1/8

[a] Year ends January 31 of following year.
[b] Based on calendar year.
Source: Standard & Poor's NYSE Stock Report, Vol. 52, No. 179, Sec. 16, September 17, 1985, p. 2243J.

CHARLES LAZARUS

Charles Lazarus, founder and chief executive officer of Toys "R" Us, started his retailing career in 1948 after serving with the armed forces. With $4,000 he opened a small juvenile-furniture store in his father's Washington, D.C., bicycle shop.

He has always been customer-oriented. Early in the business, a woman asked him for some toys to go with the crib she was buying; having none, he promptly added a few basic playthings to his stock. It was not long before a customer came to replace a toy her baby had smashed. Lazarus said, "When I realized that toys broke, I knew it was a good business."[1]

Lazarus also realized that, "Everybody enjoys buying toys." He said, "It's fun and that makes it a fun business."[2]

He boasts, "There are people who cannot afford McDonald's and people who will not go to McDonald's. If you are poor you must shop at our store because you will save money. If you're rich, it's the only place you can go to see everything, because we've got it all."[3]

He says, "What we do is the essence of America—making a business grow. If you're going to be a success in life, you have to want it. I wanted it. I was poor. I wanted to be rich."[4]

Today Charles Lazarus is indeed a rich man. In 1984 he was listed as the second highest paid executive on the *Business Week* executive compensation scoreboard. His compensation included the following:

Salary	$ 315,000
Bonus	1,098,000
Annual Total	$ 1,413,000
Long-term income	42,360,000
Total	$43,773,000

In all fairness, it should be pointed out that the long-term income is paper profit. This figure is what Lazarus would earn if he exercised his stock options at current market prices. In 1978, the Board of Directors granted key executives options for the purchase of up to 4,050,000 shares of common stock at the current market price at that time, approximately $2 a share. As of 1984, the common stock traded above $35. The author estimates that the stock has risen 20-fold in value from 1978 to 1984.

What makes Charles Lazarus tick? His wife, a well-known New York psychiatrist, asked Lazarus why he continued to grow. He said, "Because that's the enjoyment. It isn't that if you don't go uphill, you go downhill. It's the pure pleasure of the business. My ego now is in the growth of this company and to see how well we can do something, how we can continue to improve it, not just sit back and say it's good enough."[5]

An executive at Lionel Corporation, the famous maker of toy trains and toy retailer (a company recently out of bankruptcy) said Lazarus had a tremendous advantage because he loved his work whereas the Lionel executive only did it for a living.

Lazarus says he and his wife are both success-oriented people. They enjoy living in Manhattan, so Lazarus commutes daily in reverse to Toy's headquarters in Rochelle Park, New Jersey.

HISTORY OF TOYS "R" US

The first store opened in 1956. In the early years, Lazarus was intrigued by the merchandising strategies of the early "Manhattan Loft Discounters," especially E. J. Korvette. Recognizing that the same formula could work for toys, he opened his second store in 1957 as a self-service, cash-and-carry operation. In 1958, the strategy that is now synonymous with Toys "R" Us was formulated by opening store number three, a 25,000-square-foot supermarket-type outlet with broad and deep assortments sold at prices 20 to 50 percent below those of conventional retailers.

In 1966, with four stores in the Washington, D.C., area doing $12 million in annual sales, Lazarus sold the chain to Interstate Stores. The sale to Interstate allowed him operating independence and the capital backing needed to pilot the growth of his chain. By 1973, Toys "R" Us had

TABLE 4-2 Toys "R" Us Key Statistics for U.S. Market, Selected Years, 1974–1985

Year[a]	Total Number of Stores	New Stores Opened	Distribution Centers and Warehouses	Market Share of Total Toy Market (percent)
1985	223	35	14	15.5
1984	198	29	14	14.0
1983	169	25	13	12.0
1982	144	24	12	11.0
1981	120	19	11	9.0
1980	101	16	10	7.5
1979	85	3	9	6.0
1978	72	9	8	5.0
1977	63	—	7	2.0
1974	47	—	6	2.0

[a] Year ends January 31 of following year.

Sources: Company records; Standard & Poor's NYSE Stock Report, Vol. 52, No. 179, Sec. 16, September 17, 1985, p. 2243J; "Where the Dollars R," Fortune, June 1, 1981, pp. 45–46; "Toys 'R' US Earnings Spurted in 1st Quarter," Wall Street Journal, May 25, 1983, p. 15.

grown to 47 units with $130 million in annual sales (see Tables 4-2 and 4-3).

In 1974, however, Interstate Stores filed for bankruptcy under Chapter X. The following year, Interstate was forced to close its White Front and Topps discount stores. Though he might well have considered leaving the company, Lazarus stayed with the Toys "R" Us throughout the traumatic period, managing to continue the success of the toy division.

In 1978, the reorganized company emerged from bankruptcy as Toys "R" Us with Charles Lazarus as its head. It had grown to 72 stores and has added an average of 25 stores a year from 1979 to 1985 (see Table 4-2).

As previously mentioned, the international division was formed in 1983. By 1984, Toys "R" Us had 4 stores in Canada and 1 store in Singapore. During 1985, 3 more stores were added in Canada and 5 stores in the United Kingdom. By the end of 1985, the international division had 13 stores in foreign markets (see Table 4-4).

Kids "R" Us, a children's retail clothing business, began operations in 1983 with 2 stores. Eight stores were added in 1984 and 13 stores in 1985. The 23 stores are primarily located in the Philadelphia, Maryland, and metropolitan New York markets.

Currently the company has three major divisions: Toys "R" Us, Kids "R" Us, and the international division. All divisions are prospering and expanding their number of stores.

TABLE 4-3 Toys "R" Us Stores Selected Years, 1956–1966

Year	Number
1966	4
1958	3
1957	2
1956	1

Sources: Company records; "Where the Dollars R," *Fortune,* June 1, 1981, pp. 45–46.

TABLE 4-4 Toys "R" Us U.S. and International Stores, 1983–1985

Year	U.S.	Canada	Singapore	U.K.	Total
1985	233	7	1	5	246
1984	198	4	1	0	203
1983	169	0	0	0	169

Source: Standard & Poor's NYSE Stock Report, Vol. 52, No. 179, Sec. 16, September 17, 1985, p. 2243J.

FINANCIAL STATISTICS

Some Toys "R" Us financial statistics have already been mentioned. To increase one's sales from $1 billion (1982) to over $2 billion (1985) in a three-year period in this type of business is virtually unheard of. The reasons for this increase are twofold. First, there has been a rapid increase in the number of stores and, second, each individual store on the average is producing increasing sales volume. The growth of net income after taxes as well as earnings per share have also kept pace (see Table 4-1).

The percentage increase in net income for the five-year period 1981–1985 is as follows:

Year	Percent Increase in Income
1985	25
1984	21
1983	43
1982	31
1981	70

These figures are remarkable considering the brunt of a national recession occurred in 1981 and 1982.

Market share data has also kept pace. Toys "R" Us increased its share of the total toy market from 2.0 percent in 1977 to 15.5 percent in 1985. Each year it has increased its market share by at least 1 percent (see Table 4-2).

In short, Toys "R" Us has an impressive record in net sales, net income, and market share.

TOYS "R" US

The goal of Toys "R" Us is to create the first national toy discount supermarket where it is fun to shop. You are supposed to find anything and everything that kids of all ages want and need. Shopping is hassle-free and the national chain projects a friendly, local image.

Toys "R" Us has a customer base that covers the entire economic spectrum. The rich, the poor, and the middle class all shop Toys "R" Us. This is unique in the retail industry. The main thrust and appeal is to the parent who wants to go to one place to see the biggest selection at the best prices and buy all their toys (one-stop shopping). Customers know that items will be in stock, at about one-third lower than list prices, on a year-round basis. The key is to create customer awareness that Toys "R" Us is *one* place to shop for toys and games.

The merchandising strategy, which stresses the development of strong consumer recognition, is accomplished through the use of mass advertising, mostly in local newspapers. Beginning in December 1984, national television advertising was used. The merchandise assortment is broad and deep. Items sold include children's and adult's games, bicycle and wheel goods, sporting goods, electronic and video games, home computers that emphasize game playing and education features, small pools, records, books, infant and juvenile furniture, and infant's and children's clothing. Each store carries over 18,000 different items.

The stores contain 43,000 square feet of selling space. This is unparalleled in the toy industry. They are generally located in free-standing buildings enroute to shopping malls. They have ample parking space. The stores have broad shopping aisles and efficient computerized checkout counters. All stores are laid out identically so that a customer can find a Monopoly game on exactly the same shelf along the same aisle in every outlet. Like supermarkets, they are set up for self-service without much personalized service. The store layout encourages impulse buying and items such as Pampers and baby food, which are sold in large volume, are deeply discounted, especially in the off season. This strategy of using a loss leader brings in the customer. The average sale per customer is $40.

The greatest strength of Toys "R" Us is its computerized inventory control system which logs sales by item and by store each day and compares them to projections. The projections are constantly honed by actual selling experience. At Toys "R" Us, 40 percent of the products are new each year, and the short Christmas selling season is crucial. In 1980, the computer tipped off management early that hand-held electronic games were not selling well. Unlike others in the business, Toys "R" Us did not overload this item for Christmas. Merchandise buyers do not make the decision on what to rebuy; the customer makes it for them.

Sales data from stores are scrutinized daily, but all buying and pricing decisions are made at headquarters. As Lazarus said, "Nothing is done in the stores." Nothing, that is but the selling. And Toys "R" Us rewards the best store managers for following orders explicitly with rapid promotion and stock options. Few ever leave. The four top executives have been with the company an average of 20 years.

Another advantage of Toys "R" Us is its warehouse and distribution system. Every store in the chain is within a day's drive from its nearest distribution center.

As one of the manufacturer's largest customers, it gets priority on deliveries. Because it operates year-round and has extensive warehouse space, it can benefit by placing orders in February at a discount, orders that need not be paid for until the following January. Buying terms get tighter as the Christmas season approaches. Because the cost of discounting and carrying the inventory are worked into the manufacturer's prices, Toys "R" Us gets a double advantage. It gets the discounts and the easy terms; its competitors share the cost.

These early bought goods are used to learn what is gaining or losing in popularity, valuable intelligence in a business that thrives on fads. The system is simple. Buy it all and monitor sales so buyers can focus pre-Christmas orders on promising items.

Toys "R" Us also has good relations with its 1,000 suppliers because its purchasing occurs throughout the year. The company is such a volume purchaser that it even influences what will be produced. When the Christmas season comes, vendors reward it with generous shipments of the most sought-after items.

MARKETING AND PROMOTION

The ads and commercials for Toys "R" Us emphasize the huge selection of items, the low prices, the convenience of one-stop shopping, and the mascot, Geoffrey. This helps to build store image and recognition to all age groups. A variety of promotional efforts to build market acceptance on both a regional and national basis through local television, radio, four-color supplements, and regular newspaper advertisements is used.

Everyone is familiar with the Toys "R" Us mascot, Geoffrey the giraffe, used as a promotional tool to attract kids and adults. Geoffrey is seen on company trucks, ads, television, and store signs. The childish backwards "R" in the company logo is another familiar and eye-catching technique. The logo also has a distinct color scheme that assists recall of the company image.

TABLE 4-5 Retail Toy Sales by Type of Store, 1982 and 1984 (Percent of Total)

Institution	1984	1982
Toy supermarkets	22.0	15.0
Discounters (K Mart, Target, etc.)	31.0	35.0
Traditional retailers (department stores, supermarkets, drugstores)	38.2	41.0
Others	8.8	9.0
Total	100.0	100.0

Source: Fortune, October 28, 1985, p. 72.

TOYS "R" US VERSUS THE COMPETITION

Competition in the toy retail market can be classified into four categories or types of stores: toy supermarkets, traditional retailers, discounters, and others (see Table 4-5).

The major competitors among the toy supermarkets are Toys "R" Us, Child World, and Lionel Leisure. The traditional retailers are department stores, supermarkets, and drugstores. Discounters are K Mart, Target, and catalog showrooms. Others are other types of retailers and specialty toy stores.

Rapid changes have occurred in this market. While the toy retailing industry has grown 37 percent between 1980 and 1984, Toys "R" Us sales have increased 185 percent.

Table 4-5 reveals that the toy supermarkets are the only category that have increased their market share. Toys "R" Us grew from 11 percent of this category in 1982 to 14 percent in 1984, which was approximately 64 percent of all toy supermarket sales. All other categories have shown a decline.

Within the toy supermarket category, rival toy-store operators are trying two strategies. Strategy 1 is to pattern your operation after Toys "R" Us. Strategy 2 is to be as different from Toys "R" Us as possible.

The two major competitors are Child World, a 103-store chain that had sales of $435 million in fiscal 1984, and Lionel Leisure, a 52-store chain that had sales of $224.7 million in fiscal 1984. The profit margins of both chains lag behind Toys "R" Us by a considerable margin. Lionel Leisure has had the additional problem of recently emerging from bankruptcy.

Toys "R" Us enjoys the following advantages: "It invented the toy supermarket and it has the best management."[6] Toys "R" Us also has over 30 stores in the lucrative California market where its major competitors have none. Toys "R" Us has had eight years of soaring profits while its competitors, Child World and Lionel Leisure, have had erratic profits.

All three chains use the same strategy of locating along major highways or near shopping malls where the rent is low. They also offer the same merchandise at low prices.

Child World has patterned its entire operation after Toys "R" Us. Management's strategy is to be an imitator. Its large warehouse stores offer the same selection of toys, dolls, games, and bicycles at reasonably low prices.

Two chains that are following Strategy 2 of being as different from Toys "R" Us as possible are Kay Bee, a division of Manville Corporation, and Enchanted Village. Both are following a differentiation strategy. Both chains have smaller stores and higher prices.

Kay Bee, a 533-store chain, locates most of its small stores in malls. It sells and displays merchandise to attract impulse buyers. The chain pays high rents but does little advertising (just the opposite of Toys "R" Us).

Enchanted Village, a five-store chain, eschews popular toys such as G.I. Joe and Cabbage Patch dolls. The store stocks science kits, wooden trains, and prize-winning children's books and puzzles. The stores offer babysitting for kids, child-rearing classes for adults, and computer classes for both, all at a modest hourly fee. Bernard Tessler, the founder, calls his stores entertainment centers.

The discounters, traditional retailers, and other categories are all loosing market share. The discounters have not pushed toy sales and have not increased selling space. Most department stores have reduced the size of their toy departments, and the supermarkets and drugstores are pushing toy items primarily during seasonal sales such as Thanksgiving, Christmas, and Easter.

One of the major concerns for Toys "R" Us is the catalog showrooms that slash prices on toys to attract buyers for other big-ticket items. But overall, the catalog showrooms constitute a minor segment of the toy market.

Despite this complex and changing market for toys, Toys "R" Us continues to expand its market share (see Table 4-5). Some experts believe that they have just barely penetrated the United States toy market, much less the world market. In the United States alone, the chain is not represented in 4 of the top 20 retail toy and operates in only 28 states. Stores have opened in Boston, Miami, Philadelphia, and Atlanta only in 1981, 1982, 1983, and 1984. There are no stores in Manhattan. During 1985 the chain continued with national television advertising that was first used in December 1984.

Currently the chain has $2 billion of a $13 billion market, or roughly 15.5 percent. This figure is not large compared to some industries. Furthermore, it is estimated that the toy market will grow to $16 billion by 1990.

KIDS "R" US

In July 1983 Toys "R" Us branched out into brand-name children's clothing. Two prototype Kids "R" Us stores were opened—a 15,000-square-foot store in Paramus, New Jersey, and a 20,000-square-foot store in Brooklyn, New York. These stores have been attracting attention because they are quite different from anything else in the off-price children's clothing market.

They are several times larger than most clothing discounters. While most off-price clothing stores have austere, bargain basement appearances, Kids "R" Us has a carefully contrived atmosphere of color and whimsy.

> A cheerful, almost carnival mood pervades the store. Customers push their purchases in orange and green grocery-style carts. Children play with blinking electronic games hanging on the walls, one of which reveals whether the player will be president, an olympic champion, or just plain rich. Sales people are everywhere, wearing orange blazers and floppy, rainbow-colored bow ties. Several seem to do nothing more than blow up their young customers' free balloons.[7]

The kids are having a great time while mom does her shopping.

Kids "R" Us also offers a larger selection of in-season, name-brand clothing and accessories for children up to age 12, all of it at discount prices. By contrast, many off-price stores specialize in end-of-season and irregular goods.

The store is arranged into departments that are sectioned off with neon signs that read "Boys 'R' Us," "Girls 'R' Us," "Babes 'R' Us," "Tykes 'R' Us," "Infants 'R' Us," and so forth.

One department store buyer arriving at the store said it caused her instant depression.

Nathaniel Tom Mendelson, president of the Youth Fashion Guild, a New York buying office that represents more than 250 specialty and department stores across the country, said, "It's one of the most outstanding things I've seen in a long time. They have the decor, the size, and the best merchandising money can buy. They will take a lot of business away from department stores, little kiddy shops, and give Sears a run for its money."[8]

Others disagree and believe that Toys "R" Us will face much tougher competition in the clothing industry than it has experienced in toys. They also question whether manufacturers will be willing to offer a continuing supply of name-brand goods to be sold at a discount.

The giant chains like Sears, Roebuck and Company and J. C. Penney Company have dominated the children's wear market selling moderately priced apparel under their store labels. Big department stores, such as Macy's and Bloomingdale's, and neighborhood specialty shops feature the more expensive labels. These stores surrendered the toy market; they simply cut back the size of their toy departments. Speculation on how they will handle their children's clothing departments is interesting.

Clinton Clark, the chief executive of The Children's Place, a division of Federated Department Stores and the nation's largest children's wear chain said, "We're not going to run away and play dead. Wherever there's a lower price, we'll meet it."[9] The Children's Place lowered its prices at its two Paramus-area stores by 24 percent after Kids "R" Us opened. This 102-store chain is adding 15 to 20 new outlets a year.

The Children's Outlet, F. W. Woolworth's recently acquired West Coast children's apparel chain, plans to add several hundred stores between 1984 and 1989. Most of the growth will occur in the unit's off-price division, called Kids Mart.

U.S. Shoe Corporation bought a chain of children's clothing stores in the fall of 1982 and is currently expanding that chain.

None of this has prevented Kids "R" Us from adding eight additional stores in 1984 and thirteen additional stores in 1985. Charles Lazarus is convinced his stores will outperform the competition. He said, "This is the store of tomorrow. This is what the customer wants."[10]

TOYS "R" US VERSUS FEDERATED DEPARTMENT STORES AND GENERAL MILLS, INC.

In September 1983, Toys "R" Us filed suit against Federated Department Stores and General Mills, Inc. (Izod apparel division), charging both with price fixing. Toys "R" Us sought triple damages of $27 million.

The complaint alleged that Izod apparel and Federated "entered into a conspiracy" to prevent Izod apparel from being sold to Toys "R" Us new clothing division.

Toys "R" Us said in its suit that Federated and General Mills were attempting to eliminate price competition, to monopolize the distribution channels for children's apparel, and "to coerce" other manufacturers into refusing to sell to Kids "R" Us.

Charles Lazarus said, "We think many of our vendors are being coerced and frightened. We want to open up a lot of these stores and we don't want this threat hanging over our heads."[11]

Lazarus noted that Federated competes directly with Kids "R" Us through its Children's Place and children's outlet stores. Federated also runs Abraham & Straus and Bloomingdale's department stores, both of which offer brand-name clothing such as Izod at full price. Mr. Lazarus said Federated was fighting the expansion of Kids "R" Us because it brings down the prices.

Federated made headlines in June 1983 at a retail conference in New York by stating it would stop buying from vendors that sold both to department stores and to off-price outlets.

General Mills said in a prepared statement it believes that Toys "R" Us is trying to challenge its fashion group's long-standing policy of selective distribution in the sale of its primary branded products—Izod, Lacoste, Ship 'N Shore, and Monet. They cited its sale of Izod products to about 12,000 accounts and said Toys "R" Us charges of conspiracy to lessen the distribution of children's wear were absurd.

Industry observers suggested that General Mills might welcome losing the lawsuit because then they could sell to the fast-growing, off-price industry without worrying about incurring the wrath of the department stores.

Lazarus noted that Izod was being sold to Toys "R" Us Interstate Department Stores division, which consisted of four stores in New York and Michigan. When Kids "R" Us opened up, General Mills learned that Izod children's wear was being transhipped from Interstate stores to the discount outlets. On August 17, Izod terminated the Interstate account. All along, Izod has refused to sell to Kids "R" Us directly.

On December 5, 1983, Toys "R" Us dropped its suits against Federated and General Mills and Federated dismissed counterclaims.

Toys "R" Us said that changed circumstances made it prudent to terminate the litigation, but would not comment further. The suits were dismissed without prejudice, meaning they could be filed again.

Howard Goldfeder, chairman and chief executive officer of Federated, said, "It has been our position all along that this suit was without merit and we are pleased to see they are being withdrawn."[12]

FOREIGN MARKETS

In 1983, W. John Devine was named executive vice-president and director of international operations. The first group of international stores was opened in Toronto, Canada, in the fall of 1984, followed shortly thereafter by a store in Singapore (see Table 4-4). By the end of 1985, Toys "R" Us operated a total of 13 stores in Canada, Singapore, and the United Kingdom.

An agreement with Alghanim Industries provided technical assistance and buying services to that major Kuwait-based corporation in its efforts to launch toy stores throughout the Middle East. The first store was opened in Kuwait in September 1983.

CONCLUSION

Toys "R" Us has come a long way since emerging from bankruptcy in 1978. Charles Lazarus is no neophyte to the toy supermarket business. By 1986, he will have completed 30 years in this industry.

Robert J. Schweick, an analyst with Wertheim and Company, has summed up the operation as follows: "This is a company with a phenomenal record. They have succeeded with an extremely sophisticated approach to marketing toys, including strong site selection, tight operating procedures, and a fundamental consumer orientation."[13]

QUESTIONS

1. Do you feel Charles Lazarus is being overpaid? How would you feel about this issue if you were a stockholder?
2. How does the competition facing Toys "R" Us differ from the competition facing Kids "R" Us?
3. Was it a smart move to diversify to Kids "R" Us?
4. In what respects are the toy market and the children's clothing market similar and different?
5. Will the competitive strategies of (1) imitating Toys "R" Us or (2) being as different as possible be effective?
6. As Toys "R" Us continues to grow, will its centralized management continue to be effective?
7. Why is Toys "R" Us practicing the marketing concept?
8. What do we have in this company—a sales philosophy or a marketing philosophy?
9. What is Lazarus really pursuing—profits or market share? Defend your answer.
10. Discuss the issues involved in the legal suit Toys "R" Us brought against Federated Department Stores and General Mills (Izod apparel). What legislation and agencies could be involved in such a suit?
11. Discuss the Toys "R" Us Marketing Intelligence Systems.
12. What are the strengths and weaknesses of the distribution and warehouse system used by Toys "R" Us?
13. Discuss the pricing policy of Toys "R" Us.
14. Does Toys "R" Us have a good relationship with its suppliers?

NOTES

1. Stratford P. Sherman, "Where the Dollars R," *Fortune,* June 1, 1981, p. 46.
2. Subrata N. Chakravarty, "Toys 'R' Fun," *Forbes,* March 28, 1983, p. 58.
3. Ibid., p. 60.

4.   Ibid., p. 58.
5.   Ibid., p. 60.
6.   Anthony Ramirez, "Can Anyone Compete with Toys 'R' Us?" *Fortune,* October 28, 1985, p. 72.
7.   Claudia Ricci, "Children's Wear Retailers Brace For Competition From Toys 'R' Us," *Wall Street Journal,* August 25, 1983, sec. 2, p. 23.
8.   Peter Keer, "The New Game at Toys 'R' Us," *New York Times,* September 4, 1983, sec. 3, p. 7.
9.   Ricci, "Children's Wear Retailers," p. 23.
10. Ibid.
11. "Toys 'R' Us Files Suit, Claims Price Fixing on Izod Ltd. Clothing," *Wall Street Journal,* September 23, 1983, p. 10.
12. "Toys 'R' Us Drops Suits Against 3 Companies, Easing Off-Price Fight," *Wall Street Journal,* December 5, 1983, p. 25.
13. Keer, "The New Game at Toys 'R' Us," p. 7.

5

APPLE COMPUTER

HISTORY AND GROWTH

Apple Computer is viewed by many as a pioneer in the development of the personal computer. Apple develops, manufactures, and markets personal computer systems for business, education, science, industry, and the home.

Apple's history began in 1976 when Steven P. Jobs, age 21, and Stephen G. Wozniak, age 26, collaborated on building a small computer for personal use. They soon had an order for 50 of their personal computers and set up shop in Jobs's garage. Jobs was the business manager and Wozniak the engineer. The computer and the company was named Apple because an apple represents the simplicity that Jobs and Wozniak were trying to achieve in the design and use of their computer. Apple Computer was incorporated on January 3, 1977.

The first computer was sold in kit form to electronic hobbyists. Apple I was so successful the two young entrepreneurs believed they had a product with great commercial and social value. The next step was to find a professional manager.

A. C. "Mike" Markkula joined the company as their first recruit. He had been a successful marketing manager for two semiconductor companies—Intel Corporation and Fairchild Semiconductor—both growth companies.

Market research revealed that the personal computer did have a market. Plans were then developed for acquiring capital, management expertise, technical innovation, software development, and marketing. Initial financing came from venture capitalists.

Apple went public in December 1980 with an initial offering of 4.6

million shares of common stock at $22 a share. Jobs, Wozniak, and Markkula became instant multimillionaires and by December 15 the stock advanced to $36 a share.

The Apple II, the first fully assembled, programmable personal computer, was introduced in 1977. In 1982, with revenues topping $583 million, the company achieved Fortune 500 status—the first time any company had done so after only five full years of operation—with rankings of 411 in sales, 201 in profit, and 26 in return on equity.

Since its listing on the over-the-counter market, the price of Apple's stock has been volatile. When IBM entered the personal computer market in 1981 with its PC, the price of Apple's stock declined to $14. In 1983, the stock fluctuated wildly from a high of $63 in June to a low of $17 in the last quarter.

Apple Computer has been recognized as one of the fastest growing companies in American history. In the eight-year period from 1977 to 1984, it grew from a two-man operation to become an international corporation of more than 5,000 employees with 2,000 dealers and sales of $1.5 billion.

In April 1983, John Sculley became president and chief executive officer. Sculley believed his mission was to teach Apple marketing and improve its response to retailers and customers. Under Jobs, the company had acquired a near-maniacal focus on products. Jobs would frequently talk about "insanely great" new computers, and he made stars of product designers.

Sculley emphasized marketing, especially advertising, promotion, development of a company sales force, and customer and dealer relations.

Sculley took Apple through two major reorganizations. By early 1984, he consolidated Apple's divisions into just three: a sales division for all products, a division for the Apple II family of products, and one for Macintosh with Jobs as its general manager.

In May 1985, a second reorganization occurred. In the past, management had been preoccupied with explosive sales growth, but a slowdown in industry sales allowed management to focus on internal operations. The reorganization consisted of three major elements: First, three of the six manufacturing plants were closed. Second, a functional structure was adopted, replacing the former divisionalized structure in which each product division had its own general management, product development, marketing, manufacturing, finance, and management information systems staffs. Under one new structure, all product operations (development, manufacturing, and distribution) were handled by one group, all sales and marketing were handled by one group, and all finance and MIS were handled by one group. Third, as a result of the first two actions, 1,200 or approximately 20 percent of the work force, was

TABLE 5-1 Apple Computer Selected Operating Statistics and Per Share Data 1977–1985

Year	Net Sales (000s)	Net Income (000s)	Earnings per Share	Dividends	Common Stock Price Range (rounded)
1985	$1,918,000	$61,200	$ .99	None	31–14
1984	1,515,876	64,055	1.05	None	35–21
1983	982,769	76,714	1.28	None	63–17
1982	583,061	61,306	1.06	None	34–10
1981	334,783	39,420	0.70	None	34–14
1980	117,126	11,698	0.24	None	36–22
1979	47,867	5,073	0.12	None	NA
1978	7,846	806	0.03	None	NA
1977	774	84	NIL	None	NA

Source: Annual Reports.

terminated—700 in manufacturing, the other 500 spread throughout the company. No cuts were made in the research and development areas.

Apple Computer is in transition to a multiproduct, multibillion dollar corporation. Table 5-1 shows the growth of Apple. No cash dividends have been paid and the company intends to retain its earnings, for the foreseeable future, for use in the development of the business.

OUTSTANDING INDIVIDUALS

Steven Jobs, one of the two cofounders of Apple, was adopted as a baby in 1955 by Paul and Clara Jobs who lived in Mountain View, California, on the southern peninsula of San Francisco Bay. He was somewhat of a loner at Homestead High School where he took an electronics class, but he was not bashful. When he needed parts for a class project, he called Bill Hewlett of Hewlett-Packard in Palo Alto and got them. Jobs never became deeply involved with the technical aspects of electronics. He was more attracted to the practical application of technology.

After high school, his life became a little bizarre. Jobs attended Reed College in Oregon where he lasted for a semester, but he hung around the college and tried meditation, the I Ching way of life, and LSD. He then moved to a Hare Krishna house in Portland where he became a vegetarian. Finally he drifted back home and landed a job at a video game outlet called Atari. This job financed his trip to India where he sought spiritual solace and enlightenment with a shaved head and a backpack. After spending several weeks sleeping under a table in the kitchen of a commune, he returned home.

In 1975, Jobs began hanging around Wozniak and some other

friends who were involved in a discussion group called the Homebrew Computer Club. This led to their building of a home computer.

Due to the commercial promise of this computer Jobs was able, at age 21, to attract a first-class industrial public relations firm and a team of experienced managers. He organized the early manufacturing and marketing concepts of Apple. He persuaded Wozniak to leave Hewlett-Packard to form a company with him. It was Jobs's idea to name the company Apple Computer.

As cofounder of Apple, Jobs had held most of the top executive positions, including president, chief executive officer, and chairman of the board.

When John Sculley joined Apple in April 1983 as president and chief executive officer, Jobs remained as chairman of the board. In the first major reorganization in early 1984, Jobs became executive vice-president and general manager of the Macintosh group.

In the second reorganization in May 1985, Jobs was stripped of his operating responsibilities. He was given no official position or authority except chairman of the board. In July, he sold 20 percent of his Apple stock, reducing his stake in the company from 11.3 percent to about 9 percent. Between August and December 1985 he sold an additional 1.3 million shares. He is still the single largest stockholder.

On September 17, 1985, Steven Jobs resigned as chairman. In his letter of resignation, he said the reorganization "left me with no work to do and no access even to regular management reports."[1]

Jobs also announced that he had formed a new company named Next Inc. and that he had hired away some of Apple's hottest young engineers and marketers.

On September 23, 1985, Apple Computer sued Jobs, charging that he had violated his responsibility to Apple by secretly planning to form a company that would use Apple research and by recruiting certain important employees while he was still chairman.

On September 24, 1985, Jobs asserted that Apple had undermined efforts to settle the dispute over his new venture and that the company had begun a campaign to ruin his reputation. He indicated an interest in creating great new products and getting on with being productive rather than spending his time fighting Apple.

In January 1986 Apple Computer reached an out-of-court settlement of its suit against Steven Jobs. The settlement specifies that Next cannot produce computers that use Apple's proprietary technology and Next cannot bring out its first computer before July 1987, and Apple has the right to inspect it before it goes to market.

Stephen Wozniak, the other cofounder of Apple, also grew up in "Silicon Valley." His father, an engineer and graduate of California Institute of Technology, taught his son some basic electronics. Stephen attended John McCollum's class in electronics at Homestead High School and learned about computers. He was continuously involved in playing tricks with gadgets based on electronic knowledge. In fact he was arrested and expelled from school for building a dummy bomb. Wozniak wanted to be remembered as the greatest prankster Homestead ever had.

In college Wozniak was a serious student who excelled in both math and science. However, he dropped out of college and was employed by Hewlett-Packard as a technician helping to design calculators. It was at Hewlett-Packard that he developed the motherboard for a new computer. He asked Hewlett-Packard if they wanted to market it and since they were not interested, Wozniak asked and received a legal release for his design

In 1975 at the Homebrew Computer Club, Wozniak was reunited with his good friend Steven Jobs. During one meeting, they talked with Paul Terrell, the founder of Byte Shop, a chain of computer stores. Mr. Terrell offered to purchase the motherboard if they could deliver 50 a month.

Wozniak left Hewlett-Packard and joined Jobs to produce the motherboard which was named Apple I in 1976.

Jobs envisioned the commercial possibilities of Apple I and urged Wozniak to produce the Apple I as a genuine consumer product by putting the motherboard in a case with a keyboard attached. Wozniak believed it would be more profitable to design a new and improved product. Thus Apple II was born but it had a major problem.

For a computer to be easy to operate, it needed a way of loading the software easily. The first users of Apple II used cassette tapes to store their programs, but this was a slow and unreliable process. Wozniak again proved his creativeness by inventing the disk drive, a box that reads information from a whirling disk of magnetized plastic. The smallest disk drive used 30 to 40 computer chips but Wozniak used five. The redesigned Apple II and newly invented disk drive became an incredible success and Wozniak was heralded as a genius for his invention.

John Sculley joined Apple Computer as president and chief executive officer in April 1983. The courting of the 44-year-old executive, formerly president of PepsiCo, had taken 18 months.

Upon initial contact, Sculley said he was not interested in the job but he "did have a lot of interest in meeting Jobs and Markkula, a couple of guys who took a company that six years ago didn't exist and built it to $1 billion."[2]

Sculley had an outstanding record as president of PepsiCo where he earned $500,000 a year. He was known as an outstanding marketing man and was credited with a number of innovations including the introduction of large plastic bottles, promotion of caffeine-free cola drinks, and

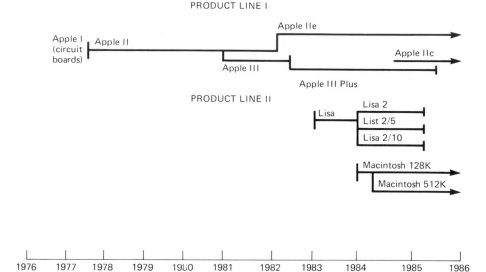

PRODUCT LINE I

Apple IIe

Apple I (circuit boards) Apple II

Apple IIc

Apple III

Apple III Plus

PRODUCT LINE II

Lisa 2

Lisa

List 2/5

Lisa 2/10

Macintosh 128K

Macintosh 512K

| 1976 | 1977 | 1978 | 1979 | 1980 | 1981 | 1982 | 1983 | 1984 | 1985 | 1986 |

FIGURE 5-1 Apple Computer Family of Products, 1976-1986

development of the "Pepsi Challenge." He had developed a strong sense of loyalty among subordinates and bottlers, and Pepsi had prospered under his presidency.

Jobs and Markkula had told the executive recruiting firm that they wanted someone with broad domestic and international management and marketing experience who could adapt to Apple's loosely structured environment.

Although Sculley admitted that his first meeting with Jobs and Markkula was exciting and had awakened something in him, he constantly reiterated that he did not want the job. Even though Jobs offered him $1 million, Sculley turned him down. Sculley knew that in three years he had a good chance of becoming chairman of the board at Pepsi upon the retirement of Donald Kendall.

Finally Steven Jobs offered him $2 million in salary and bonus the first year, $1 million guaranteed severance pay, options on 350,000 shares of Apple stock, and help in buying a house. At this point Sculley gave in, moved to Apple, and commenced its first reorganization.

Sculley reorganized Apple into two major divisions: Apple II, which includes all versions of the Apple II and III; and Macintosh, encompassing the compatible Mac and Lisa groups (see Figure 5-1).

Sculley brought discipline, organization, and structure to Apple. He also believed that Apple's touted culture was the source of its creativity and that innovation and technical knowledge count for a great deal. Sculley was adept at mastering the technical aspects of the computer industry.

Before Sculley arrived, marketing was not given serious consideration. It was regarded as an expense rather than an investment. Sculley increased the advertising budget from $2 million in 1983 to $80 million on advertising and promotion in 1984.

MARKETING MIX

The Apple Product Line. The Apple II line is the most popular personal computer line ever sold. Between 1977 and 1984, this line with its modified versions sold over 1 million units. Initially the Apple II was purchased by hobbyists and computer freaks. By mid-1979, personal computing for fun shifted to personal computing for profit. As systems were upgraded with printers and disks, small business, professional, and educational applications became the major focus. The Apple II became an all-purpose personal computer serving homes, schools (primary, secondary, and college), and small businesses (see Table 5-2).

By 1982, despite attempts (discussed below) to market an Apple III model, Apple II was the company's only successful product. This model was the sole reason for Apple's rapid increase in sales and revenues. It was responsible for the company's expansion and development of new products. It has been called Apple's cash cow.

At this point, however, the Apple II was six years old and becoming obsolete. Dealers were disturbed that the company had not developed successful new products. They were fearful that they would not be able to sell Apple II much longer.

The modification of the Apple II line continued with the introduction of the Apple IIe in 1982 and the Apple IIc in April 1984.

TABLE 5-2 Product Line I: All Versions of Apple II and Apple III, 1976–1986

Product	Life Span[a]	Price Range	Market Served
Apple I (circuit board)	1976	$549	Hobbyists
Apple II	1977–1982	$1,200–$1,500	Homes Schools (primary & secondary) Small businesses
Apple IIe	1982–1986[a]	$995–$1,500	Businesses Schools
Apple IIc	1984–1986[a]	$1,295	Homes
Apple III	1981–1982	$4,000–$8,000	Offices Small businesses
Apple III Plus	1982–1985	$3,244	Professionals in specialized markets

[a] End date of 1986 indicates model still in production at press time.
Source: Company literature.

TABLE 5-3 Product Line II: Lisa and Macintosh Groups, 1983–1986

Product	Life Span	Price	Market Served
Lisa	1983	$9,995	Corporate market
Lisa 2	1984–1985	$3,495	
Lisa 2/5	1984–1985	$4,495	Small and medium-sized businesses
Lisa 2/10	1984–1985	$5,495	
Macintosh 128K	1984	$2,495	Small and medium-sized businesses
Macintosh 128K (revised)	1984–1986[a]	$2,195	Departments of large offices College students
Macintosh 512K	1984–1986[a]	$3,195	Large accounts

[a] End date of 1986 indicates model still in production at press time.
Source: Company literature.

The Apple IIe was an updated version of the Apple II directed at the same market. There were some technical improvements but it was not a revolutionary new type of product. It was marketed well and package deals that effectively cut the list price by about 25 percent kept its sales up.

The Apple IIc may be the final transmutation in the Apple II line. This portable is a direct attack on the IBM PC. It has a number of accessories including printer, mouse, monitor, monitor stand, carrying case, second power pack, and disk drive. A disk drive is required for compatibility with its base of 10,000 programs. Its major market is the home user.

In 1981, the company had attempted to expand its product line with the Apple III, a more powerful version of the Apple II. With a price range of $4,000 to $8,000, the Apple III was directed to small businesses and corporate accounts. This was a new market for Apple, who had little experience selling to corporate accounts. The Apple III was a product failure. It had design flaws and had to be recalled. The redesigned unit was terminated in 1982. The Apple III Plus took its place, obtained only modest sales, and was terminated in mid-1985.

In January 1983, Apple announced a revolutionary new product named Lisa whose start-up costs were $50 million. Lisa was designed for the noncomputer business executive and was very easy to use. A device named a mouse told the computer what to do. In other words, Lisa was extensively preprogrammed to eliminate most of the computer commands that previously had to be typed into personal computers. (See Table 5-3.)

When Lisa was introduced, dealers and users praised its capabilities but said its $9,995 price was too high and complained about the lack of adequate software support. Apple also missed the benefits of the publicity surrounding Lisa's debut because the company took almost six months to ship the product after its announcement.

In early 1983, Steven Jobs said, "Lisa's technology will be Apple's technology base for the '80s."[3] He predicted the machine would be phenomenally successful in its first year, but it was not. In 1984, three revised Lisa models were marketed at a considerably reduced price. In May 1985, the Lisa line was dropped.

The Macintosh was introduced in January 1984. Two of its advertising slogans were, "If you can point you can use a Macintosh," and "The computer for the rest of us." This computer is very user friendly. It has a mouse and uses much of Lisa's technology. It is good with both words and pictures and has an extraordinary ability to mix text, graphs, and freehand drawings.

The Macintosh is aimed primarily at small and medium-sized businesses and at university students. It is currently available in two models, Mac 128K, priced at $2,195, and Mac 512K, priced at $3,195.

As of October 1985, Apple marketed four models: Apple IIe, Apple IIc, Macintosh 128K, and Macintosh 512K. The Apple II line has been the most successful. The Apple III line and Lisa line failed to penetrate the corporate and small business market and were terminated.

Historically, two weaknesses have existed in Apple's product strategy—the lack of peripheral products to accompany its computers, and its attempt to be completely independent from IBM.

In 1985, Apple began to correct these weaknesses by introducing "The Macintosh Office" and announcing a strategy to coexist with IBM.

"The Macintosh Office" is a series of products that tie into Macintosh technology to enhance work-group productivity. The principal market for these products is small and medium-sized businesses. Distribution is through Apple's established dealers.

In 1985, three new products were introduced: AppleTalk, the LaserWriter, and a hard disk—based file server.

AppleTalk is a low-cost network that can connect up to 32 Macintosh personal computers and related peripheral devices within 1,000 feet of each other and assists in sharing information and using bridges and gateways to link to other networks.

The LaserWriter is a high-resolution laser printer that can print many kinds of documents. It ties into the personal computer work stations and the AppleTalk network.

The hard disk—based file server is an electronic filing cabinet that can be shared by everyone on the AppleTalk network.

The strategy to coexist with IBM is a complete reversal of previous strategy. Apple had previously stated that its strategy was to be an alternative to IBM, and Apple sold only two IBM hookups that had limited capabilities. During 1986 and 1987 Apple and other firms started marketing devices that would allow Apple to plug into IBM networks.

Promotion.   Under John Sculley, Apple's promotional expenditures are soaring. From the last quarter of 1984 through the end of 1985 the company spent $200 million to advertise its computers—more than double the amount spent in the two previous years.

The Macintosh promotional strategy provides a good example of how Apple promotes its products. For months before Macintosh was introduced, Apple executives met with reporters and editors of magazines and newspapers giving interviews and letting newspeople experiment with the machine. All agreed not to publish details learned at these sessions before the official press release. A few limited stories were published based on information from inside sources.

The press release was timed to attract coverage by weekly and monthly magazines. Macintosh received 12 cover stories because of this timing. A few days later, the product was formally introduced at Apple's annual meeting.

IBM has a much lower-key approach. Reporters are given a day's notice before a press conference. The announcements are straightforward and clear. There is no misunderstanding.

Many personal computer companies leak information to stir up interest and play on press rivalries. They believe the controlled leakage will generate some preannouncement excitement.

In early 1984, Apple ran advertisements for Macintosh in business and general interest publications. The *Wall Street Journal* ran a number of single-page ads. The March 3, 1984, edition of *Business Week* ran a 20-page advertising insert.

In November 1984, a $10 million advertising campaign began. The theme was "Test Drive a Macintosh." Customers were allowed to take the computer home overnight and experiment with it. This program was coupled with a sales contest in which 12 top producing salespeople won the use of a 1985 pearl-white Porsche for one year and $3,000 in cash to cover gas and other expenses.

Apple specializes in what it calls Event Marketing. This means having a highly visible event accompany a product introduction. An example was the $3 million spent to buy every inch of advertising space available in the November 1984 election week issue of *Newsweek* to introduce Macintosh and the "Test Drive a Macintosh" campaign.

Another example of Event Marketing was the introduction of the Apple IIc at San Francisco's Moscone Center. The all-day show gained considerable press coverage and highlighted Apple's new portable computer.

Apple wants its promotional campaigns and new product announcements to be daring. It is matching IBM almost dollar for dollar in advertising expenditures. Apple is raising the stakes not only on advertising expenditures but on shock value. Sculley has said Apple wants to have the most talked about advertising in the industry.

In 1984, the company terminated agreements with independent manufacturers' representatives and hired and trained a sales force of 350 to work closely with its dealers. Apple's national direct sales force of 65 to 70 people who call on corporate accounts is minuscule compared to IBM's force, estimated at 6,000 to 7,000 persons.

Distribution.   Apple distributes its products through 2,000 dealers consisting of independently owned and operated stores, franchisers, members of large chains, and department stores.

As with most distribution systems, disputes have occurred. In July 1982, Apple had a dispute with Computerland, a big franchise chain, because Apple wanted the right to approve new Computerland locations. Apple was seeking to protect its existing dealers, generally small independent retailers. When Computerland refused to go along, Apple stopped supplying its products to Computerland—though it continued to sell directly to some Computerland franchisees. These differences were eventually resolved.

In 1984, two weeks before the Macintosh introduction, Apple attempted to reconcile differences with its dealers. Sculley, Jobs, and 50 members of the Macintosh division visited with 3,000 dealer representatives to promote the new product. Jobs said, "We just openly told the dealers: we have no plans to open stores, we have no plans to sell direct to corporations, you are our future."[4]

This show of top-level support has pleased the dealers. Apple is doing business with Computerland again as well as with other chain retailers. The Macintosh and Apple II lines are also distributed through Sears Business Systems Centers and through Businessland, which caters to an exclusive business clientele.

However, small as it is, the national direct sales force of 65 to 70 people still alienates the independent dealers who provide most of Apple's revenues. The dealers accuse Apple salespeople of elbowing them out of markets by offering low-cost Macs to potential corporate customers at prices the dealers cannot match. The dealers obtain their Macs at 30 to 40 percent below suggested retail prices, and big corporate customers pay approximately the same.

Pricing.   Price competition in this industry is keen. During 1984, both manufacturers and retailers cut prices drastically. It is believed that by 1988 the IBM PC and the Macintosh will sell for $500 to $1,000. Demand in the industry is price elastic. If prices for home computers fall by 50 percent by 1988, a truly mass market will be created.

Apple's only error in pricing strategy occurred when it originally priced its IIc portable at $1,295 compared with $995 for the bigger but less powerful IIe. The seeming discrepancy between the higher price for the IIc and ads touting its portability confused consumers who did not want to pay more money for a product that looked smaller and therefore less capable than the IIe. This created a pricing fiasco because the extra value that was provided at the higher price did not come across to the consumer.

APPLE'S MAJOR COMPETITORS

Apple Computer pioneered the personal computer industry and was instrumental in creating a market for this product. The industry was literally started by Jobs and Wozniak working out of Jobs's garage. It is interesting to note that none of the big electronic firms such as ITT, National Cash Register (NCR), Hewlett-Packard, IBM, Texas Instruments, Minneapolis-Honeywell, AT&T, SONY, or a host of others developed the home computer. Many of these firms were involved with mainframe computers and small hand-held calculators. In fact, Hewlett-Packard gave its employee Steve Wozniak a release on his motherboard for a new computer because the company did not see its commercial possibilities.

Apple had immediate success and quickly gained the largest market share. By 1979, other manufacturers had entered the market. In 1981, IBM began marketing its highly successful PC. By 1984, IBM had become the dominant force in the market with a 24 percent market share. Steven Jobs said, "IBM wants to wipe us off the face of the earth."[5]

During 1983 and 1984, a number of manufacturers declared bankruptcy. This did not prevent a major new contestant from entering the field. In September 1984, AT&T began marketing the AT&T Personal Computer.

Table 5-4 shows the market share for personal computers based on the number of units sold in North America from 1981 to 1984.

IBM is Apple's major competitor. Both companies have products in just about every price range. Both companies now advertise extensively, although Apple began to do so only recently. Both companies are willing to cut price. The major differences occur in their methods of distribution and the products themselves.

Apple relies solely on its dealers (retailers). IBM uses dealers but also has an experienced direct sales force that calls on corporate accounts, and IBM Product Centers that were sold to NYNEX in July 1986.

Until 1985, Apple touted a philosophy of incompatibility with IBM. None of its products were similar to IBM's or compatible with IBM

TABLE 5-4 Market Share for Personal Computers Sold in North America, 1981–
1984 (Percent of Total Units)

Company	Year			
	1984	*1983*	*1982*	*1981*
Apple	25	26	27	40
IBM	37	35	27	7
Tandy (Radio Shack)	8	9	10	16
Hewlett-Packard	7	5	4	10
AT&T	2	0	0	0
Others	21	25	32	27
Total	100	100	100	100

Source: Author's best estimate based on average figures from various market research firms. Market share figures for each company vary among the individual firms.
Note: Percents are based on units ranging in price from $1,000 to $12,000.

software. Apple attempted to create a second industry standard. It stressed technology and how user friendly its computers are.

Beginning in 1985 with "The Macintosh Office," Apple announced a strategy of coexistence with IBM. It implemented technology that would allow Apple equipment to inferface with IBM personal computers.

COUNTERFEIT MODELS

In recent years, manufacturers in some Asian countries have become notorious for their complete indifference to trademarks, copyrights, and patents. In fighting these imitators, a company must contend with copyright and patent laws that vary among countries and are often only erratically enforced.

In 1982, Apple filed suits in Taiwan, Hong Kong, and New Zealand against counterfeiters who were producing clones of the Apple II. Taiwan was the largest producer with an estimated 2,000 to 4,500 units produced each month.

Shortly after the cloned Apple II appeared, Apple went after these small operators in an attempt to discourage larger, better-financed operators from entering the market. As of June 1982, Apple estimated that the clones had captured half the Asian market.

In January 1984, Apple was successful in protecting its software. A Taiwan court sentenced six computer company executives to eight-month prison terms for copying Apple software.

The infringement problem also exists in the United States. On August 2, 1982, Apple was denied a preliminary injunction to stop Franklin Computer Corporation from making a machine that could run all Apple II software. Apple fought Franklin for two years and eventually won a $2.5 million settlement. Franklin entered bankruptcy proceedings in July 1984.

THE EDUCATIONAL MARKET

Apple derives approximately 25 percent of its business from the educational market. Its educational marketing division is active at the primary, secondary, college, and university levels. On May 11, 1983, Apple launched its program to donate a personal computer system to every eligible public and private school in California. Many newspapers ran articles mentioning that Apple would donate computers to over 9,000 schools in California. The company maintained that its motive was philanthropic—the desire to make sure that American children are computer literate.

Training sessions for teachers and school administrators started in July to coincide with the shipments of Apple IIe computer systems. The program, which was named "The Kids Can't Wait," grew out of a year-long effort by Apple to help train students in today's technology.

Apple has also done well in the college and university market. The Apple University Consortium, a group of 24 prestigious colleges and universities, including Stanford, the University of Michigan, and the entire Ivy League, plans to order $50 million worth of Macintoshes.

Drexel University in Philadelphia also agreed to buy 3,000 Macintoshes, a large number of which would be sold to students for about $1,000.

Apple prices its products attractively for the educational market and works closely with its dealers to provide instruction and support for the educational market.

CONCLUSION

Apple Computer has been a very successful company; however, it has had two major product failures, the Apple III and Lisa. Its cash cow, the Apple II line (Apple IIe and Apple IIc), will eventually become obsolete. If Apple's new products, the Macintosh and "The Macintosh Office," are not successful, the company could be in trouble.

With the resignation of Steven Jobs and with John Sculley in control, the corporate environment may change. It could become more organized and structured, losing its entrepreneurial and innovative spirit.

It is also clear that Apple must remain a technological leader and coexist with rather than isolate itself from IBM.

QUESTIONS

1. Discuss the characteristics that make Steven P. Jobs an entrepreneur. Was Jobs a good manager?
2. Why did Steven Jobs and Stephen Wozniak make a good team for Apple?
3. Why or why not is John Sculley the right president for Apple?
4. Describe the corporate culture at Apple Computer. Is it important for a firm to have its own corporate culture?
5. Apple II has been described as a cash cow. What is a cash cow?
6. Is Macintosh important for Apple Computer's future?
7. Before John Sculley arrived at Apple, advertising was treated as an expense rather than an investment. What does this mean?
8. Has Apple won its marketing war with IBM?
9. What areas need attention if Apple aims not only at the small business market but also at the corporate market? How have Apple's markets changed over a period of time? Is Apple as successful as IBM in the business market? Why or why not?
10. Who has the best distribution system—Apple or IBM?
11. Why did AT&T enter the personal computer market in September 1984?
12. Do you prefer Apple or IBM? Why?
13. What should Apple do about the Asian counterfeit Apple II?
14. Is it a good strategy for the Apple Educational Fund to practice philanthropy towards the primary and secondary schools?
15. Discuss Apple's formula for success and how it has recently changed.

NOTES

1. John D. Cox, "Apple's Chairman Resigns," *Sacramento Bee,* September 15, 1985, p. C14.
2. Janet Guyon, "Apple Lured President from Pepsi with Patient Persuasion and Cash," *Wall Street Journal,* April 15, 1983, sec. 2, p. 29.
3. Carrie Dolan, "Apple's New Macintosh Computer Is Seen as Critical to Firm's Future," *Wall Street Journal,* December 8, 1983, sec. 2, p. 29.
4. Ann M. Morrison, "Apple Bites Back," *Fortune,* February 20, 1984, p. 91.
5. Ibid., p. 86.

6

CALIFORNIA ALMOND GROWERS EXCHANGE/BLUE DIAMOND

INTRODUCTION

All almonds commercially grown in the United States are produced in California. In 1918, California produced less than 3 percent of the world's almond crop which accounted for 25 percent of U.S. almond consumption.

Tables 6-1 and 6-2 reveal that the U.S. percentage of worldwide production of almonds has increased dramatically since 1950. By the early 1980s, California produced 60 percent of the world crop; Spain produced 20 percent; Italy, 8 percent; and all others, 12 percent.[1] The United States currently imports less than 0.5 percent of its yearly production—a dramatic reversal from 1918 when 75 percent of the almonds consumed in the United States were imported from abroad.

The California Almond Growers Exchange (hereafter called CAGE) is an agricultural cooperative formed in 1910 for the purpose of processing and marketing almonds. Its membership represents over 70 percent of the California almond growers who account for 50 percent of California's production. CAGE currently exports 60 to 70 percent of its yearly production. Most Americans are familiar with CAGE through its famous Blue Diamond label.

Over the years, the Blue Diamond growers have enjoyed an excellent rate of return. This is attributed to CAGE's excellent management and its progressive marketing strategies. However, this high rate of return and tax considerations have encouraged the planting of thousands of new acres of almonds. In 1961, 120,000 acres of almonds were under cultivation; in 1971, 255,000 acres; in 1981, 407,000 acres; and by 1985, 440,000 acres.[2]

The productivity per acre has also increased dramatically. During

TABLE 6-1 Foreign Production and U.S. Marketable Commercial Production of Almonds, 1950–1984 (Millions of Shelled Pounds)

Five-Year Averages	Foreign	U.S.	World Total	U.S. Percent of World Total
1980–1984	234.6	360.9	595.5	61
1975–1979	193.7	244.8	438.5	56
1970–1974	185.8	160.4	346.2	46
1965–1969	187.0	92.9	279.8	33
1960–1964	170.7	65.6	236.3	28
1955–1959	146.2	47.6	193.8	25
1950–1954	167.2	40.0	207.2	19

Source: Almond Board of California.

TABLE 6-2 Foreign Production and U.S. Marketable Commercial Production of Almonds, 1976–1985 (Millions of Shelled Pounds)

Year	Foreign	U.S.	World Total	U.S. Percent of World Total
1985	279.4	470.0	749.4	63
1984	202.4	563.6	766.0	74
1983	215.6	221.8	437.4	51
1982	241.9	330.8	572.7	58
1981	303.0	383.1	686.1	56
1980	210.4	305.1	515.5	59
1979	150.9	348.5	499.4	70
1978	242.4	162.4	404.8	40
1977	163.4	284.8	448.2	64
1976	228.4	258.1	486.5	53

Source: Almond Board of California.

the 1930s, the average yield per acre was 215 pounds; by 1950, it had risen to 462 pounds; by 1960, to 587 pounds; by 1970, to 876 pounds; by 1980, to 991 pounds; and by 1984, to 1,546 pounds per acre (see Table 6-3). The major reason for the exceptionally high yield per acre in 1984 was the perfect weather conditions for almonds in California.

The increased acreage coupled with a dramatic increase in productivity per acre has resulted in a continuous increase in the supply of California almonds. Between the five-year periods 1950–1954 and 1960–1964, the California supply of marketable almonds increased 39 percent; between 1970–1974 and 1980–1984, it increased 80 percent.

The marketing department of Blue Diamond did an excellent job in increasing domestic consumption and exports in the 1960s and 1970s. New products, new markets, and new uses were developed to absorb the

TABLE 6-3   California Almonds Produced per Acre, Selected Years, 1920–1984

Year	Shelled Pounds per Acre
1984	1,546
1983	679
1982	1,038
1981	1,249
1980	991
1975	755
1970	876
1965	759
1960	587
1955	473
1950	462
1940	220
1930	209
1920	187

Sources: California Crop and Livestock Reporting Service; U.S. Department of Agriculture.

ever increasing production, although supply did generally exceed demand.

It became increasingly evident by the late 1970s that the disparity between supply (production) and demand (consumption) was widening.

In 1981, California and foreign production peaked at a record high. World total consumption did not keep pace, resulting in the largest yearly surplus to date (see Table 6-4). This situation was temporarily alleviated in 1982 and 1983 when both foreign and U.S. production was substantially reduced due to unfavorable weather. In 1983, the industry experienced one of the poorest years in yield per acre in recent U.S. history.

Weather was excellent in 1984 and production in California soared to an all-time high of 564 million marketable pounds, an increase of 109 percent over 1983 production of 221 million pounds (see Table 6-2). Domestic consumption in 1984 was 131 million shelled pounds and exports accounted for an additional 267 million shelled pounds for a total consumption of 398 million shelled pounds. This resulted in a 1984 U.S. surplus of 166 million pounds (see Table 6-5).

In 1985, world production continued at a high level but world consumption took a quantum leap. In an unexpected move, the Soviet Union purchased approximately 10 percent of the California statewide harvest from Blue Diamond. This purchase reduced the 1985 world surplus. Without the Soviet purchase, the surplus would have surpassed 100 million pounds for two consecutive years, 1984 and 1985.

The trends that are causing increased production could result in world production of 1 billion shelled pounds by 1990. California would produce 700 million pounds and foreign production would total 300

TABLE 6-4 Total World Commercial Production and Consumption of Almonds, 1977–1985 (Millions of Shelled Pounds, Rounded)

Year	Total World Production	Total World Consumption	Surplus (Deficit)
1985	749	690	59
1984	766	590	176
1983	437	530	(93)
1982	573	550	23
1981	686	505	181
1980	515	470	45
1979	499	450	49
1978	405	400	5
1977	448	410	38

Source: Production data from Almond Board of California. Consumption data are estimates from the Almond Board of California.

TABLE 6-5 Marketable Production and Consumption of the California Almond Crop, 1984 (Millions of Shelled Pounds, Rounded)

Production		564
Consumption		
Domestic	131	
Export	267	
Total		398
Surplus		166

Source: Almond Board of California.

million pounds. California production as a percent of total world production would then increase from an average of 60 percent to 70 percent.

In the 1960s and 1970s, CAGE was capable of reasonably equalizing production and consumption. To repeat this task in the 1980s and 1990s will be very difficult.

Roger Baccigaluppi, president and chief executive officer of CAGE, acknowledges that he is concerned that almond farmers may be overplanting. He refers to this problem as "an opportunity to develop new products, to pioneer new markets."[3]

In early October 1985, Blue Diamond stopped accepting new members because of record 1984 and 1985 crops. Steve Easter, vice-president of member and government relative of CAGE, said, "We wanted to send a message to growers that the almond industry has more than enough supply, and it would be a mistake to plant new acreage."[4] This announcement occurred shortly before substantial new Russian purchases considerably reduced the surplus.

The Blue Diamond challenge for the remainder of the 1980s and 1990s is to expand existing markets and find new markets for an impending surplus of almonds.

In a recent annual report, CAGE has described the nature and scope of its activities as follows:

DESCRIPTION OF CALIFORNIA ALMOND GROWERS EXCHANGE

"The California Almond Growers Exchange is the largest almond processing and marketing organization in the world. It is a grower-owned cooperative that markets almonds, hazelnuts, pistachios, and macadamia nuts under the world-famous Blue Diamond label. Almonds are marketed through the Exchange on a cooperative basis, while the other nuts are marketed under the Blue Diamond label on a fee basis.

The largest almond processing plant in the world is located at its world headquarters in Sacramento, California. The Exchange owns the world's second largest almond-processing plant in Salida, California, and it leases a plant in Fullerton, California. The Exchange receives its almonds from growers who deliver at strategically located receiving stations within California's Central Valley between Red Bluff and Bakersfield. The Exchange also owns a hazelnut-processing plant in Salem, Oregon.

For marketing purposes, the Exchange has offices in Leonia, New Jersey, and in Tokyo, Japan. A network of nearly 200 brokers in the United States and abroad sell 2,000 different forms of Blue Diamond almond products and the other nuts marketed by the Exchange. Almond Plaza retail stores, which feature hundreds of gift pack items, are operated in eight locations.

Since the cooperative's inception in 1910, over half of California's total production is under the Blue Diamond label. Within the last 30 years, 88 foreign markets have been opened by the Exchange to make almonds California's leading food export."[5]

Highlights in CAGE's history are shown in Table 6-6.

OUTSTANDING INDIVIDUALS

Blue Diamond has produced two outstanding individuals, Jack Axer and Roger Baccigaluppi.

Jack Axer worked for CAGE for almost 50 years. Beginning in the Sacramento plant in 1930, Axer worked in production, doing field test grading at area receiving stations, and then in member relations until 1936 when he transferred to the sales department in New York.

After World War II, Axer came back to Sacramento to join the domestic sales department. Axer spent the next 30 years traveling worldwide to open new markets.

TABLE 6-6 California Almond Growers Exchange Highlights, 1910–1985

Year	Highlights
1910	CAGE formed by J. P. Dargitz.
	Headquarters located in San Francisco.
1913	Land purchased in Sacramento, California.
1915	Receiving and packing shed built.
1918	Blue Diamond label used on burlap bags of unshelled almonds.
1920–1930	Sacramento processing plant completed to expand shelled almonds.
1930–1940	Consumer pack expanded to East Coast.
	Shelled almonds sold in cellophane packages.
	Scientific test grading established.
	Growers assured of equitable return for quality.
1949	Blue Diamond® Almond Gift Brochure (first catalog) issued.
1940–1950	Production doubled.
1950s	Almonds exported to Japan for chocolate bars only.
1950–1960	Production doubled again.
	Smokehouse®, diced, blanched, and slivered almonds introduced as consumer products.
1961	Roger Baccigaluppi joined CAGE as a sales representative.
1966	Almond Plaza®—California's first specialty food store—opened.
1968	American Airlines adopted small foil packets of Smokehouse®-flavored almonds.
1969	Sales of almonds to Japan reached $3 million.
1969	Quaker Oats began using almonds in 100% natural cereal.
1960–1970	Mechanized harvesting and advanced agricultural practices doubled per acre output.
1970	Blue Diamond became one of the top ten food mail order businesses in the United States.
1973	Almonds exported to India.
1975	First full time consumer salesperson hired.
	Almonds used in granola bars.
1979	Sales of almonds to Japan reached $30 million.
1981	Bio-mass cogeneration plant to burn almond shells for steam and electricity became operational.
1981	Almond Research Center established.
	CAGE began marketing hazelnuts produced by Oregon Filbert Growers, "Blue Diamond Hazelnuts."
	H. J. Heinz began marketing Blue Diamond products for CAGE to institutional market (restaurants).
1982	Department of Military Sales established.
1982	CAGE began marketing pistachios produced by Pistachio Producers of California, "Blue Diamond Pistachios."
1982	Blue Diamond began marketing macadamia nuts.
	U.S. school lunch program established.
	Almond butter program revived.
1983	Almond Plaza® Visitors Center opened.
1985	The Soviet Union became the second largest export market and took 10% of California crop (17% of total exports).

Source: California Almond Growers Exchange/Blue Diamond.

In 1960, he was named vice-president and export manager, a position he held until his retirement in 1974. He has been a marketing consultant at CAGE since 1974.

Axer is part of a team that has analyzed domestic and foreign markets for all types of commercial nuts, including almonds, hazelnuts, cashews, walnuts, and pecans. Extensive information has been gathered on producers, processors, marketing systems, distributors, users, and consumers. His series of articles titled "Competitive Tree Nuts," which appeared in *Almond Facts,* a CAGE publication, provides insights as to the depth of the studies.

For example, in discussing the interaction of almonds and hazelnuts in the German market, he points out that Germans thought of edible nuts as almonds and hazelnuts. Walnuts were a secondary nut and Germans possessed minimal knowledge of peanuts, cashews, or pecans.

Almonds were utilized in the form of almond paste. Hazelnuts, until recently, were used as a component of chocolate bars and as an in-shell nut. Their secondary usage was as a sweetened paste that possessed a different taste and texture than almond paste. This detailed analysis and interpretation of data was done on all markets that Blue Diamond entered.

Axer personally opened each of the 88 foreign markets. His 50 years with Blue Diamond have given him more experience in the industry than any other individual in the Western Hemisphere.

Roger Baccigaluppi, president and chief executive officer, joined CAGE in 1961 as a sales representative. He has a bachelor's degree in business administration from the University of California at Berkeley, and an M.B.A. from Columbia University. Baccigaluppi's former career was in advertising in San Francisco. His first accomplishment was persuading supermarket managers to stock Blue Diamond's six-ounce cans. He was instrumental in convincing American Airlines to adopt the small foil packets of Smokehouse almonds. He established the first Almond Plaza, Blue Diamond's Sacramento retail store. He assisted in the development of the Japanese market. His corporate rise has paralleled Blue Diamond's spectacular growth over the past two decades. He and his team are responsible for developing new products and nontraditional markets. New products have included specially flavored almonds (snack foods), almond butter, almond paste, almond candy, almond cooking oil, and others. Nontraditional markets include both foreign markets, especially Western Europe and the Far East, and new domestic markets such as airlines, Almond Plaza stores, fund-raising organizations, the military, and others.

Baccigaluppi travels abroad extensively. Between 1968 and 1981, he made 22 trips to Japan alone. He has served in the following capacities at Blue Diamond from 1961 to the present: sales representative, manager of advertising and sales promotion, vice-president of marketing, senior vice-president, and president and chief executive officer.

MAJOR COMPETITORS

Blue Diamond's two largest competitors are Tenneco West, a division of Tenneco Oil in Bakersfield, California, and the T. M. Duche Nut Company of Orland, California. Market share figures are difficult to arrive at because all firms are highly secretive and each has a different Standard Industrial Classification Number. Best estimates are that Blue Diamond has a 50 to 60 percent market share; Tenneco, 15 to 20 percent; and Duche, 10 to 15 percent. These three firms control approximately 95 percent of almond sales in the United States.

All three firms are marketing a new product called almond butter. Almond butter is similar to peanut butter but retails at twice the price. Roger Baccigaluppi believes that almond butter manufacturers could eventually purchase about half the domestic total for almond consumption. Major peanut butter manufacturers are currently reluctant to take on this new product until the supply of almonds is increased. Another problem is its price. In 1984, shelled almonds used for processing in other products sold for $1.20 a pound. Almond butter processors were charged $0.60 a pound. It appears that the almond industry is willing to subsidize almond butter until a market is developed for this new product.

CAGE began test marketing its Blue Diamond almond butter in February 1984. Two flavors are produced, plain and honey-cinnamon, in both smooth and crunchy versions. Retailers are having trouble keeping almond butter on the shelf although CAGE's Northern California peanut butter maker is producing 40,000 pounds of almond butter a week.

Tenneco West, which produces the Sun Giant brand and runs a chain of House of Almonds specialty stores, has four versions of almond butter—smooth and crunchy, with or without salt. Tenneco began selling all four in January 1984 through its 33 House of Almonds stores and its gift catalog, and has achieved success comparable to Blue Diamond's. The company's new five-year plan will expand its House of Almonds chain from 33 to 250 stores. Tenneco will continue to produce and market its own house brand of almond butter.

Duche offers its Gourmet Nut Center brand of almond butter in about 50 stores in California and Hawaii. Its major strategy is to promote the spread as an ingredient for manufacturers and processors in the United States and abroad. Duche will concentrate its efforts on the candy, bakery, cereal, yogurt, and ice cream markets.

Tenneco West's new products in addition to almond butter are a line of almond oil–based salad dressings, and beauty products ranging from shampoos to shaving creams. Tenneco has the most ambitious plans of the three in the new product development area.

DOMESTIC MARKETING

Blue Diamond almonds are used in more than 2,000 products in 88 countries. About 50 products are sold under the Blue Diamond label.

Blue Diamond segments its product lines into the following three market segments:

Consumer (retail)
Food service (wholesale)
Industrial (processors and manufacturers)

Its retail market (Blue Diamond label) has grown rapidly in recent years. Major retail outlets are supermarkets, discount houses, variety stores, drug stores, and others. Its first company store, which opened in 1966, was California's first specialty food store. Currently there are eight retail stores called Almond Plazas. Its gift pack outfit, which was established in 1949, is one of the ten largest food mail order operations in the United States.

Blue Diamond's retail market is further divided according to package type and user.

Tin   Airplane
Foil   Fund raising
Cello   Food service
Glass   Military
Gift Pack
Bulk
In-shell

In 1981, CAGE purchased the Oregon Filbert Growers and began marketing their hazelnuts under its Blue Diamond label.

In 1982, CAGE entered into an agreement with the Pistachio Producers of California, a cooperative, to market Blue Diamond pistachios for a fee. A similar agreement was concluded in 1982 with Mac Farms of Hawaii to market macadamia nuts under the Blue Diamond label.

Although retail is a growth segment and more visible than products sold in bulk to food manufacturers, it should be remembered that the majority of sales are still to buyers who use almonds as an ingredient (see Table 6-7).

TABLE 6-7 U.S. Almond Consumption by Product Category (Percent of Total)

Product Category	1990[a]	1983	1970
Confectionary manufacturers	18.0	25.0	38.0
Nut salters	14.0	15.0	23.0
Ice cream	12.0	12.0	11.0
Bakers	2.0	2.0	10.0
Food processors	8.0	9.0	8.0
In shell	2.0	3.0	6.0
Food service institutions	12.0	6.5	4.0
Almond butter	10.0	4.5	0.0
Consumer products and health food	22.0	23.0	0.0
Total	100.0	100.0	100.0

[a] Estimated.

Source: California Almond Growers Exchange/Blue Diamond.

Wholesale markets have also been expanded and new wholesale markets have been developed among manufacturers of cookies, ice cream, pastries, processed vegetables, granola bars, cereals, candy, cheese logs, and other products.

Following are some of Blue Diamond's important recent product and market accomplishments:

1968	American Airlines began serving almonds to its customers.
1969	Quaker Oats began using almonds in its 100 percent Natural cereal. Today cereal manufacturers are among CAGE's ten largest customers.
1975	Granola Bars began using almonds.
1981	H. J. Heinz Company began marketing Blue Diamond almonds for CAGE to restaurants and the institutional trade.
1982	U.S. school lunch program was established.
1982	Almond butter program was revived.

Blue Diamond's basic forms of promotion consist of advertising and personal selling. Advertising is almost totally print, namely, newspapers and magazines. It is segmented to reach the appropriate consumer—retail, wholesale, institutional, and industrial market.

The sales force is led by a director of sales for the United States and a director of sales for foreign markets. Both individuals report to the vice-president of marketing.

The domestic sales force is small, consisting of approximately 15 people. CAGE uses food brokers to sell its extensive line of products, believing this to be the best and most economic method. Personnel work closely with brokers to monitor, review, and guide them in protecting existing markets and building new ones. These long-term relationships are based on mutual assistance, cooperation, and benefit to both parties. Even though it uses food brokers, CAGE's staff knows every customer personally and deals directly with large, long-term customers (key accounts) such as Hershey's.

In November 1983, CAGE opened a new Almond Plaza Visitors Center in Sacramento, California. This major tourist attraction contains a permanent exhibition of the history, cultivation, and uses of the almond. The complex also includes an Almond Plaza Gift Center, a cooking and recipe center, a 230-seat film and theater facility, and an International Center with multilanguage translation facilities.[6] Guests are taken on a free factory tour and can sample free almond tastings. The new center showcases the cooperative's role as exporter to 88 nations. The old center received 25,000 visitors in 1982. The new center hopes to double that.

FOREIGN MARKETS

General Characteristics. CAGE exports to 88 countries and has 88 strategies. To analyze this situation is beyond the scope of this case. After discussing foreign markets in general, the profile of two countries will be emphasized: Japan and India. When dealing with exports, it is important to note the various controlling laws of the countries involved, the duties that must be paid, and the monetary rate of exchange.

There are fundamentally two markets for almonds determined by quality or price. CAGE pursues the quality market in its strategy and allows all its competitors to fight over the price markets. One other generality can be made about all 88 markets: the greatest percentage of exports is for industrial usage. This is primarily because the duties on processed goods range from 100 percent to 300 percent higher than those on unprocessed goods.

Table 6-8 shows exports of California almonds by destination in percentage from 1976 to 1985.

Western Europe is the largest consumer of export sales and the greatest competitive arena. The European product line is similar to that in the United States with three exceptions: a larger quantity of lower-quality almonds are used, most almonds sold must be blanchable, and ice cream manufacturers will not use nuts. Food brokers are used. They negotiate with customers and communicate with CAGE by telex.

West Germany is the largest export market with 25 percent of CAGE's total exports. Japan has historically been second, and France third. In a rather unexpected move, the Soviet Union entered the market in 1984–1985 to become second. The Soviets had switched their purchases from hazelnuts to almonds, due to a short hazelnut supply in Turkey.

The European Community (Common Market) is primarily a price market and CAGE has a policy of nonintervention in price wars. It

TABLE 6-8 Exports of California Almonds by Destination, 1976–1985 (Percent of Total)

Destinations	1984–1985	1983–1984	1982–1983	Five-Year Average 1976–1981
West Germany	24	23	25	35
Japan	12	19	16	12
France	6	8	8	8
USSR	17	—	1	5
Canada	5	7	7	5
India	2	1	2	1
All Others	34	42	41	34
Total	100	100	100	100

Note: Years run from July through June.
Source: Almond Board of California.

attempts to keep its prices uniform worldwide. Spain has been successfully selling to the European market but its production and marketing systems are inefficient and this offsets the transportation advantage it has over CAGE. As a result, Spain offers a lower-quality almond at approximately the same price.

Other competitors in the European market are Duche and Tenneco. They do not have the resources for market innovations and use a follow-the-leader strategy. CAGE has left the price market in the European Community to its competitors since it is already entrenched in the quality market.

Almonds are elastic in demand and CAGE's successful marketing efforts have increased almond consumption. Competitors know they can increase sales by lowering prices.

The relative strength of the United States dollar compared to other currencies has a direct effect on almond exports. During the 1970s, exports to most countries showed a substantial increase. The dollar declined in value against other currencies and this made it easier for foreign citizens to purchase almonds.

This situation reversed itself by 1980 when a weakened export market developed, especially in Germany and France. As the dollar strengthened, the absolute price of almonds rose. For example, in August 1980 a pound of almonds, which cost $1.88 in U.S. dollars, cost 3.4 German marks; in 1982, however, a pound of almonds, which cost $1.57 in U.S. dollars, cost 4.1 German marks or approximately 20 percent more despite a decline in the dollar price of 16 percent.

In the 1982–1983 annual report year, industry shipments of California almonds in pounds to Western Europe were down 20 percent over the previous year. Shipments to West Germany were down 32 percent and in France shipments declined by 12 percent. A strong dollar forced many buyers to purchase more than the usual supply of almonds from Spain and Italy.

In Asia, the story is very different. Asia is strictly a quality market and a newer expanding market for California almonds. Also, the dollar's strength was not as pronounced against some of the Asian currencies during this period. In the 1982–1983 annual report year, industry shipment of California almonds in pounds to Asia were up 14 percent over the previous year. In Japan, shipments were up 22 percent; in Taiwan shipments were up 25 percent; however, in India shipments were down 26 percent.

By mid-1985, the dollar had again weakened and exports soared. The 1984–1985 year saw California almond exports increase worldwide by 56 percent, with Western Europe up 37 percent, and Asia up 9 percent with no change for Japan. In the 1983–1984 year, shipments to the Soviet Union were nil. In the 1984–1985 year, the Soviet Union became the second largest importer of almonds following West Germany.

Japan. Japan and the USSR are now the fastest-growing major markets in the world for California almonds. Almond consumption in Japan has been steadily rising and the Japanese now consume at an average annual rate of one-quarter pound per person. In 1955, almonds were almost unknown in Japan—except in the chocolate trade. Almonds were not grown and imports were insignificant. As the Japanese traveled abroad in the 1950s and 1960s, they tasted almonds in a new way through desserts, entrees, and pastries. Thus, demand grew slowly.

The first shipment of almonds to Japan was in 1955. The Nisson Trading Company served as agents. The decision to sell almonds to Japan was part of an overall strategy to develop a new market—not simply to dump surplus almonds. At that time, CAGE was experiencing record sales overseas because a European crop failure had reduced an important source of almonds. CAGE made a strategic decision to commit to the Japanese market by fulfilling two essential requirements of that market: quality almonds and assured supply at stable prices.

Although the Nisson Trading Company had exclusive rights to market Blue Diamond products, they were ineffective in some markets; therefore, exclusive rights to market Blue Diamond products were given to several trading companies who specialized in compatible food areas. This agent system had its weaknesses. It was adequate for servicing existing market sectors, but did little in terms of further developing or expanding those markets. To remedy this situation, CAGE opened a market development office in 1969 in Tokyo under the direction of Masuo Koga.

This office currently employs 54 Japanese staff members and is charged with coming up with ideas and techniques to develop more almond consumption in Japan. The employees are divided into teams according to their assigned areas which include bulk sales, retail snack sales, and advertising and market development. This office is credited with a major distribution breakthrough in the snack market sector in 1975 when Masuo Koga persuaded Kinki Coca-Cola Bottling Company of Osaka, said to be Coca-Cola's largest bottler in the world, to take on the Blue Diamond line. By 1984, all 17 of Japan's Coca-Cola Bottling Companies sold almonds directly to supermarkets and other retail outlets, thereby bypassing the costly distribution channels.

In 1972, CAGE/Japan was established with Masuo Koga as senior managing director. This organization is the marketing arm of CAGE in Japan. The market development office is located in Japan and marketing functions such as research, pricing, advertising, sales, product promotion, and special events are performed by this office. CAGE does not use brokers in Japan; it maintains its own sales force.

Distribution in the Japanese market is costly and complex because of the numerous middlemen involved in getting products from the processor to the numerous users or consumers. CAGE's response has been to use different distribution strategies for the three market sectors, confectionery (40%), baking (40%), and snack (20%).

In the confectionery and baking sectors, CAGE sells almonds to different trading companies that resell to numerous wholesalers or distributors who serve their respective markets. CAGE's general sales manager in Tokyo works directly with industrial customers who buy large quantities in bulk. This strategy has spurred innovation and the development of new markets.

An interesting aspect of marketing almonds in Japan is the role that food plays as a social and cultural event. All young girls go to special cooking schools as does anyone planning to make a career in the food industry. CAGE employs ten full-time cooking instructors, and Blue Diamond almonds are part of the curriculum of the 900 Japanese cooking schools. Every year CAGE sponsors over 60 cooking students to travel to California. This event is filmed and 60 million Japanese citizens view it upon their return. The exchange sponsors TV cooking shows, contests, and many other events. Almonds are part of the Japanese school lunch program and are promoted as a highly nutritional basic ingredient.

The Japanese are the most innovative importers of almonds.

The list of new products developed in the Japanese market seems endless. As in the United States, the majority of almonds are sold as an ingredient in other products. These include chocolate products, bakery goods and cookies, rice cracker products, granola bars, cheese and ice cream with almonds, a spread filling for the Japanese school lunch program, a ready-to-fry frozen fish with almonds, Chinese noodles with almonds, sausages, curried rice, almond milk, and almond soap and cosmetics.[7]

There are even almond salami rolls, almond spagetti sauce, and almond-flavored tofu.

Japanese consumers respond to almonds because they have Western glamour, California glamour, and a high nutritional profile.

The Japanese Trade Center in San Francisco cites Blue Diamond as one of America's most successful exporters to the Japanese market. The 1953 market of less than 100 tons (200,000 pounds) grew to 32 million pounds a year by 1985. This market is expected to double by 1990 and surpass West Germany and the USSR to become CAGE's major export market. CAGE's Tokyo office is also targeting South Korea and Taiwan as future big markets.

India.   India's 1985 population of 700 million people makes it the second most heavily populated country in the world. This could make India one of the almond industry's largest markets.

The mystique surrounding the almond in India is interesting. Many Indians think of the almond as a brain food. Because almonds are thought to sharpen the intellect, businessmen and government officials frequently soak a half dozen or so of the nuts in water the night before an important meeting and consume them in the morning. Almonds also serve as indicators of prestige and status. They are used as a snack, for baking, as a refreshing drink, in confections, as a cosmetic, and in pharmaceutical products. The almond provides a nutritious alternative to India's generally vegetarian diet.

The two major obstacles that have prohibited the expansion of this potentially large market have been quotas and import duties (tariffs). In 1977, when India removed all restrictions on the amount of almonds that could be imported, the purchase of California almonds doubled to 2 million pounds.

In 1984, the import duties were reduced from 185 percent to 130 percent. CAGE said the effect was a reduction in the wholesale price of California almonds of better than 33 percent.

The effect of the tariff reduction coupled with a weaker dollar caused exports to India to increase 64 percent in 1984–1985 with a market value of $14 million.

Import duties are important to the Indian government because they generate 85 percent of its revenues. Although a 130-percent import duty may seem unreasonably high to some, a further reduction will require creative negotiations by CAGE, the U.S. Agricultural Counselor and trade representatives, and Indian government officials.

CONCLUSION

Almonds are California's largest food export. Every single export market enjoyed by the almond industry today was opened by Blue Diamond. An average of 60 percent of the California crop is exported and this figure will rise to 70 percent by 1990. Had it not been for the export market, the almond industry in California would not be what it is today.

CAGE has aided in achieving a 50-percent reduction in almond duties worldwide and is an avid supporter of free trade. That CAGE has become one of the world's leading exporters is due to three factors:

1. Careful long-range planing
2. Aggressive marketing practices
3. Excellence in brand promotion

By 1990, California will produce 70 percent of the world's almonds. CAGE has excelled in finding new uses and markets for almonds; however, the spread between supply and demand remains. CAGE's major effort should be to increase consumption in both the domestic and export markets.

QUESTIONS

1. What is an agricultural cooperative?
2. Why does CAGE use food brokers in the United States and its own sales force in Japan?
3. Is Roger Baccigaluppi qualified to be president of CAGE?
4. Why did CAGE enter into an agreement with H. J. Heinz to have them market Blue Diamond products to the institutional market (restaurants)?
5. Why did CAGE add hazelnuts in 1981 and pistachios and macadamia nuts in 1982?
6. Draw some conclusions about consumer behavior in the export market.
7. Would a lower duty on almonds entering India be in the best interest of the Indian government and its citizens?
8. How would a weaker dollar affect almond export sales?
9. Tenneco plans to expand its House of Almond specialty stores from 33 to 250. Should CAGE increase its number of stores?
10. CAGE must expand consumption. Should the primary emphasis be placed on the domestic or export market?
11. What barriers does CAGE face when entering foreign markets?
12. What conclusions can be drawn on the development of the Japanese market for almonds?

13. Almond butter costs almost twice as much as peanut butter. Why is the industry pushing almond butter?

NOTES

1. Almond Board of California.
2. Almond Board of California.
3. Mike Dunne, "Cans of Nuts Brings Sacks of Dollars," *Sacramento Bee,* July 20, 1981, p. C1.
4. "Almond Co-op Stops Taking New Members," *San Francisco Chronicle,* October 12, 1985, p. 52.
5. 1982–1983 California Almond Growers Exchange Annual Report, p. 1.
6. "Best New Show in Town" (advertisement), *Sacramento Bee,* November 13, 1983, p. B4.
7. 1982–1983 Annual Report, p. 10.

7

United States Football League (USFL)

INTRODUCTION

The sports world is filled with big money makers and big money losers. This is the story of a possible loser, the United States Football League (USFL), whose teams lost more than $163 million in its first three years—1983, 1984, and 1985.

Football is big business in the United States. The National Football League (NFL) was founded in 1920. It currently consists of 28 teams, 14 in the National Football Conference and 14 in the American Football Conference. Over the years, the league has been very successful, with total team revenues staying comfortably ahead of their expenses. In 1984, however, conditions began to change. With the arrival of the USFL, player salaries began to escalate and team player expenses began to exceed combined broadcast revenues, which account for more than 60 percent of total revenues.[1] With gate receipts, NFL teams are still able to show a profit.

The first new league to challenge the NFL was the American Football League (AFL), which was founded in 1960. The AFL was successful right from the beginning. Most of the teams were located in cities that did not have an NFL franchise. Game attendance was good as were TV ratings. The NFL was televised on CBS, and the AFL was on NBC. In a short period of time, the AFL became so good that Joe Namath and the New York Jets beat the Baltimore Colts of the NFL 16 to 7 in an upset in the Super Bowl playoff of 1969. In 1970, the 11 teams of the AFL merged into the NFL to form a single league. This new league dominated the TV networks, using CBS and NBC as well as ABC for Monday night football that began in 1970.

The revenues, salaries, and value of an NFL franchise are significant. The 1985 network television contracts returned $15 million per year for each team in the league.

Salaries are also impressive; a handful of superstars earned over $1 million a year. The average salary is $130,000. Randy White, the All-Pro defensive tackle of the Dallas Cowboys, earns $700,000 a year. In 1984, salaries increased by an average of 23 percent.

An NFL franchise is expensive. In 1984, the Dallas Cowboys were sold for $60 million and the Denver Broncos for $45 million. The original owner of any NFL team has seen a tremendous appreciation in the value of his franchise. He has been able to accelerate depreciation charges (a player is an asset that can be depreciated) and most teams have shown consistent profits.

In 1974, another league was born. The World Football League (WFL) consisted of 12 teams. Its season ran from June to November and a number of its rules differed from those of the NFL. Its contract with CBS netted each team $100,000, a small sum considering that the average NFL team averaged $1 million per season in 1974.

Play started in July to give the WFL a jump on the NFL and college games. Nothing went right. A scandal surfaced when officials of the Philadelphia Bells and Jacksonville Sharks confessed to inflating attendance figures. Some 44,000 freebees were handed out to Shark fans for the team's first two home games. A whopping 100,000 tickets went to Bell spectators. The press discovered that other teams engaged in the same practice and the league lost its credibility.

In 1974, every team had huge losses. A number of teams moved their franchises during the year, and two teams, the Detroit Wheels and Chicago Fire, went broke. Most players were never paid and superstars tried to break their contracts.

The league was reorganized and WFL II began in July 1975. Attendance was very low. Players remained unpaid, and in some cases, gate receipts could not even cover fixed expenses such as stadium rental. At midseason, the league went into bankruptcy. Attendance for the last week of play averaged 13,371.

Football's most recent arrival is the USFL, which consisted of 12 teams in 1983. Its season ran from February to July and its game and rules were very similar to those of the NFL.

A major difference between the WFL and USFL was that the USFL teams were well financed. Each team contributed $1.5 million to a league kitty that would be used to protect the league and financially troubled teams. Another $4.5 million was set aside by each team to cover anticipated losses. First-year franchises sold for $1.5 million. Original estimates were that each team would lose $6 million over the first three years. This league planned for heavy losses in its introductory stage.

Estimated losses for 1983 were $40 million.[2] The league champions,

TABLE 7-1 United States Football League Key Statistics, 1983–1985

	1985	1984	1983
Number of teams	14	18	12
Losses (millions)	$60	$63	$40
Average loss per team (millions)	$ 4.3	$ 3.5	$ 3.3
Average attendance (regular season)	24,494	27,126	24,824
TV ratings[a]			
ABC Sports	4.1	5.5	6.0
ESPN	2.0	2.9	3.3

[a] Each rating point = 900,000 viewers.
Sources: USFL; ABC Sports; ESPN.

the Michigan Panthers, incurred a $6 million loss. Only one team, the Denver Gold, had a minimal profit.

In 1984, the USFL was expanded to 18 teams. Six of the original 12 teams changed hands and 6 new teams joined the league. Second-year franchises sold for $6.25 million. Ownership of the New Jersey Generals exchanged hands for $6 million, followed by the Chicago Blitz for $7 million and the Washington Generals for $8 million.

Despite a 9-percent increase in average attendance during the regular 1984 season, the average loss per team continued to increase and TV ratings continued to decrease (see Table 7-1).

The only team to turn a profit was the Tampa Bay Bandits who earned $800,000. Even the league champions, the Philadelphia Stars, lost $2 million. The combined losses of the USFL in 1984 were $63 million.

The 1985 season was even more dismal. It began in February with 14 teams. Midway through the season, the league bailed out the financially troubled Los Angeles Express for the rest of the season. Average attendance decreased 10 percent and the average loss per team continued to increase. Network TV ratings decreased about 30 percent and the combined losses of the USFL in 1985 were $60 million (see Table 7-1).

HISTORY

Origins of the USFL. The entrepreneur behind the USFL was David F. Dixon, a 59-year-old New Orleans art dealer who observed that this country had an insatiable appetite for football. Dixon began his quest in 1980 and put the USFL together from the ground up. He spent 1981 and 1982 searching for owners, often accompanied by his son, Shea, an attorney, or John Falston, a former NFL coach who was the league's first full-time employee.

Dixon informed the would-be owners how much they could lose, but he also told them that an investment of $1.5 million could someday be worth $50 million. A substantial number of the original investors were very wealthy and the league had a stronger financial base than the defunct WFL.

The original goals of the USFL were clearly defined and understood. The premise was to establish a competitive but minor-league summertime diversion to provide a relatively low-cost type of television programming. The USFL-televised games were to replace some of the marginal spring sports. The league was to limit itself to players no higher than an NFL fourth-round draft choice. It was not to raid or entice players away from the NFL with huge salaries. Its TV revenues, which were substantially higher than the WFL's, but nowhere near the NFL's, were to cover player salaries (see Table 7-2).

The formation of the USFL was announced at a press conference in New York City on May 11, 1982. The franchise areas include Los Angeles, New Jersey, Chicago, Denver, Oakland, Philadelphia, Tampa Bay, Arizona, and Birmingham.

The opening game was March 6, 1983. Between May 11, 1982, and March 6, 1983, the following list of significant events occurred.

1. USFL and ABC Sports entered into a two-year television agreement.
2. Chester R. Simmons was named commissioner of the USFL.
3. USFL teams hired "big name" coaches such as Chuck Fairbanks, "Red" Miller, George Allen, and John Ralston.
4. USFL and ESPN entered into a two-year national cable agreement.
5. USFL teams signed agreement to play in major sports stadiums such as the Liberty Bowl, Superdome, and Silverdome.
6. Commissioner Simmons announced plans for a territorial drafting system for college athletes.
7. Heisman Trophy winner, Herschel Walker, was signed to USFL.

United States Football League, 1983 Season.   By the end of the first year, many people characterized the league as being shaky. The use of many marginal collegiate players and former NFL players made the game sloppy and unexciting. The league lost $40 million with only the Denver Gold showing a modest profit. The TV rating of 6.0 was sufficient for the ABC network to earn a profit (5.0 was the break-even point), but below the desired 7.0 rating. Average attendance was 25,000—lower than the desired 35,000.

The ground rules were broken with the signing of Herschel Walker, which resulted in escalating player salaries.

Table 7-3 outlines the USFL structure in 1983.

1984 Season.   The 1984 season began with a number of changes. Six new franchises were added to bring the total to 18 teams with 6 teams changing ownership. Several big-name players were signed, including

TABLE 7-2 Comparison of Marketing Mix and Other Selected Factors for the NFL, WFL, and USFL

	NFL	WFL	USFL
Number of teams	1973 26 1985 28	1974 12 1975 12	1983 12 1984 18 1985 14
Market potential of U.S. population (target market)	1974 60% 1985 70%	1974 35% 1985 0	1983 40% 1984 35% 1985 25%
Average paid attendance (customers)	1975 50,000 1984 60,000	1974 20,000 1975 15,000	1983 24,824 1984 27,126 1985 24,494
Average TV revenue per team	1974 $1 million 1985 $15 million	1974 $100,000 1975 $100,000	1983 $1.5 million 1984 $2.3 million 1985 $2.5 million
Time	Fall	Fall	1983–1985 Spring-Summer 1986 Fall
Rules of the game (product)	Standard	Different from NFL	Basically, same as NFL
Location (distribution)	Big cities Large TV markets	Mostly NFL cities	1983 Most NFL cities 1985 Only 5 NFL cities
Players (product)	Superstars, 12–15 blue chip players, 30 fill-ins	Raided NFL for superstars, 2–3 blue chip players; rest fill-in	Raided NFL & colleges for superstars, Heisman Trophy winners, 2–3 blue chip players; rest fill-ins
Promotion	Strong	Strong	Strong
Pricing	Competitive	Competitive	Competitive

Sources: National Football League; World Football League; United States Football League.

TABLE 7-3 United States Football League Structure, 1983

Team	Owner	Coach	Stadium & Capacity (rounded)
Arizona Wranglers	Jim Joseph	Doug Shively	Sun Devil Stadium (70,000)
Birmingham Stallions	Gradford Liebman Marvin Warner	Rollie Dotsch	Legion Field (75,000)
Boston Breakers	George Mathews	Dick Coury	Nickerson Field (21,000)
Chicago Blitz	Ed Diethrich	George Allen	Soldier Field (65,000)
Denver Gold	Ron Blanding	Red Miller	Mile High Stadium (75,000)
Los Angeles Express	Bill Daniels	Hugh Campbell	LA Coliseum (93,000)
Michigan Panthers	Alfred Taubman Max Fisher	Jim Stanley	Silverdome (81,000)
New Jersey Generals	J. Walter Duncan	Chuck Fairbanks	Giant Stadium (77,000)
Oakland Invaders	Tad Taube	John Ralson	Oakland Coliseum (55,000)
Philadelphia Stars	Myles Tanenbaum	Jim Mora	Veterans Stadium (72,000)
Tampa Bay Bandits	John Bassett	Steve Spurrier	Tampa Stadium (72,000)
Washington Federals	Berl Bernhard	Ray Jauch	RFK Stadium (55,000)

Source: USFL Media Guide.

Mike Rozier and Steve Young. Team payrolls leaped from an average of $1.8 million to $2.8 million, representing 40 percent of the average team's budget.

Despite the attraction of more superstars, the TV rating fell to 5.5, which was a disappointment to the owners and players but still allowed ABC to earn a modest profit. ABC was not too disturbed because all three networks had experienced a decline in ratings in virtually all sports programming since 1981.

Despite average attendance increasing 9 percent from 24,824 in 1983 to 27,126 in 1984, the combined losses of the league was $82 million (see Table 7-1).

Table 7-4 outlines the USFL structure in 1984.

1985 Season.   The significant preseason events were the signing of Doug Flutie with the New Jersey Generals, the appointment of Harry Usher as the new league commissioner, and the reduction of the league from 18 to 14 teams. The following changes caused the reductions and name changes:

1.   Michigan merged with Oakland.
2.   Oklahoma merged with Arizona.
3.   Pittsburg merged with Philadelphia and moved to Baltimore.
4.   Chicago Blitz was not playing in 1985, but technically was not closed.
5.   New Orleans moved to Portland.
6.   Washington moved to Orlando.

Table 7-5 shows the 1985 location cities and the season tickets sold by the USFL prior to the opening of the season. Table 7-1 illustrates the continuing eroding statistics of the league.

1986 Season.   In 1986 the USFL was scheduled to field only eight teams. Gone are the Los Angeles Express, operated in 1985 at league expense, the Oakland Invaders, losers in the 1985 title game, the San Antonio Gunslingers, and the Portland Breakers. The Denver Gold merged with the Jacksonville Bulls, and the Houston Gamblers were purchased by Donald Trump and merged with the New Jersey Generals.

The remaining eight teams for the 1986 season were:

Arizona Wranglers
Baltimore Stars
Birmingham Stallions
Jacksonville Bulls
Memphis Showboats
New Jersey Generals
Orlando Federals
Tampa Bay Bandits

TABLE 7-4 United States Football League Structure, 1984

Team	Owner & Coach	Key Players	Stadium & Capacity (rounded)
New Jersey Generals	O Donald Trump	QB Brian Sipe	Giant Stadium
	C Walt Michaels	RB Herschel Walker	(77,000)
Philadelphia Stars	O Myles Tananbaum	QB Chuck Fusina	Veterans Stadium
	C Jim Mora	RB Kelvin Bryant	(72,000)
Pittsburgh Maulers	O Edward Debartalo	QB Blenn Carano	Three River Stadium
	C Joe Pendry	RB Mike Rozier	(59,000)
Washington Federals	O Berl Benhard	QB Reggie Collier	RFK Stadium
	C Ray Jauch	RB Craig James	(55,000)
Birmingham Stallions	O Marvin L. Warner	QB Cliff Stoudt	Legion Field
	C Rollie Dotsch	WR Jim Smith	(77,000)
Tampa Bay Bandits	O John Bassett	QB John Reaves	Tampa Stadium
	O Bert Reynolds	RB Gary Anderson	(72,000)
	C Steve Spurrier		
New Orleans Breakers	O Joe Canizaro	QB Johnnie Walters	Superdome
	C Dick Coury	RB Marcus Marek	(73,000)
Memphis Showboats	O William Dunavan	QB Walter Lewis	Liberty Bowl
	C Pepper Rodgers	DE Reggie White	(50,000)

Team		Owner/Coach	Pos	Player	Stadium
Jacksonville Bulls	O	Fred Bullard	QB	Matt Robinson	Gator Bowl (80,000)
	C	Lindy Infante	DT	Don Latimer	
Michigan Panthers	O	Alfred Taufman	QB	Bobby Hebert	Silverdome (81,000)
	C	Jim Stanley	WR	Anthony Carter	
Chicago Blitz	O	Dr. James Hoffman	QB	Vince Evans	Soldier Field (65,000)
	C	Marv Levy	DB	Mark Rush	
Houston Gamblers	O	Bernard Lerner	QB	Jim Kelly	Astrodome (51,000)
	O	Dr. Jerry Argovite	RB	Mark Rush	
	C	Jack Pardee			
Oklahoma Outlaws	O	William Tatham	QB	Doug Williams	Skelly Stadium (41,000)
	C	Woody Widenhofer			
San Antonio Gunslingers	O	Clinton Manges	QB	Rick Neuheisel	Alamo Stadium (32,000)
	C	Gil Steinke	WR	Danney Buggs	
Arizona Wranglers	O	Dr. Ted Diethrich	QB	Greg Landry	Sun Devil Stadium (70,000)
	C	George Allen	RB	Tim Spender	
Los Angeles Express	O	William Oldenburg	AB	Steve Young	L.A. Coliseum (93,000)
	C	John Haci	DT	Eddie Weaver	
Oakland Invaders	O	Tad Taube	QB	Fred Besana	Oakland Coliseum (55,000)
	C	John Ralston	RB	A. Whittington	
Denver Gold	O	Ron Blanding	DE	Dave Stalls	Mile High Stadium (75,000)
	C	Craig Morton			

Source: USFL Media Guide.

95

TABLE 7-5   USFL Season Tickets Sold through February 18, 1984 and 1985

Team	1985	1984	Change Number	%	Stadium Capacity (rounded)
Arizona	12,000	18,500	(6,500)	(35)	70,000
Baltimore[a]	16,000	15,477	523	3	45,000
Denver	18,000	23,000	(5,000)	(22)	75,000
Birmingham	16,401	17,094	(693)	(4)	77,000
Houston	10,200	10,200	0	—	51,000
Jacksonville	23,100	23,500	(400)	(2)	80,000
Los Angeles	6,000	10,000	(4,000)	(40)	93,000
Memphis	20,000	18,174	1,826	20	50,000
Oakland	15,000	25,000	(10,000)	(40)	55,000
New Jersey	36,000	35,000	1,000	3	77,000
Portland[b]	13,500	14,000	(500)	(4)	33,000
Orlando[c]	18,506	10,000	8,506	85	50,000
San Antonio	10,500	4,500	6,000	133	32,000
Tampa Bay	37,500	32,600	4,900	15	72,000

[a] Played 1984 season in Philadelphia.
[b] Played 1984 season in New Orleans.
[c] Played 1984 season in Washington, D.C.
Source: USFL records.

An 18-game fall schedule beginning September 14 and ending with a championship game February 1, 1987, was planned.

An agreement was reached on a TV contract with ESPN; the USFL would also syndicate games independently.

On August 4, 1986, the team owners suspended play for the 1986 season because the USFL lost its antitrust case against the NFL.

COMPETITION

One of the major reasons for the spring-summer schedule of the USFL was to avoid direct competition with the NFL. This schedule provided a better opportunity to obtain favorable programming with ABC television. Television ratings are key to the success of most professional sports. This helps to explain why 8 out of the 12 franchises were placed in the eight top television markets in 1983.

Table 7-6 compares some key variables between the NFL and the USFL for 1984. Other factors were compared in Table 7-2.

The NFL is not the USFL's only competition. By playing in the spring, the USFL had to contend with other professional sports such as hockey (National Hockey League), basketball (National Basketball Association), and major league baseball. Although their schedules are not identical to the USFL, the overlap is considerable with many televised

TABLE 7-6 Comparison of Key Variables of the NFL and USFL, 1984

	NFL	USFL
Average attendance	59,811	27,126
Average TV ratings	14.0	5.5
Average annual TV revenue per team	$14 million	$2.3 million
Average cost for 30-second commercial	$125,000	$35,000
Average annual profit (loss) per team	$2.5 million	($3.5 million)

Sources: NFL; USFL.

games. If the USFL had implemented its 1986 fall schedule, the nature of its competition with the NFL would have been dramatically altered.

MARKETING

Market, Marketing Research, and Image. The idea to play football in the spring was the brainchild of David Dixon. To investigate the feasibility of this idea, he hired Frank N. Magid, a top broadcast marketing research firm to conduct a survey. Magid's assignment was to find Joe Sportsfan and ask him, "Would you like to watch football in the spring?" The results were yes by a three-to-one margin.[3]

Dixon then proceeded with the development of a league. He set his priorities in the following ranked order:

1. The right owners
2. The right cities
3. The right stadiums
4. The right coaches
5. The right players

Lamar Hunt, one of the original founders of the old AFL and a respected director of the NFL, said the main problem was one of conditioning people to spring-summer football—sports fans would not attend games just because it was football and it would be difficult to change people's habits.

Hunt believed that the USFL would have difficulty establishing its identity. Selling names like the Generals, Federals, and Invaders would be more difficult than selling names like the Rams, Cowboys, or Giants. However, Hunt believed that it could be done, just as the old AFL was able to overcome a similar problem.

Product. The now-defunct WFL had differentiated its game from the NFL. The rules were modified to make the game more interesting. The kick for the extra point was eliminated. A touchdown was worth seven points, and an extra point could be made by running or passing the ball into the end zone. The goal posts were moved back to make the field goal more difficult. One foot in bounds was allowed for a completed pass, and a back could move toward the line of scrimmage before the ball was swapped. A black and gold ball was used to make it easier to follow.

Unlike the WFL, the USFL set out to look like the NFL, adopting essentially the same game rules. In fact, the only major differences are the option to attempt a two-point conversion after a touchdown and the two-pass interference penalties. An unintentional call results in a 15-yard penalty and a first down. A flagrant call results in the ball being marked at the point of the infraction. In general, the USFL plays the same game, with the same ball, according to the same clock, and on the same fields as the NFL.[4]

The USFL took two steps to improve its image and credibility as a professional league. First, they hired a number of famous NFL coaches such as Chuck Fairbanks, George Allen, and John Ralson. Second, they went after some of the top college players, including the following Heisman Trophy winners: Herschel Walker in 1983, Mike Rozier in 1984, and Doug Flutie in 1985. Other top collegiate players to join the USFL were Steve Young and Jim Kelly. The league was also able to attract a number of current and former NFL stars.

In 1983, the typical USFL team had two or three blue-chip players. The NFL's best teams have about 12 to 15 blue-chip players along with 30 fill-in types. The USFL's fill-ins are as good as the NFL's fill-ins because the country is full of players who can play in either league—but real quality is hard to find. If each USFL team adds a couple of quality players each season, by 1988 they will be on a par with the NFL.

By October 1985, over 70 USFL players had defected to the NFL. This raises the question that perhaps the USFL had a better product than was generally assumed.

Place. In 1983 the USFL played in 12 stadiums; in 1984, 18; in 1985, 14; and in 1986, were scheduled to play in 8.

The original place strategy of the USFL was to locate in highly successful football cities. In 1983, 9 of the 12 teams were located in NFL cities. The other three cities, Phoenix, Birmingham, and Oakland have been described as football-starved cities. Phoenix and Birmingham had continually sought membership in the NFL and Oakland took the Raiders to court in an attempt to prevent their exodus from Oakland to Los Angeles.

Market forces, changing conditions, and reality have forced the USFL to abandon its original place strategy. By 1985, only five of the 14 USFL teams were located in NFL cities.

The mergers and relocation of franchises have resulted in the league losing Philadelphia, Chicago, Detroit, Pittsburgh, Boston, Washington, D.C., and New Orleans by 1985. These are large television markets. Although the USFL has entered new markets, its total market potential declined 15 percent between 1983 and 1985. Approximately 25 percent of the public would be able to attend a game if they so desired.

If the USFL had moved to its fall schedule in 1986, only two of the remaining eight franchises would have been located in NFL cities, and the total market potential would have declined by more than 60 percent from the 1985 season.

Price. Price is not a crucial variable for the success of the USFL. Season tickets and individual tickets have been competitively priced.

Promotion. The first promotional task was to sell the USFL to the networks. Robert Landau Associates, the league's agent, was successful in signing contracts with ABC and the Entertainment Sports Programming Network (ESPN), a cable television network, that returned $1.5 million to each team in the league for 1983.

The revised 1985 contract increased this to $2.5 million per team, a significant improvement but still considerably below the $15 million each NFL team receives from the networks.

The signing of the television contracts made the USFL feasible and gave credibility to the league. Landau then began to license and promote the USFL logo. Companies put the USFL logo on everything in sight: key rings, pajamas, pennants, mugs, bookends, towels, shirts, jackets, and so forth. The extensive licensing push was used to gain exposure. For the right to promote the USFL logo on products, the charge was the same as the NFL, 7 percent of wholesale against guarantees.

Large corporations spent around $1 million each to launch their promotions. Pan Am, the USFL's official airline, gave away footballs and showed game films on board their Boeings. Dodge gave away a Charger to every team at every other home game, plus contributing a few hundred thousand dollars to the league's substance abuse program. Miller, the league's official beer, paid for the right to mention the USFL in every print ad it ran during the season. Pony became the league's "official shoe."

Estimates are that each team received $1.5 million from television rights, $200,000 to $300,000 from licensing, and another $250,000 from local radio rights in 1983.

Individual teams also engaged in promotion and special events. In 1983, actor Burt Reynolds, part-owner of the Tampa Bay Bandits, had his girl friend, actress Loni Anderson, pose for a publicity shot for Tampa Bay. In 1984, Reynolds hosted a party for 25,000 season ticket holders at

Tampa stadium. Dr. James Hoffman, the owner of the Chicago Blitz, budgeted $1 million for marketing—complete with free buses to the games, beer garden parties, and concerts—to reverse the 1983 lackluster attendance.

The USFL has received considerable publicity. The league, as well as most of the teams, have spent heavily on promotion and special events.

Perhaps the most effective promotion has been the publicity surrounding the signing of collegiate superstars such as Walker, Young, and Flutie to multimillion-dollar contracts.

LEGAL ISSUES

Professional sports in the United States has been partially exempt from the antitrust laws. Baseball has had limited protection since the 1920s. Another exemption occurred in 1960 when a merger between the NFL and AFL was permitted.

Donald Trump, owner of the New Jersey Generals, has described the NFL as a "great monopoly." Others have described the monopolistic behavior of the NFL. Since its merger with the AFL in 1970, the NFL has expanded only twice, allowing the cities of Seattle and Tampa Bay to join in 1974. Every year, four or five cities have been denied a league franchise, although new owners have been able to meet league requirements and standards.

The NFL wants to exclude additional city expansion in order to protect its television revenues, which are evenly divided among the 28 teams. Increasing the number of franchises in the league would dilute the average revenue per team. Thus, it is in the league's best interest to exclude others from joining.

Recently a number of franchises have relocated. In 1983 the Oakland Raiders moved to Los Angeles, and in 1985 the Baltimore Colts to Indianapolis. League officials strongly opposed the Raiders move but the courts favored the owner. This freedom of movement has enhanced the monopolistic power of the NFL.

In 1985, Congress introduced a bill that would grant the NFL further antitrust exemption by allowing league officials to restrict the movement of teams.

Donald Trump testified that to give the NFL wider antitrust exemption would only strengthen the NFL and could hurt the USFL. He said a limited exemption would be reasonable but only in regards to franchise movement.

A shift by the USFL from a spring-summer schedule to a fall schedule for 1986 left the league without a TV network, except for ESPN. ABC televised USFL games on Sunday during 1983, 1984, and 1985, and has an option for 1986. But the network stated that it would not pick up that option if the USFL switched from its spring-summer schedule.

In 1986, the USFL filed a $1.3 billion antitrust case against the NFL. This case went to trial in the U.S. District Court in New York on May 12, 1986.

The USFL pleaded monopoly. The league contended that the NFL conspired to pressure the three major networks into keeping USFL games off television in 1986, thus closing off its largest source of potential income, and to sabotage its efforts to operate franchises in large cities.

The NFL argued that it conspired with no one and did nothing to harm the new league, that the USFL was really suing to force a merge, and that the USFL is in financial trouble through its own doing—poor management and excessive spending.

On July 29, 1986, the United States Football League won a hollow victory against the National Football League. The federal court jury ruled that the NFL did have a monopoly on the overall professional football market. It also concluded that the NFL did not monopolize the market for fall football telecasts and did not exert pressure on the three major television networks to stop them from offering a contract to the USFL for a 1986 fall schedule of games. The jury awarded the USFL only $1 in damages, asserting that the USFL's problems stemmed mostly from its own blundering.

This very controversial verdict will be appealed and the league will seek an injunction requiring the NFL to drop one of its three network contracts.

On August 4, 1986, the team owners suspended play for the 1986 season and will attempt to field a more powerful, larger league in the fall of 1987.

During 1985, the networks (ABC, NBC, and CBS) paid approximately $420 million to the NFL. This constitutes approximately 60 percent of their gross revenues.

The real contest with the NFL will come in 1987 when the NFL television network contracts expire. The NFL will be asking for billions in new contracts and the USFL would like to compete in the bidding.

ABC has been reluctant to move with the USFL to a fall schedule, a move that would place the USFL in direct competition with NBC for stadiums, TV contracts, and the public.

The USFL has already driven up player salaries. The NFL has resisted merger efforts and would like to remain a 28-member league with its exclusive fall schedule and renewable television contracts.

CONCLUSION

The USFL survived its first three seasons, but was in financial trouble. In 1985 only two teams, Tampa Bay and New Jersey, had sold over 30,000 season tickets and only one team, Tampa Bay, earned a profit.

With Los Angeles, Houston, Chicago, San Antonio, Oakland, and Denver out of the league it was difficult to envision its survival. Its Fall 1986 schedule with only eight teams had a vastly reduced market potential.

Many believe that its $1.3 billion antitrust case against the NFL was a desperation move. Having effectively lost this case, the league decided to postpone its 1986 season and will attempt to field a more powerful, larger league in 1987.

The controversial antitrust verdict will be appealed and the league has filed an injunction requiring the NFL to drop one of its three network contracts.

QUESTIONS

1. Discuss three nonfinancial criteria that are appropriate in measuring the success or failure of the USFL.
2. Choose one of the following as the best strategy for the USFL and defend your choice: (a) continue with a spring-summer schedule; (b) compete directly with the NFL by adopting a fall schedule; (c) attempt to merge with the NFL.
3. Discuss the original positioning strategy of the USFL as compared to the NFL and WFL. Has this strategy changed?
4. Develop a profile of the current image of the USFL.
5. Does the USFL have credibility? What does a professional sports organization need to do to establish its credibility?
6. There are 28 teams in the NFL and 8 teams in the USFL for a total of 36 professional football teams. Has the USFL entered an already saturated football market? Defend your answer.
7. Why is a television contract important for a professional football team?
8. Identify and discuss five marketing concepts or principles that can be related to a sports organization.
9. The NFL has been described as a monopoly. How do you feel about this issue?
10. The USFL has filed a $1.3 billion antitrust suit against the NFL. Discuss what you think the charges are. What act would you prosecute under? Why?
11. Has the USFL stayed with its original goals and objectives?

NOTES

1. John Merwin, "Who's Getting Clipped?" *Forbes*, November 5, 1984, p. 39.
2. "Fourth and Long, But the USFL Goes for It," *Business Week*, February 27, 1984, p. 108.
3. Larry Filser, "They Play Football Don't They?" *Sport*, March 1983, p. 52.
4. Ibid., p. 52.

8

BRANIFF INTERNATIONAL

INTRODUCTION

By 1930, the passenger airline industry in the United States was well established. Most of the major carriers that the public is familiar with today had their beginning in the 1920s and 1930s. Braniff was founded in 1928 and was one of the U.S. airline pioneers of the 1930s.

This industry eventually became highly regulated. The Civil Aeronautics Board (CAB), the watchdog of the industry, was established in 1938. Interstate airlines that came under its purview needed CAB permission for almost everything. This included changes in fares and all route change applications. Competition came to be based not on price, but on scheduling and on in-flight amenities.

The CAB adopted a policy of protecting existing carriers and keeping newcomers out. For example, between 1950 and 1974, the CAB received 79 applications for routes from companies that wanted to enter the airline industry. All were rejected. The CAB also had the final say on mergers and acquisitions.[1]

The other major regulatory agency in the field of air service is the Federal Aviation Administration (FAA) whose primary concern is air safety.

The passage of the Airline Deregulation Act of October 1978 completely changed the way airlines operated. It imposed a degree of competition and free enterprise on the airlines that was inconceivable a few years ago. But just how well deregulation has served the public, airlines, and passengers depends on whom you are asking.

It has fostered competition in the industry. Prior to 1978, there were 36 certified carriers. By December 1984, there were 125 carriers including the reorganized Braniff. Between 1980 and December 1984, 28 carriers went out of business. Most of these carriers were new entrants to the industry with the exception of Braniff and Continental. Braniff declared bankruptcy in May of 1982 and Continental in September 1983.

Current assessment of the industry is that many airlines are living on borrowed time. There has been an acceleration in the airline bankruptcy rate and investors are leery of contributing to finance struggling carriers or to provide capital for new ones.

Many of the new airlines have insufficient capitalization, haphazard marketing, and weak management. If the coming years bring a recession or decline in air passenger mileage, some of the marginal airlines would fail.

On May 13, 1982, Braniff International was shut down by its own management. The company filed for bankruptcy under Chapter XI. This provision protects a company from having to pay any outstanding debts while it tries to reorganize and come up with a plan for paying its creditors.

During 1979, 1980, and 1981, Braniff operated at a loss. The cash flow problem became so severe in 1982 that Braniff could not pay its current bills for salaries, food, and fuel. Some blamed its demise on deregulation. Others said it was the recession, high fuel prices, and poor management. Braniff was the first major airline since the 1930s to file for bankruptcy. The impact of its demise was not severe since it carried only 3.5 percent of U.S. air passengers.[2] Its routes and markets were easily absorbed by other airlines.

The reorganization period lasted from May 13, 1982, to March 1, 1984, or approximately 22 months.

On March 1, 1984, a pared-down revitalized Braniff Airways, Inc., began operations again. It sustained losses of $70 million for the ten-month period remaining in 1984.

HISTORY AND BACKGROUND, 1926–1979

Braniff Airlines was founded in 1928 by Tom and Paul Braniff. By 1980 it became the eighth largest U.S. airline.

In 1952, Braniff merged with Continental Airlines and acquired many additional route miles. In 1967, it purchased Pan Am Grace Airways and extended its routes throughout Latin America. By 1968, it had a route structure of 30,000 miles.

Between 1928 and 1965, Braniff served routes mostly in the Midwest and in Latin America. In 1965, Harding Lawrence became president and expanded Braniff's routes. At its peak, it employed over 15,000 people.

Braniff's hub city and home base was Dallas, Texas. In the late

1970s, headquarters were built at the new Dallas/Ft. Worth International Airport.

For a while, Braniff prospered. Harding Lawrence was innovative, improved aircraft utilization, and created a flashy new image for the airline. Up until 1979, Braniff made a profit. It has sustained losses ever since.

THE BRANIFF LEADERSHIP

The most outstanding individual at Braniff was Harding Lawrence, who directed Braniff from 1965 to December 1980. Lawrence was born in Perkins, Oklahoma, in 1920. He received his bachelor's degree in business from the University of Texas in 1942 and his law degrees from Southern Texas College of Law and the University of Portland. Almost all of his business career was spent in the airline industry. From 1947 to 1955, he was a director of Pioneer Airlines. From 1955 to 1957, he was vice-president of sales for Continental Airlines and was then promoted to vice-president and executive administrator from 1957 to 1958. From 1958 to 1965, he was executive vice-president and director of Continental Airlines. He came to Braniff in 1965 as a seasoned, experienced executive. From 1965 to 1968, he was director and president of Braniff Airways, Inc. From 1968 to 1980, he was chairman of the board and president of Braniff International.

Harding Lawrence was a colorful and ambitious executive. In 1967, he married Mary Wells, chairperson of Wells, Rich, Green Advertising Agency in New York City. Wells was the best-known, most successful woman in the advertising industry. She was very creative and took on Braniff as an account. Braniff's conservative image was changed to a trendy, prestigious one. Braniff's stewardesses were decked out in Pucci-styled uniforms. The airplanes were painted in seven pastel colors and artist Alexander Calder was paid handsomely for his designs. The slogan of the late 1960s was, "When you've got it, flaunt it."[3]

In 1978, Lawrence used the Airline Deregulation Act to progressively expand Braniff. Service was added to a host of new cities. In December 1978, Braniff began flying 16 new routes and added many more after that in the United States, Europe, and Asia. It borrowed millions of dollars at high interest rates to buy 747 jumbo jets to fly the new routes. Customer demand on these new routes was weak and could not generate the necessary revenue to pay for the cost involved. Concurrent problems were a weak economy and rising fuel prices. Because of severe losses, Lawrence resigned in December 1980. He was replaced on a temporary basis for nine months by his vice-chairman at Braniff, John L. Casey.

In mid-1981, Howard Putnam became chairman of Braniff International. He had received his M.B.A. in Marketing at the University of

Chicago in 1966 and had held leadership positions in the airline industry. His strategy to save Braniff involved slashing ticket prices to generate revenue in the short run, selling unprofitable routes to cut costs, and reducing the number of employees. Despite these efforts, Braniff went under.

THE AIRLINE DEREGULATION ACT OF 1978

Deregulation actually began in early 1977 when the CAB, with a mandate from the Carter Administration, began to ease airline controls. The board allowed some airlines to introduce deep discount fares. It also loosened the restrictions on the operation of point-to-point charter flights. This resulted in the major airlines responding with bargain fares. Soon to follow were supersavers and other promotional offerings.

The Deregulation Act officially became law in October 1978. By December 1981, the CAB relinquished all control over domestic routes; by January 1, 1983, it lost control over domestic fares and its authority over domestic mergers and interlocking relationships among airlines.

On December 31, 1984, the CAB closed its doors after 46 years. It was the first federal regulatory agency ever to go out of business.

One of its last major decisions was to allow tickets to be sold to almost anybody, including supermarkets and department stores.

The CAB's consumer-protection functions—resolving overbooking problems, finding lost luggage, and enforcing nonsmoking rules—were taken over by the U.S. Department of Transportation.

Braniff was a proponent of deregulation. It saw deregulation as an opportunity to apply aggressive marketing. The airline engaged in vigorous price competition and pursued a policy of building market share by entering many widespread areas.

Braniff was first in applying for "automatic market entry," which were unused routes that the CAB made available in the initial experimentation with deregulation. Braniff shared the industry's worry that the CAB would halt its move toward deregulation and return to the old system; therefore, the airline acquired as many new routes as quickly as possible.

The Airline Deregulation Act encouraged a number of new entrants into the market. Most of these airlines were low-cost operators with discount prices. A number of them, such as People Express, have been successful and they have become known as the no-frills airlines.

Another major change occurred in the distribution and sale of tickets. Before deregulation, travel agents accounted for 50 percent of total ticket sales. By 1982, they booked an estimated 70 percent of the airline's tickets. Many consumers were shopping for the best price. Instead of calling on a single airline, they would use the services of a travel agency or ticket agent.

TABLE 8-1 Braniff's Profits and Losses, 1977–1981

Year	Profit (Loss) (millions)
1981	$(161)
1980	(131)
1979	(44)
1978	48
1977	37

Source: Moody's Transportation Manual.

THE DIFFICULT YEARS, 1979–1982: AN ASSESSMENT

Braniff chose the wrong strategy in attempting to expand its market share. The newly acquired routes were not profitable and Braniff offered limited schedules for these routes. The company also had difficulty in establishing its image and developing a strong customer identity in the new markets.

The reason that so many unused routes were available was their lack of traffic. Other airlines avoided these routes but Braniff saw them as a way to expand its business.

In order to service the new routes, Braniff purchased many new planes. These planes were financed by increasing the company's long-term debt at high interest rates.

This overexpansion coupled with changing environmental conditions resulted in Braniff's precipitous collapse.

Table 8-1 illustrates Braniff's profit and loss position from 1977 to 1981. Table 8-2 shows the increase in its long-term debt during the same period.

Figure 8-1 illustrates Braniff's fluctuation in capacity of total available seat miles from 1977 to 1981.

Figure 8-2 illustrates the relationship between the passenger load factor and the break-even point from 1977 to 1981.

TABLE 8-2 Braniff's Total Long-Term Debt, 1977–1981

Year	Long-Term Debt (millions)
1981	$591
1980	663
1979	665
1978	398
1977	321

Source: Moody's Transportation Manual.

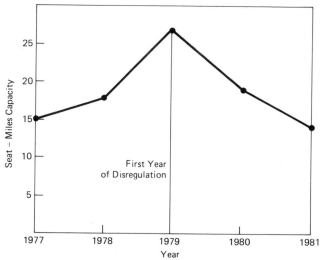

FIGURE 8-1   Braniff's Total Available Seat-Miles Capacity, 1977–1981 (Billions)

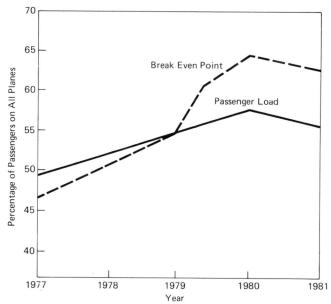

FIGURE 8-2   The Relationship between the Passenger Load Factor and the Break-even Point, 1977–1981

TABLE 8-3 Key Data on Major U.S. Airlines for the Quarter Ending March 31, 1982 (Millions)

Airline	Income	Profit	Current Ratio	Long-Term Obligations
American Airlines	$ 911.4	$(59.1)	0.96	$1,571.4
Braniff International	253.4	(43.2)	0.55	545.9
Continental Airlines	276.1	(23.1)	0.40	151.7
Delta Airlines	888.0	(45.8)	0.88	373.3
Eastern Airlines	908.4	(21.5)	0.88	1,861.2
Northwest Airlines	413.0	(36.1)	0.73	50.0
Pan American	796.6	(108.3)	0.74	1,208.4
Republic Airlines	372.7	5.1	0.71	748.0
Trans World	635.4	(108.7)	1.20	579.0
United Airlines	1,056.4	(106.2)	0.80	1,456.0
U.S. Air	279.2	(4.9)	1.07	292.0
Western Airlines	248.7	(6.4)	0.43	432.3

Source: Civil Aeronautics Board.

COMPARISON WITH COMPETITORS

The entire domestic airline industry faced severe problems in 1981 and 1982. Operating losses of the 12 major airlines in the first quarter of 1982 reached $558.2 million, the largest quarterly loss ever. In 1981, the major airlines lost more than $800 million.[4]

Table 8-3 reveals the following facts for the first quarter of 1982: Pan American, Trans World, and United each lost over $100 million. Delta, traditionally one of the most profitable airlines, reported a quarterly loss. Only one, Republic, showed a profit. Only two had adequate current assets to cover their current liabilities. Most had crucial financial problems and many sold off assets to raise cash.

The biggest difference between Braniff and the others was that Braniff ran out of cash and the others did not.

Most of the problems were due to price competition, overcapacity, recession, continued servicing of unprofitable routes, and high interest costs. The air controllers' strike also curtailed travel.

THE RETURN OF BRANIFF, MARCH 1984–SEPTEMBER 1984

In September 1983, the wealthy Pritzker family of Chicago acquired Braniff. This family owns Hyatt Corporation, which it built up from a single hotel in Los Angeles into a 41,500-room nationwide hotel chain. The family also owns a host of other well-known companies. Jay Pritzker, the son of the founding father, had a reputation of near infallibility in buying troubled companies and turning them around. He assessed Braniff as having a 60-percent chance of becoming successful.[5]

TABLE 8-4 Comparison of Old Braniff and New Braniff

	Braniff May 1982	*Braniff March 1984*
Hub base	Dallas/Ft. Worth	Dallas/Ft. Worth
Employees	9,200	2,200
Aircraft (727s)	75	30
Airports	54	18
Countries	13	USA only

Sources: Company records; *USA Today*, February 28, 1984, p. B1.

The reborn Braniff began operations on March 1, 1984. It should be pointed out that putting 30 planes into the air on the start-up date is a complex operation. A comparison of the old Braniff and new Braniff is shown in Table 8-4.

The new Braniff was approximately one-third the size of the old Braniff. It had three strengths: a low-cost structure, a good union contract, and Hyatt, a high-image profitable hotel chain.

Table 8-5 shows market share data in the Dallas/Ft. Worth area for 1982, when old Braniff ceased operations, and 1984, when new Braniff reentered the market.

American Airlines had always been the dominant carrier in the Dallas/Ft. Worth market, but during the 1970s, Braniff was a keen competitor. After Braniff's demise in 1982, American emerged as the dominant force in the market. As one travel agent said, "American just runs Dallas."

In March 1984, flights originating in the Dallas/Ft. Worth market were as follows: Braniff had 82 daily flights to 18 destinations; American had 280 daily nonstops to 82 U.S. cities; and Delta had 120 daily flights and nonstop service to 41 cities.

American had a convenient schedule and an active frequent-flyer program.

Braniff's marketing strategy was to go after the full-fare business travelers. The airline offered high-quality business cabin service similar to first-class but at a lesser cost. More room and storage space was available for the business traveler. There were no more Alexander Calder–painted planes, no international routes, and no crystal glassware.

TABLE 8-5 Market Share in Dallas/Ft. Worth Market (Percent)

	May 1982	*February 1984*
Braniff	35	0
American	40	63
Delta	10	21
Others	15	16
Total	100	100

Source: Business Week, February 27, 1984, p. 7.

Braniff did not plan to be a cut-rate carrier or offer special introductory fares—except for a 90-day charitable program offering up to 10 percent off the price of a ticket to the March of Dimes.

The initial $10-million advertising campaign was based on two themes: "The new Braniff is up and running," and "We're building the new Braniff around you." Complementing the ads was a frequent-flier deal linked with United Airlines.

In March 1984, the new Braniff had a cost reserve of $90 million. It projected a loss of $14 million the first year. In the airline's first seven months of operation, its losses ran between $7 and $11 million a month and its passenger load factor rarely exceeded 50 percent.

SEPTEMBER 1984–DECEMBER 1984

On September 7, 1984, Braniff changed its operating strategy and became a full-fledged discount carrier. Although the load factor had risen to a high of 58 percent in August, it was insufficient to make Braniff profitable. Costs were also cut by laying off approximately 500 employees.

In October, Braniff considered redeploying some of its planes to Detroit or Denver as alternate hub cities.

On November 5, Braniff scaled down its operations. Its fleet was cut from 30 to 10 planes. The number of cities served was cut from 20 to 10. The work force was again dramatically reduced.

On December 19, a minihub was opened at the Houston Hobby Airport, the old downtown airport close to the central city. Two daily round-trip flights to New York's LaGuardia Airport were scheduled. Braniff's main competitor was People Express, the only other low-cost carrier flying from Hobby to the New York area.

In late December 1984, Braniff reported it had $27 million in cash, enough to keep it operating through the winter and early spring. Twenty million dollars of this cash came from the sale of nine Braniff gates at the Dallas/Ft. Worth Airport to American Airlines.

Braniff's load factor from November 5 through the remainder of the year was 64.3 percent, slightly below its new break-even point. Losses for November and December 1984 had declined to $500,000 per month.

CONCLUSION

Braniff renewed operations March 1, 1984, as a full-service air carrier, catering primarily to the business segment. The renewed operation was well financed. Prices were competitive and amenities were offered. On September 8, 1984, a new strategy was implemented. Braniff became a full-fledged discount carrier. At this time, the possibilities of relocating to other hub cities was considered. On November 5, 1984, Braniff's operations were scaled down. Assets such as gates were sold to raise additional capital. As of December 1984, Braniff was a very small carrier operating 10 planes to 10 cities.

Its stock, which was issued at $10.50 a share in March, had fallen to $2.00 by December 1984.

QUESTIONS

1. Braniff quickly applied for "automatic market entry." These were unused routes. Discuss the weaknesses and strengths of this expansion strategy.
2. Discuss the implications of the Airline Deregulation Act on the following parties: (a) the airline industry, (b) Braniff, (c) airline passengers, (d) the general public, (e) investors, and (f) ticket agents.
3. State four different marketing strategies that were available to Braniff as of March 1, 1984.
4. Describe the marketing strategy that Braniff should have used as of March 1, 1984.
5. Discuss the pros and cons of using the Braniff name again.
6. Should another city besides Dallas have been used as the hub city?
7. How ready do you think the Dallas/Ft. Worth market was to welcome a new competitor like Braniff in March 1984?
8. Suggest a strategy for American Airlines and Delta Airlines to counter Braniff's reentry into the market.
9. Why did ticket agents and travel agents increase their share of airline ticket sales after deregulation?
10. Discuss Figure 8-2. Why did the break-even line rise so rapidly between 1977 and 1980? Diagram two other examples of break-even analysis.
11. Which of the following options should Braniff implement: (a) relocate to another hub city; (b) merge with another airline; (c) pare down operations; (d) liquidate?

NOTES

1. Paul Grimes, "Airline Deregulation Act, 2 Years old, Fosters Competition, Free Enterprise," *Sacramento Bee,* October 19, 1980, travel sec., p. 3.
2. John S. Demott, "Bankruptcy at Braniff," *Time,* May 24, 1982, p. 63.
3. Ibid.
4. Daniel C. Cuff, "Major U.S. Airlines Are Facing a Severe Financial Squeeze," *New York Times,* May 14, 1982, p. D3.
5. Laurie P. Cohen, "Rough Flight, Pritzkers of Chicago Adept at Turnarounds Face Failure at Braniff," *Wall Street Journal,* Western ed., October 11, 1984, pp. 1 and 24.

9

F. W. WOOLWORTH

INTRODUCTION

F. W. Woolworth Company is one of America's oldest retailers. It is the fourth largest merchandiser. The company is the outgrowth of a single store established in 1879 in Lancaster, Pennsylvania. In 1982, Woolworth was our twelfth largest retailer. At its peak in 1980, there were 7,000 stores and 197,000 employees.

Incorporated in New York on December 15, 1911, the company and its various subsidiaries operate 5,124 stores and leased departments in the United States, Puerto Rico, the U.S. Virgin Islands, Canada, Germany, and certain other countries.

This retailer has run the cycle of retailing. It began as a variety store. In 1962, the Woolco Division, a discount department chain, was founded. During the 1960s and 1970s, Woolworth further diversified by purchasing a number of specialty retail chains.

Recently the company has fallen on hard times. In 1982, the Woolco Division was closed, casting off some $2 billion in sales and shrinking the company nearly 30 percent. Also shed was the company's 52.6-percent interest in some 1,000 Woolworth stores in Britain.

Although Woolworth's growth has stagnated in recent years, management established the following strategic priorities in order to fulfill its mission and achieve its financial objectives.

To restructure, reformat and revitalize businesses which can meet the company's objectives within a reasonable time span and to redeploy assets away from those which cannot.

To accelerate expansion of successful specialty retailing formats and to develop new ones.

To acquire compatible specialty retailing companies having actual and potential rates of profit growth and return on investment higher than those of F. W. Woolworth Co.[1]

BRIEF HISTORY BEFORE INCORPORATION, 1879–1911

Frank W. Woolworth, Woolworth's founder, provided the inspiration and pattern for an entirely new field of retail merchandising which was the 5-and-10-cent store. His idea for this type of store came from his experience as a clerk in a dry goods store. A table of miscellaneous goods labeled with a sign, "Anything on this table, 5¢," was almost cleared the first day. This convinced Woolworth that a whole store devoted exclusively to 5-cent items would prove successful.[2]

The first store opened in Utica, New York, and was successful for a period of time but eventually had to be closed. The second store, established in Lancaster, Pennsylvania in 1879 was very successful. Stores 3 and 4 had to be closed. The fifth store in Scranton, Pennsylvania, established in 1880, proved to be equally successful.

At this point, Woolworth was convinced that the concept of a 5-and-10-cent store was basically sound, provided you had the right location. He also believed that a number of stores was necessary for success; a single store had limitations.

Store expansion continued rather slowly. Finding promising locations was time consuming. Hiring and training trustworthy managers was also difficult. One method used to accelerate expansion in the early days was to add partners who had capital.

By 1900, 59 profitable stores were in operation. In 1904, growth was further accelerated by the purchase of 21 stores.

Because Woolworth was successful, other imitators began similar types of stores and most of the variety store chains in existence today had their origins in the 1890–1910 period.

TABLE 9-1 Woolworth Merger of 1911

Company	Stores
F. W. Woolworth & Co.	318
S. H. Knox & Co.	112
F. M. Kirby & Co.	96
E. P. Charlton & Co.	53
C. S. Woolworth	15
W. H. Moore	2
Total	596

Note: From Godfrey M. Lebhar, *Chain Stores in America 1859–1962*, 3rd ed. (New York: Chain Store Publishing Corp., 1963), p. 39. Reprinted with permission from Chain Store Publishing Corp., 425 Park Ave., New York, N.Y. 10022.

In 1905, Frank Woolworth incorporated the stores he owned outright to form F. W. Woolworth & Company. By 1911, the company operated 318 stores. In addition, there were a number of associate stores that Frank Woolworth held in partnership with others. This group ratified a merger in 1911 and the F. W. Woolworth Company was born. It consisted of 596 stores whose sales totaled over $52 million and was by far the largest variety store chain in the industry (see Table 9-1).

BRIEF HISTORY AFTER INCORPORATION, 1912–1984

From 1912 to 1933, the Woolworth Company expanded rapidly by entering Canada, Cuba, Mexico, Germany, and England. British Woolworth opened its first store in Liverpool in 1909. Its success led to the rapid development of the British chain. These stores were known as "3d and 6d" shops—three pence and six pence being the nearest equivalent to nickels and dimes. Although the company had less than half as many stores as its American parent, opening its one thousandth store in 1958, its net profits for many years were greater than its American parent. The profits began to slip in 1981 and a loss occurred in 1982, so Woolworth sold its interest in its British subsidiary to raise cash and to reduce the parent company's debt.

German Woolworth began in Bremen in 1927 and by 1984 operated 219 stores. The Mexican affiliate was formed in 1956.

The number of U.S. stores rose from 1,111 in 1920 to 1,938 in 1949. By the end of 1929, American Woolworth either owned or controlled 2,247 stores worldwide. Table 9-2 illustrates the growth of the chain and its major competitors from 1920 to 1949.

For many years, the company did strictly a 5-and-10-cent store business. In the spring of 1932, a 20-cent line of merchandise was added and, on November 13, 1935, directors discontinued selling price limits in order to take advantage of distress merchandise and exceptional buys during the Depression.

In 1962, the company formed the Woolco Department Stores Division to operate discount department stores in the United States and Canada separately from the company's variety stores.

In 1963, the company acquired G. R. Kinney Corporation, a shoe retailing and manufacturing subsidiary of Brown Shoe Company. The Kinney Shoe Corporation operates family shoe stores and other specialty stores—misses' sportswear (Susie's Casuals), high-fashion ladies' footwear (Fredelle), athletic footwear (Foot Locker and Lady Foot Locker),

TABLE 9-2 Growth of the Nine Leading U.S. Variety Store Chains by Number of Stores, 1920–1949

Chain	1920	1925	1930	1949
Woolworth	1,111	1,420	1,881	1,938
Kresge	184	306	678	702
Kress	145	166	212	256
McCrory	156	181	242	201
Murphy	53	88	166	218
McLellan	43	94	277	230
Grant	38	77	350	480
Newberry	17	86	335	482
Neisner	4	13	75	121
Total	1,751	2,431	4,216	4,628

Note: From Godfrey M. Lebhar, *Chain Stores in America 1859–1962*, 3rd ed. (New York: Chain Store Publishing Corp., 1963), p. 56. Reprinted with permission from Chain Store Publishing Corp., 425 Park Ave., New York, N.Y. 10022.

and factory outlets (Frugal Frank's). Canadian and Australian stores also used these names.

In 1969, Richman Brothers, a manufacturer and retailer of men's clothing, was acquired. Men's and boys' clothing is sold through 210 Richman stores, and family apparel is sold through 105 Anderson-Little shops.

J. Brannam stores, which were opened in 1979, consist of 38 off-price stores selling brand-name clothing and household linens. This chain was closed in 1986.

Little Folk Shop, which was acquired in August 1983, is a specialty retailer operating under the names Kids Mart and Little Folk Shop. There are 120 stores.

In October 1984, plans were announced to further diversify by opening an unnamed deep-discount drugstore chain.

In summary, the major divisions of F. W. Woolworth Co. are as follows:

U.S. Woolworth
Woolworth Canada
Woolco Canada
Activeworld, Canada
Woolworth Germany
Kinney Shoe Corporation
Richman Brothers
Little Folk Shop

Contributions of the major divisions to sales and profits are shown in Table 9-3.

TABLE 9-3 Sales and Profits for Woolworth's Major Divisions, 1983 (Percent of Total)

Division	Sales	Profits
U.S. Woolworth	33	25
Woolworth/Woolco Canada	26	19
Woolworth Germany	13	15
Kinney Shoe Corp.	23	39
Richman Brothers	4	3
J. Brannam	1	−2
Total	100	100

Source: Standard & Poor's NYSE Stock Report, Vol. 51, No. 200, Sec. 23, October 16, 1984, p. 2500.

In the late 1970s and early 1980s, the company fell on hard times. The resulting retrenchment followed:

1977	Sold trade receivables of $216 million.
1980	Discontinued operations in Spain.
1981	Sold 51 percent of its Mexican affiliate; retained 49 percent interest.
1982	Sold its remaining interest of 52.6 percent in British Woolworth.
1982	Closed Woolco Division—336 stores.

Although large in sales, Woolco was never highly profitable. In 1981 and 1982, Woolco became such a drain on Woolworth that Edward F. Gibbons, the chief executive officer, decided to close the Woolco Division. Table 9-4 shows Woolco's sales and profits or losses from 1977 to 1982. Some of the reasons for the Woolco failure were the following:

1. Management's inability to recognize and call Woolco a discount store. Woolco was always referred to as a department store.
2. Weak commitment to Woolco's growth in its early history.
3. Lack of direction.

TABLE 9-4 Sales and Profits (Losses) of Woolco Division, 1977–1982

Year	Sales (billions)	Profits (Losses) (millions)
1982[a]	$2.0	($40)
1981	2.2	(19)
1980	2.0	12
1979	1.9	25
1978	1.7	28
1977	1.5	11

[a] Accounted for as discountined operations since September 24, 1982.

Sources: F. W. Woolworth Company, Annual Reports; *Business Week,* October 11, 1982, p. 118; *Wall Street Journal,* September 27, 1982, p. 8.

4. Too widely dispersed geographical markets. Avoidance of a market-by-market development with too few stores in many markets.
5. A blurred image.
6. A hostile retail economy.

COMPARISON WITH VARIETY STORES

Since 1911, F. W. Woolworth has been one of America's largest merchandisers. Relative to other retailers, it has declined in recent years. In 1955, *Fortune* ranked Woolworth seventh in sales; by 1970 it was eighth and by 1982 it was twelfth. However, in the variety store category, which it pioneered, it has always been the largest in sales and number of stores (see Tables 9-2 and 9-5).

Table 9-5 shows how Woolworth compared with its competition in 1958 in the variety store group. Woolworth operated 10.2 percent of all variety stores and accounted for 23.8 percent of their combined sales. Woolworth's major competitors were the nine next largest chains. Collectively, these stores constituted what the industry referred to as "The Big Ten." The nine chains operated 16.4 percent of the stores and accounted for 49.1 percent of the sales, approximately twice the sales of Woolworth.

The remaining 15,000 stores, or 73.4 percent of total stores, accounted for 27.1 percent of total sales. The variety store category has always been competitive. Woolworth has been successful in this market.

Woolworth's direct competition as covered by Table 9-5 does not tell a complete story. Indirect competition from traditional retailers such as department stores, general merchandise stores, drug stores, apparel stores, supermarkets, and discount stores intensified as these stores extended their scrambled merchandising practices. New retail formats such as off-price retailers, barn operations, super drug stores, and superstores have also affected sales of the variety store category.

TABLE 9-5 Variety Store Group, Number of Stores and Sales, 1958

Group	Number of Stores	Percent of Total	Sales (millions)	Percent of Total
Woolworth	2,152	10.2	$ 864.6	23.8
9 Next Largest Chains	3,456	16.4	1,777.6	49.1
All Other Chains[a]	2.399	11.4	290.0	8.0
Independents	13,010	62.0	689.0	19.1
Total	21,017	100.0	$3,621.2	100.0

[a] With four stores or more.

Source: U.S. Department of Commerce, Census of Business, 1958.

TABLE 9-6 F. W. Woolworth Selected Operating Statistics and Per Share Data, Selected Years, 1962–1986

Year	Net Sales (millions)	Net Income (millions)	Earnings per Share	Dividends	Common Stock Price Range
1986[a]	$6,400	$191	$5.97	$2.00	89–45
1985	5,958	177	5.50	2.00	63–36
1984	5,737	141	4.45	1.80	39–29
1983	5,456	118	3.72	1.80	40–22
1982	5,124	82	2.63	1.80	30–15
1981	7,223	82	2.64	1.80	28–17
1980	7,218	161	5.30	1.80	30–21
1975	4,650	100	3.34	1.20	23–9
1970	2,528	77	2.52	1.20	39–25
1965	1,443	70	2.41	1.00	33–26
1962	1,110	48	1.67	0.83	32–18

[a] Estimates as of May 1986.
Source: Annual Reports.

WOOLCO VERSUS K MART: NO COMPARISON

Before 1962, Kresge and Woolworth were arch rivals and the main battle for the consumer's dollar was fought in downtown areas. In 1962, both companies expanded into the discount department store arena. Woolworth had more than three times the number of variety stores and had almost three times more in net sales than Kresge. By 1970, K Mart's sales of $2,559 million surpassed Woolworth's sales of $2,528 million (see Tables 9-6 and 9-7). Lester A. Burcham, chairman of the board of Woolworth, insisted in 1970 that his company's more moderate approach to discounting was the right one, "not just for the immediate time, but for the long pull. We decided at the outset that our Woolworth Company was too valuable an asset to just go in one direction."[3]

By 1982, 20 years after both companies had entered the discount field, K Mart sales had increased 35-fold compared to Woolworth's 4.6-fold increase. K Mart's earnings per share had increased 23-fold compared to Woolworth's 1.5-fold increase. K Mart had 2,117 discount stores versus Woolco's 120 remaining Canadian stores (see Tables 9-8 and 9-9). Woolworth closed 336 Woolco stores in the United States in 1982. K Mart had clearly outperformed its arch rival.

Woolworth made a number of mistakes. In 1962, the Woolco and Woolworth stores were separated into different divisions. As a result, a tug of war developed between the new Woolco and the old Woolworth stores. Woolco took a back seat to Woolworth. In 1971, management reversed its decision and the two operations were integrated. Considerable friction between the two camps was reduced but a major weakness evolved. The same company buyer purchased goods for both stores.

TABLE 9-7 K Mart Selecting Operating Statistics and Per Share Data, Selected Years, 1962–1985

Year	Net Sales (millions)	Net Income (millions)	Earnings per Share	Dividends	Common Stock Price Range
1985[a]	$22,745	$221	$1.73	$1.36	42–30[b]
1984	21,408	499	3.84	1.20	38–26
1983	18,884	492	3.80	1.06	40–21
1982	16,942	262	2.06	.99	28–15
1981	16,679	220	1.75	.95	24–15
1980	14,343	261	2.07	.90	26–15
1975	6,884	201	1.64	.24	35–20
1970	2,559	68	.62	.14	20–11
1965	851	22	.22	.08	5–4
1962	483	9	.09	.08	3–2

[a] Year ends January of following year.

[b] Calendar year.

Source: Annual Reports.

Customers could obtain similar merchandise in both stores. It was commonplace for Woolworth's artificial flowers, ceramic vases, and other items to appear on Woolco's shelves. The buying operations of the two divisions should have been separated.

Woolworth did not make a full commitment to discounting. Its pace of opening new discount stores was much slower than K Mart's (see Table 9-8). The locations also differed. Woolco stores were located in shopping centers, whereas K Mart preferred free-standing buildings. Woolco also failed to cluster its stores and develop the enterprise market by market. Instead, the stores were scattered across the United States, but mostly in

TABLE 9-8 Number of K Mart and Woolworth Stores, Selected Years, 1962–1983

	1962	1967	1974	1977	1979	1982	1983
K Mart Corp.[a]	33	216	803	1,397	1,688	2,117	2,160
Kresge[b]	788	614	422	329	296	253	201
Jupiter[b]	30	113	101	86	85		
Total	851	943	1,326	1,782	2,069	2,370	2,361
Woolworth[c]	2,760	2,088	1,993	1,901	1,800	1,665	1,641
Woolco	2	67	328	381	426	120[d]	121[d]
Total	2,762	2,088	2,321	2,282	2,226	1,785	1,762

[a] K Mart figures are for total worldwide stores, almost all in the United States.

[b] Kresge and Jupiter are variety stores.

[c] Woolworth figures are for total worldwide stores, including approximately 200 Canadian and 200 German stores; British Woolworth is not included.

[d] Remaining Canadian Woolco stores.

Sources: K Mart Annual Reports; F. W. Woolworth Company Annual Reports.

TABLE 9-9   Increases in Key Statistics for K Mart and Woolworth, from 1962–1982

	Net Sales (millions)	Earnings per Share	Dividends	Price of Common Stock
K Mart	$35.1	$22.9	$12.4	12.2
Woolworth	4.6	1.5	2.2	1.2

Source: Compiled from Tables 9-6 and 9-7.

the Southeast and South Central states. K Mart would cluster many stores in a Standard Metropolitan Statistical Area.

Woolworth's management further diversified by establishing or acquiring the following specialty retailers:

1963	Kinney Shoe Corporation
1969	Richman Brothers
1979	J. Brannam
1983	Little Folk Shop
1984	RX Place, deep-discount drugstore chain
1985	Frame Scenes, specialty frame store
1985	Afterthoughts, boutique—jewelry, handbags, accessories
1985	Herald Square Stationers, stationary

K Mart's diversification strategy began in 1980. It has cafeterias and other retail units. In 1984, K Mart purchased the 850-store Walden Books chain for $300 million. Also in 1984, it entered the off-price apparel business with Designer Depot, its only specialty retailing operation, developed internally. In January 1985, plans were announced to purchase Pay Less Drug Stores Northwest, Inc., for $500 million. This chain operates 164 drug stores. As of 1983, K Mart stores contributed 97 percent of K Mart's sales and profits. Officials predict that by 1989, 20 percent of its revenue and profit will come from other than its K Mart discount stores.

F. W. WOOLWORTH COMPANY:
SUCCESS OR FAILURE?

The success of Woolworth came mostly in the early years of its existence. The highly profitable stores allowed it to expand and establish itself as the leading variety store chain. Its foreign operations were also successful in its early days.

Few observers 20 years ago would have predicted the demise of Woolco and survival of Woolworth. At that time, most retailers were jumping into discounting, the newest retail revolution.

Woolco was a failure. Key indicators were increased losses while sales were increasing (see Table 9-4). Inventory turnover ratios for Woolco in 1981 at 2.2 times were far below the industry average of 3.5. Also, with average sales per square foot at $70, Woolco stores lagged far behind the industry average of $100.

Management could have turned Woolco around in a three- to five-year period with a large infusion of capital but had no guarantee of a reasonable rate of return or investment.

Management believed investment of this capital would better serve its mission and financial objectives if deployed to other projects. In short, it was not worth saving Woolco.

An examination of Table 9-3 reveals that Woolworth Germany is the best performing Woolworth division. Kinney Shoe Corp. is the most successful division.

The specialty retailers such as J. Brannam, Frugal Frank's, Fredelle, Lady Foot Locker, Little Folk Shop, and others are in the introductory or early development stage. It may be too early to assess their level of success or failure.

CONCLUSION

F. W. Woolworth is at a crossroad. Management must decide if the company's future lies with its variety store chain or specialty retail chains or both.

The variety store chain should be reformulated. A modernization program is necessary, as is a complete review of the profitability of all locations. The size of the stores, merchandise assortment, store layout, food service, and electronic point-of-sale devices should be reexamined.

The number of stores in most of the current specialty retail chains should be increased. If Woolworth purchases or develops too many new retail formats, its business could become fragmented. It would be difficult to develop a cohesive strategy and management could fall into the trap of buying and selling businesses based on profitability and return on investment. Long-range planning and development of their other current businesses would suffer. The company would become large and complex but only nominally profitable.

QUESTIONS

1. Do variety store chains such as Woolworth, Kresge, and Murphy's have a future?
2. Have any variety store chains closed?

3. Suggest a comprehensive strategy for revitalizing Woolworth's variety store chain.
4. What methods did Frank Woolworth use to expand his chain in its early history?
5. Suggest some other methods that chains use to expand.
6. In its early history stores 1, 3, and 4 were closed; yet stores 2 and 5 were successful. Why?
7. Was closing Woolco a correct decision?
8. K Mart began its diversification program much later than Woolworth. Why was this a wise decision?
9. Is it common for retailers to operate stores throughout the world?
10. What is Woolworth's future in foreign markets?
11. Who are Woolworth's variety store competitors?
12. Discuss Frank Woolworth's contributions to retailing and marketing.
13. Woolworth's financial statistics for 1984, 1985, and 1986 are impressively healthy. Why is Woolworth currently a success or failure?

NOTES

1. F. W. Woolworth Co., 1983 Annual Report, p. 7.
2. Godfrey M. Lebhar, *Chain Stores in America, 1859–1962*, 3rd ed. (New York: Chain Store Publishing Corp., 1963), p. 36.
3. "How Kresge Became the Top Discounter," *Business Week*, October 24, 1970, p. 63.

10

DELOREAN MOTOR COMPANY

INTRODUCTION

John DeLorean, an engineer turned entrepreneur, nearly succeeded in launching a new automobile company in the United States despite overwhelming odds.

His task was doubly complex. First he had to build a company and then he had to build an automobile. For an individual to undertake such an operation is truly astounding. He raised nearly $240 million in funding and built and staffed a factory (assembly operation) in Northern Ireland in less than two and one-half years.

Experts estimate the start-up cost of a complete automobile manufacturing facility at $3 billion. An assembly operation that uses components from the outside would cost $300 million. Few major corporations would risk such a challenge.

The DeLorean Motor Company (DMC) made a $6 million profit in its first five quarters. Some experts believe that survival would have been possible had DMC remained small and grown slowly. Instead, John DeLorean ordered that production be doubled in January 1982 when sales were slipping. He ignored market demand and market conditions.

The Northern Ireland assembly operation was built to start big and be expanded. Because of its size, the project may have been doomed from the start.

McKinsey & Co., a management consulting firm evaluating the project, gave it a one-in-ten chance of succeeding. DeLorean was also aware of the risks associated with the project. He said that if successful, "it will be the most incredible accomplishment in the last 100 years."[1]

The mid-1970s were an inauspicious time to begin a new automobile company. The Arab oil embargo and the rapid increase in the price of gasoline brought about a complete upheaval in the industry. The first DeLorean cars reached the United States in June 1981, but by December 1981 the recession and a very severe winter affected sales.

Past history shows that the track record for new car companies has been abysmal. There has not been a successful start up of a major car company in the United States since Walter P. Chrysler founded the Chrysler Car Company in 1925. Henry Kaiser began the Kaiser-Frazer Company in 1945 and managed to stay in business until 1955, when the company closed after losing $100 million. Preston Tucker produced a modernistic, streamlined car named the "Tucker Torpedo" in 1946. He sold $40 million of stock in his company but only 51 cars. Malcolm Brinklin built a sports car. His Canadian plant was partially financed with a $20 million loan from the Canadian government. The cars were stylish and exciting, but poorly engineered. Quality is an important aspect in automotive manufacturing. After one year, the plant closed.

Ford itself had one of the costliest new product failures in history. The Ford Edsel is estimated to have cost the company over $200 million. Only a large corporation could absorb such a loss.

The odds against John DeLorean were not favorable. Since 1900, there have been some 2,500 attempts to launch new car companies in the United States. By 1973, only the big four and a handful of small producers—Excaliber, Avanti, and Checker—remained.

JOHN DELOREAN

John DeLorean's entire career has been in the automotive industry. He grew up in Detroit, the oldest of four sons of a Ford foundry worker. His parents were divorced when John was 13 and he stayed with his mother in Los Angeles during the school year. In the summers he returned to Detroit to work at a Chrysler assembly plant.

His formal education consisted of an undergraduate degree in engineering from Lawrence Institute in Michigan in 1948, a master of science degree from the Chrysler Institute in 1952, and an M.B.A. from the University of Michigan in 1956.

He began his career with Chrysler in 1948 and moved to the Packard Motor Company in 1952 where he became that company's chief of engineering. When Packard folded in 1956, he joined General Motors.

DeLorean had a brilliant 17-year career with General Motors. In 1965, at 40, he became the youngest general manager of a General Motor division when he took over Pontiac. His engineering credits include Pontiac's wide-track styling, stacked headlights, concealed windshield wipers, radio antenna, and several cars—the GTO, Grand Prix, and Firebird.

In 1969 DeLorean was named General Manager of the Chevrolet Division. By 1971, Chevy sold more than 3 million cars and trucks. This was a record for all manufacturers. DeLorean was promoted to vice-president of car and truck operations in 1972, one step away from the presidency. He was 48, earned $650,000 a year, and was the heir apparent to the General Motors presidency.

In 1973, DeLorean resigned from General Motors. He believed that Detroit was closed to new ideas and innovations, lacked concern for the safety and finances of the consumer, and put undue emphasis on profit.

After a year of heading the National Alliance for Businessmen, he asked General Motors dealers if they might be interested in a new kind of car—a sports car unlike anything in the General Motors line. It would be safe, fuel efficient, affordable, and durable. He called it the "ethical car." The response was positive and he founded the DeLorean Motor Company in 1975.

The capital for this firm came from a number of different sources. Of the total, $8.6 million came from 345 automotive dealers and $18 million from 134 limited partners. The government of Northern Ireland gave $200 million in grants and subsidies for a new assembly plant to be located outside Belfast, Ireland. By one estimate, DeLorean put up only $20,000 of his own money, yet wound up with more than 80 percent ownership of the company that bore his name.[2]

As an entrepreneur, DeLorean was an outstanding fund-raiser. Yet, experts believe that the firm was undercapitalized from the beginning.

DeLorean also pursued an extravagant lifestyle. Some questioned whether the point of the company was to build a car or to maintain the founder's lifestyle and illusions.

DeLorean had difficulty focusing on his central objective, which was to launch a successful automobile company. Funds and energy went to dubious projects and goals.

John DeLorean became involved in a myriad of projects. Money was moved around from one account to another to finance these projects. The legality of many of these transactions is being questioned in the courts.

In November 1978, $18.8 million went to GPD, a Swiss-based company that was supposed to do development work on the DeLorean car. GPD was a one-room office in Geneva, was not Swiss registered, and had nothing to do with making cars.

A $6 million loan from the Continental Illinois Bank in Chicago was used to purchase a Utah-based company that made equipment for grooming slopes at ski resorts. This loan was partially paid off with a check drawn on a Swiss bank.

Another $500,000 was paid in legal fees to figure out how to buy the Chrysler Corporation.

Meanwhile, a talented and experienced management team was

assembled and DMC's start-up went well. The dealer network, plant, quality assurance center, and car financing arrangements were all handled by experienced automotive executives.

The company broke ground in Northern Ireland for the assembly plant in October 1978. Two and one-half years later, the first commercially produced cars were manufactured. They reached the United States in June of 1981 and sold quickly.

During the first six months, 3,500 cars were sold. Unit sales then fell from 650 in December to 350 in January. This was not a problem since the company was producing 30 to 35 cars a day—an output the market could absorb and allow the company to break even.

At this point, John DeLorean ordered that production be more than doubled. His executives tried in vain to persuade him to cut back on production. They explained the numerous problems that would result from a doubling of production. DeLorean woud not listen. Some 1,200 untrained workers were hired and production increased as he had ordered.

In February 1982, the British government declared DMC insolvent and asked for $22 million. On October 19, 1982, their demand unmet, the government officially closed the facility. Seven hours later, John DeLorean was arrested in a hotel room in Los Angeles in connection with a cocaine deal that would have netted $24 million.

THE MARKET AND COMPETITION

John DeLorean left Detroit concerned with two of its business practices— the yearly model change and the American automobile's relatively short physical life. He believed that these practices cost the American consumer too much money.

Therefore, he decided to build a car his way. Consumers would be sold what DeLorean thought they needed. The "ethical car" built by the ethical company would have no annual model changes. It would be immune to rust and corrosion.

The car as originally conceived was a quality personal sports car. It was to have a molded plastic body using a process that DeLorean had developed at General Motors. Its major competitor was Chevrolet's Corvette. It was to retail in the $14,000 range (1981). Its target market would be successful professional males who would not be affected by economic swings. DeLorean believed that, despite the depressed U.S. economy, a market did exist for his car.

Analysts estimated that 6,000 to 8,000 cars a year could be sold. The company needed sales of 10,000 to 12,000 cars a year to break even. DMC's marketing department said it could sell at most 12,000 cars if it drew customers away from Porsche, Mercedes, Cadillac, and other high-class makes. The major sports car competitors were Porsche, Corvette, and Datsun Z.

Sales taken from competition would not be sufficient to make the venture profitable. The DeLorean auto (the DMC) had to be more than a sports car. It had to be an exciting new concept in style, design, content, and philosophy. It had to draw customers from more than the limited sports car market.

As the car neared the production stage, high inflation in Britain and a declining U. S. dollar shifted the retail price from $14,000 to $26,000. As the DMC grew more expensive, its market became more limited.

THE MARKETING MIX

Product. The DMC was a traditional two-seater sports car. The engine was in the rear, driving the rear wheels. The standard transmission was a five speed with an automotic shift as the only option. Fuel economy was 19 miles per gallon better than that of most sports cars.

Although more efficient than the Corvette, the DMC was not quite as zippy on takeoff. It handled well and traveled fast enough to be fun to drive.

Since General Motors would not give a release on DeLorean's plastic-molding process, stainless steel was used.

Among the DMC's unique features were its gull-winged doors and stainless steel body. The gull-winged doors made an attention-getting humming noise when opening. Stepping out of the car into a crowd of bystanders was what the DeLorean image was all about.

The car was also durable, safe, and comfortable. Although aimed at people who liked sportiness, it was inexpensive to maintain. Many sports cars had a reputation for being temperamental and expensive to maintain. DeLorean described the DMC as the ethical sports car.

Distribution. DeLorean personally signed dealers to distribute the car. Each dealer became an investor in the company, adding the DMC to his existing line of cars. Dealers were required to purchase a DeLorean sign and a basic supply of parts and tools. They were to send at least one technician to a special training school. The dealers agreed to purchase between 50 and 150 cars the first year. Originally 345 dealers invested in the company. The network would eventually have 400 dealers.

Pricing and Demand. In the introduction months, so much pent-up demand existed for the car that dealers were able to sell it at several thousand dollars over list price. The car listed for $26,000 but the average sales price was $30,000.

Promotion. The DeLorean was to be synonymous with style and quality. Avrett, Free & Fischer, a small advertising agency that thought up Contac's "tiny time pills" and the Meow Mix catfood "dancing cat," was selected to handle the account.

It was decided to capitalize on the dream aspect of the DMC. This was John DeLorean's dream. It could be yours. The theme, "Live the Dream," was chosen.

The first television commercial, a 30-second spot, appeared in the fall of 1981 during the U.S. Open Tennis Championship. It showed the car alone by the seashore with gulls flying in the background. The doors swung up and closed and the car raced along the coast and finally stopped. A voice said, "The most awaited car in history," and closed with, "Live the dream today." Advertisements appeared in a select group of magazines whose audience it was believed would identify with the dream.

It may not have been necessary for the company to spend the millions of dollars on advertising that it did. Demand had built up before the car arrived. Dealers had back orders for 7,000 cars. The nation's press was so enthralled with the DeLorean adventure that newspapers and television carried many stories about the man, the car, and the company. They showed the first boatload of DMCs arriving at Long Beach, California, as well as the first car to arrive at a dealer. Later, celebrities and other early purchasers were frequently shown with their DMCs.

DELOREAN'S LIFESTYLE AND ETHICS

In 1956, John DeLorean had been hired by Bunkie Knudsen, the general manager of Pontiac Division, to head research and development. Knudsen said, "He was a pretty square fellow when I hired him."[3]

In his 17-year career with General Motors, DeLorean rose rapidly through the ranks. The sales records established by the Pontiac and Chevrolet Divisions under his leadership still stand today and DeLorean is recognized as a talented engineer who holds more than 100 patents.

One trait that surfaced during DeLorean's rise was his ability to appear as the star of a project. He was always in the limelight and viewed General Motors' successes as his personal accomplishments.

As he moved up the corporate ladder, his behavioral patterns and lifestyle changed. In 1969, he divorced his secretary-wife of 14 years and married Kelly Harmon, the 20-year-old daughter of former football star Tom Harmon.

He started to look much less corporate. His clothes ran more to turtlenecks and Nehru suits rather than buttondowns and pinstripes. He dyed his hair black and wore it long. He had a facelift and started lifting weights to preserve his physique. His circle of friends went beyond the

General Motors clique to include film stars and sports celebrities. In 1973, he married Christina Ferrare, a fashion model half his age. Later that year he quit his $650,000 a year job. He left General Motors as a modishly attired corporate renegade.

John DeLorean was arrested on October 19, 1982, and charged with conspiracy to possess and distribute cocaine. On August 16, 1984, he was acquitted of all counts in the alleged cocaine-smuggling conspiracy, despite hours of videotape evidence secretly recorded by the government. The key defense in this case was "entrapment." District Judge Robert M. Takasugi told jurors, "That entrapment meant that the defendant was guilty of a crime, but that he wouldn't have committed it without improper coercion by government agents."[4]

A number of former DMC company executives, when questioned as to the motive for DeLorean's becoming involved in the alleged drug deal, said that he was out to save himself, his reputation, his ego, and perhaps most of all his glamorous style of living. Only one executive believed he was using the alleged drug deal to raise money to save the firm.[5]

During the 1960s, Cristina Ferrare became a born-again Christian. During the trial she persuaded her husband to join her in that faith. At a baptism ceremony attended by 200 other Christians, the two of them were baptized in their swimming pool behind their Bedminster, New Jersey, mansion.

Shortly after DeLorean was acquitted in mid-September 1984, he and his wife separated.

On November 8, 1984, DeLorean took out a full-page advertisement in a Los Angeles newspaper to solicit contributions to help pay the remaining legal fees incurred in the cocaine case.

The advertisement asked that contributions of $5, $10, $20, or $100 be sent to the John DeLorean Defense Fund, Inc. The fund was described as a nonprofit organization.

The headline on the ad, which ran in other newspapers as well, said, "It's a Horror Story." The ad said his life has been virtually destroyed by an outrageous pattern of police abuse and he tried to escape from the frameup and entrapment. As a born-again Christian, he wanted to devote the remainder of his life to his Christian ministry and his children.

John DeLorean faces a number of legal suits. A federal grand jury in Detroit is investigating creditors' allegations of bankruptcy fraud in the DeLorean Motor Company case. In addition, creditors and investors in various DeLorean concerns are bringing civil law suits.

Meanwhile, DeLorean's personal assets of more than $20 million are tied up by court order.

CONCLUSION

John DeLorean was successful as a rising young executive at General Motors but failed as an entrepreneur. DeLorean ignored marketing research that showed his car to have a limited market. He insisted on expanding production against the advice of his executives. Some questioned whether DeLorean was seriously interested in DeLorean Motors or was simply using it as a means of supporting his extravagant lifestyle.

QUESTIONS

1. Why would the British government invite John DeLorean to locate his assembly operation in Northern Ireland?
2. Would the assembly operation have been better off to locate in the United States?
3. Why did John DeLorean believe that the U.S. automobile industry was not socially responsible?
4. Why was the DMC called the "ethical" sports car?
5. What major marketing concept did John DeLorean violate?
6. Demand for a new product is very difficult to measure. How would you measure demand for the $26,000 DMC?
7. Give a product definition of the DMC.
8. Discuss the strengths and weaknesses of this company's marketing strategy.
9. Develop a profile of the DMC owner.
10. Discuss John DeLorean's shortcomings.

NOTES

1. Craig R. Waters, "John DeLorean and the Icarus Factor," *Inc.*, April 1983, p. 35.
2. Ibid., p.38.
3. Ann M. Morrison, "John DeLorean's Long Downhill Ride," *Fortune*, November 15, 1982, p. 62.
4. Scot J. Paltrow, "DeLorean Is Acquitted of All Counts in Cocaine Smuggling Conspiracy Case," *Wall Street Journal*, Western ed., August 17, 1984, p. 3.
5. Morrison, "John DeLorean's Long Downhill Ride," p. 61.

11

THE GREAT ATLANTIC & PACIFIC TEA COMPANY (A & P)

INTRODUCTION

The Great Atlantic & Pacific Tea Company, Inc., is an American institution. In 1986 this company was 127 years old. Its major contribution to retailing is the concept of a chain. In 1930, there were 15,737 A & P stores scattered across the United States, by far the largest number of stores ever assembled in a corporate chain. For over 100 years, A & P was ranked number one in sales for all retailers. In 1973, Safeway passed A & P to become the largest food retailer; in 1964, Sears, Roebuck and Company became the number one retailer (see Table 11-1).

A & P has met many challenges during its history and has radically transformed itself to meet these challenges. Lately the company has fallen on hard times. Only 6 out of the 11 years from 1974 to 1984 were profitable. Dividends have been practically nonexistent.

In 1979 the Tenglemann Group, the second largest food retailer in West Germany, purchased a 42-percent interest in A & P. Today this group has 51 percent control.

For a while, it appeared that the Tenglemann Group had purchased a real lemon. A & P was headed for bankruptcy. However, by controlling costs, negotiating favorable labor contracts, and shedding unprofitable operations, A & P may again be a winner. Its $56 million profit in 1985 was the largest in the company's history. Its percent return on sales put A & P right in line with the traditional 1-percent industry average.

Despite this rebound, it is too early to classify A & P in the turnaround category. Bankruptcy has been avoided but good merchandising is necessary for long-term survival and profitability.

TABLE 11-1   Ranking of A & P by Sales among Food Retailers and All Retailers, Selected Years, 1963–1985

Year	Food Retailers	Year	All Retailers
1985	6	1985	16
1984	6	1984	17
1982	6	1982	13
1981	5	1981	10
1980	3	1978	6
1973	2	1973	3
1972	1	1972	2
1964	1	1964	2
1963	1	1963	1

Source: Fortune, "The Top 50 Retailers," June 9, 1986, p. 136; July 13, 1983, p. 168; July 12, 1982, p. 140; July 13, 1981, p. 122; July 1974, p. 120; July 1973, p. 128; August 1965, p. 176; August 1964, p. 158.

EARLY HISTORY OF A & P

1859–1911.   A & P had its beginning in a small store in New York City in 1859. It was not a grocery store and was not yet named the Great Atlantic & Pacific Tea Company. The founders believed they could make tea available to the public below the prevailing price by importing directly from China and Japan and eliminating the middleman.

By 1865, there were 25 stores and the name Great American Tea Company was used. At this time, a line of groceries was added. Management believed that if tea could be sold at reduced prices so could other items. The concept and principles of a chain organization had become operational and successful.

The Great Atlantic & Pacific Tea Company name was chosen in 1869 because the company had spread westward. By 1900, 41 years after its foundation, the chain had 200 stores. Its rate of growth was modest, with an average of five stores opening per year.

1912–1930.   A major store expansion program began in 1912. A successful new type of store was developed and management decided to open as many of these stores as rapidly as possible.

The new stores were called "economy stores." They were designed to sell groceries as cheaply as possible on a cash-and-carry basis. The old services of making deliveries and extending credit were eliminated. These were common practices with most food retailers of the day.

The new stores were small, low-rent, one-man operations, with modest fixtures, all making for low operating costs. They were to be satisfied with minimal profits that would be offset by increased volume.[1] In size they rarely exceeded 1,500 square feet.

Because of their low prices, these stores could prosper practically anywhere and everywhere. Over 100 stores were opened in 1913. Between 1920 and 1925, almost 10,000 new stores were opened (see Table 11-2). This averaged to 2,000 stores a year and nearly 40 stores a week. This incredible store explosion remains unequaled in the realm of retailing.

1931–1950. The explosion came to an end in 1930 when A & P had 15,737 stores, its all-time high. A new revolution occurring in the grocery field brought about by the introduction of the supermarket in the early 1930s. This store was much larger than the combination stores that immediately preceded it. The combination stores added fresh meats, fresh fruits, and vegetables to its grocery lines.

The supermarkets were four to five times larger than the traditional grocery stores. Many of these new stores had 10,000 square feet. They emphasized the new concept of self-service and had checkout counters at the front of the store. Although orginally established by independents, the chains eventually adopted their format.

A & P was slow in reacting to its first major threat, but eventually started the conversion process. Three to four "economy stores" were closed for each new supermarket opened. A & P witnessed a drastic shrinkage in number of "economy stores" and by 1941 only 4,576 remained (see Tables 11-2 and 11-3). The company had weathered its first major challenge. A single "economy store" remains in operation today in the French Quarter of New Orleans. It is a novelty and popular tourist attraction.

TABLE 11-2 Number of A & P Stores, Selected Years, 1859–1984

Year	Stores	Year	Stores
1984	1,015	1940	7,000
1983	1,021	1935	14,926
1982	1,040	1930	15,737
1981	1,055	1927	15,671
1980	1,543	1925	14,034
1979	1,542	1920	4,621
1978	1,771	1916	2,866
1977	1,905	1915	1,817
1976	1,978	1914	991
1975	2,074	1913	585
1974	3,468	1912	480
1971	4,400	1900	200
1960	4,351	1880	100
1955	4,150	1865	25
1950	4,500	1859	1
1945	5,600		

Source: Annual Reports.

TABLE 11-3 A & P Conversion of Economy Stores to Supermarkets, 1935–1941

Year	Number of Supermarkets	Number of Economy Stores	Total Number of Stores
1941	1,594	4,576	6,170
1940	1,396	5,834	7,230
1939	1,119	8,081	9,200
1938	771	10,129	10,900
1937	282	13,032	13,314
1936	20	14,726	14,746
1935	0	14,926	14,926

Source: Company records.

1951–1971. After World War II, A & P ceased being an innovative merchandiser. It became a follower rather than a leader. It lagged in introducing nonfood items such as apparel, hardware, health and drugs, beauty, toys, china, and other household items. It also lagged in the area of sales promotion, being one of the last chains to accept trading stamps.

Other changes were occurring in food merchandising. Various kinds of discounting and discounting stores were evolving. The convenience food stores were also expanding rapidly. Some supermarket chains even set up a separate convenience food store division to compete against the independent national chains such as 7-Eleven and to protect their own business. The fast-food business also affected the sales volume of the supermarket chains.

During the 1950s and 1960s, A & P stabilized at 4,400 stores. Sales in the 1950s were in the $3 to $4 billion range and profits were $30 to $40 million. During the 1960s, sales were in the $4 to $5 billion range and profits were $40 to $50 million. The company had matured. It was also paying out a rather high percentage of its earnings per share in dividends as compared to other supermarket chains.[2] In 1969, A & P was 100 years old. It was still the largest food retailer. It was stable, profitable, and in trouble. The giant of the industry had lost its innovativeness and was at a standstill.

WEO CAMPAIGN OF 1972

In 1972, the new president, William J. Kane, decided to convert A & P to a superdiscount chain. Sales had leveled off and profits were slowly dropping in the late 1960s. Market share was the major concern. In 1950, A & P was estimated to have 15 percent of the market; in 1960, 10 percent; and by 1970, 6 percent.[3]

In 1971, Safeway almost edged out A & P in sales to take the number one position. Kane wanted to shake A & P from its lethargy. He wanted to return A & P to what it was—good food at low prices. The way to do this, he believed, was to cut prices. This would increase sales, reinstate higher profitability, and recapture the lost market share.

WEO stands for "Where Economy Originates." During this campaign, the number of items in the stores was reduced from 11,000 to 8,000. Prices were lowered from 8 to 12 percent on 90 percent of the merchandise. Extensive in-store promotion and heavy advertising in newspapers, radio, and television broadcast the message that A & P's prices were lower than those of competitors. WEO stores became known as "Warehouse Economy Outlets." By August 1982, 90 percent of the stores were WEOs. The results were disastrous. Sales increased 13 percent, market share remained about the same as 1970, but A & P posted the first deficit in its history, $51 million (see Table 11-4).

The problems facing A & P were later identified as follows:

1. Location: Too many inner-city stores, too many free-standing stores, and not enough stores in neighborhood shopping centers.
2. Size of stores: 1970 average for A & P of 14,000 square feet compared to industry average of 20,000 square feet.
3. Store maintenance: Run-down, unkept, and crowded conditions, poor service.
4. Work staff: Many employees too old.

TABLE 11-4 A & P Sales, Profits (Losses), and Dividends, Selected Years, 1960–1985

Year	Sales (millions)	Profits (Losses) (millions)	Dividends
1985[a]	$6,615	$56	$0.10
1984	5,878	51	None
1983	5,222	31	None
1982	4,608	21	None
1981	6,227	(232)	None
1980	6,990	(43)	None
1979	6,684	(4)	None
1978	7,470	(52)	0.05
1977	7,289	3	0.15
1976	7,236	14	None
1975	6,538	3	None
1974	6,875	(157)	0.45
1973	6,748	12	None
1972	6,369	(51)	0.80
1971	5,508	15	1.30
1970	5,664	50	1.30
1960	5,240	55	1.25

[a] Year ends February 28 of following year.

Sources: Annual Reports; Standard & Poor's NYSE Stock Reports, Vol. 53, No. 17, Sec. 10, January 24, 1986, p. 1052.

5. Private labels: Too much emphasis placed on private labels and not enough prominence given to national brands.

Overall, A & P had developed a poor image. Its customers on the average were older and it was not attracting the young suburbanite families. Management's solution was to cut prices.

JONATHAN L. SCOTT, 1975–1980

When Jonathan L. Scott took over A & P, it was a very backward company. It lacked the financial controls of a modern corporation. Its cost structure had become very high. Labor costs, which represent over 60 percent of the total operating costs, ran to 12.4 percent of sales compared to the industry average of 10.1 percent. Administrative costs were 2 of sales percent compared to the industry average of 1.25 percent. A & P had been late in following its customers to the suburbs and there were too many small, inefficient stores tucked away in deteriorating urban neighborhoods. Stores were overstocked with A & P's private-label merchandise (notably Jane Parker and Ann Page brands) which were consequences of the company's excessive emphasis on its manufacturing plants.

In 1973, Safeway Stores became the nation's number one grocery chain in total sales.

Scott implemented the following program in his four-year tenure:

1. Replaced nearly all of top management.
2. Closed one-half of the 3,468 stores.
3. Closed 27 of the 46 food processing plants.
4. Closed 9 warehouses.
5. Closed two divisions—Dallas and Buffalo.
6. Invested hundreds of millions of dollars in new facilities.
7. Purchased 62 stores from National Tea in Chicago in 1976.

In essence, the strategy was major surgery—cut out the unprofitable operations. However, a major mistake was made in the closing of the stores. The problem was deciding which stores to close and which to save. Scott's choice was to close down the company's worst operating units, store by store, warehouse by warehouse, plant by plant. This decision called for immediate closing of 1,250 unprofitable or marginal stores as well as certain warehouses and manufacturing plants. To cover the estimated cost of the program, A & P set up a $200 million reserve taken as a charge against earnings in the fourth quarter of 1974. The result was an after-tax loss of $157 million for the year (see Table 11-4).

The decision was a mistake. Instead of concentrating on individual units, the company should have concentrated on operating divisions and markets, retreating completely from geographical areas where they were weak. The store-by-store approach left A & P spread too thin in some areas, sacrificing economies of scale that are inherent in geographical concentration.

The 1976 purchase of 62 stores for $22 million in Chicago from National Tea, which had decided to withdraw from that market, was another poor decision. A & P did not know which National Tea Stores to close and which ones to integrate into their system. Labor and advertising costs as a percent of sales did not decrease as anticipated. In 1981, the Chicago market was closed. Capital had been poorly deployed.

THE TENGLEMANN GROUP, 1979

In 1979 the Tenglemann Group of West Germany bought A & P. Erivan Haub, its president, had his own ideas on how to run A & P. He wanted the retrenchment program stopped and ordered the following:

1. Turn the current stores around. Make them profitable. Stop closing stores.
2. Make the Horseheads processing plant work. Stop closing processing plants.
3. Stop closing divisions.
4. Expand the PLUS chain.

The PLUS chain concept was developed in Europe where it was very successful. Haub believed that the concept could be transplanted to the United States and that the American housewife would save money. PLUS would absorb the excess capacity of the Horseheads plant, the largest food processing plant in the world.

PLUS is a limited-assortment, no-frills store that sells 1,000 or so items at a discount, but no meat, dairy products, or fresh produce (see Table 11-5). A & P switched over to PLUS many of its smaller outdated city stores.

TABLE 11-5 Number of PLUS Discount Food Stores, 1979–1984

Year	Number of Stores
1984	0
1983	25
1982	40
1981	55
1980	78
1979	32

Source: Annual Reports.

JAMES WOOD, 1980 TO PRESENT

In April 1980, James Wood became president of A & P. Although hired by Erivan Haub, Wood was opposed to many of his decisions. Wood wanted to close PLUS and the Horseheads plant. By 1981, PLUS had costs around $40 million and its stores were losing more than $4 million a year. The decision was made to phase out the chain.

The Horseheads plant was built in the mid-1960s in the expectation that A & P's sales would grow to $16 to $18 billion a year. The plant processed many of A & P's private labels. Production never ran over 50 percent of capacity and sometimes approached 20 percent. The plant generally lost between $5 and $10 million a year. When the decision was made to retrench on the private label and phase out PLUS, Horseheads became more vulnerable. It was closed in April 1982

James Wood finally prevailed over Haub and was given the go ahead to run A & P as he saw fit. In 1981 he took the following actions:

1. Closed out 500 stores or one-third of the remaining stores.
2. Got out of manufacturing.
3. Phased out PLUS.

The store closings resulted in a loss of $232 million, the greatest in A & P's history. This time, however, the surgery was done right: whole divisions and geographical areas were closed.

Wood was also successful with the unions. He wangled relief Scott had never been able to get. By this time, average industry wages were 11 percent of sales; A & P's were 13 percent. The unions renegotiated many contracts to the advantage of A & P and the company promised to close no more stores.

In Philadelphia, A & P instituted a closely watched experiment.[4] It closed the division and reopened as Super Fresh stores emphasizing fresh produce. In exchange for getting their jobs back, union members relinquished 25 percent of their wages and benefits. They gained the right to share decisions on what to stock. They will divide 1 percent of the store's annual sales, providing labor costs are 10 percent of sales or less. In the former A & P stores, labor costs had run to 15 percent of sales. The Super Fresh stores had a profit of $10 million in 1982 versus a $12 million loss as A & P stores in 1981. In 1983 and 1984, many new Super Fresh stores were opened in the Philadelphia market.

Wood also decided to open a number of Super PLUS Warehouse stores (see Table 11-6). These stores have 75,000 to 100,000 square feet and are four to five times the size of a supermarket. Prices are considerably below most supermarkets on most goods all the time. The stores carry a wide variety of merchandise, including an extensive assortment of perishable goods.

TABLE 11-6 Number of Super PLUS Warehouse Stores, 1981–1984

Year	Number of Stores
1984	8
1983	6
1982	3
1981	1

Source: Annual Reports.

Both Scott and Wood took $200 million write-offs when they drastically reduced the number of supermarkets. Three years of profitability followed each retrenchment. Scott's operation then turned to a deficit. Hopefully, Wood will be able to retain profits.

James Wood knows how to turn a company around. Knowing how to run one after it has been turned around is a different story. In order for A & P to remain profitable and regain its lost innovativeness, it must become a merchandiser again.

CONCLUSION

The food industry has undergone many changes during A & P's long history. In its early history, A & P was the innovator and leader in the retail food industry. Its major contributions were the implementation of the chain concept, economy stores, and self-service.

Since the 1930s, A & P has been a follower. It has not pioneered new concepts with the exception of the PLUS stores, a European innovation that did not work in the United States. A & P has reacted to changes in its environment and the new concepts and technologies introduced by its competition. Its history can be divided into the following periods:

1859–1930	Innovator
1930–1970	Maturity
1970–present	Decline

A & P remained the number one food retailer for well over 100 years until relinquishing that position to Safeway in 1973. At its height, it employed over 140,000 people. Today it employs 40,000.

If A & P is to survive and prosper, it must become efficient on a market-to-market basis. Its major competition is strong regional and local chains.

The environment that A & P operates in today has vastly changed from past years. As the retail revolution progresses, it will provide some opportunities and challenges in A & P's future.

QUESTIONS

1. Discuss the characteristics of a chain store. What are its advantages and disadvantages?
2. A retail revolution has occurred in food retailing. It began in 1859 and continues today. In your discussion of how food retailing has changed from 1859 to the present (a) list and describe the various types of stores that sell food; (b) identify and describe new marketing principles or concepts that were used; (c) identify and discuss five major changes in the environment that affected food retailing; and (d) discuss three technological changes that affected food retailing.
3. Many of A & P's closed stores were reopened by independents. What have these entrepreneurs done to make the reopened stores successful?
4. Suggest the strategies that the competition used to effectively offset A & P's WEO campaign.
5. What steps did James Wood take to control costs at A & P?
6. A & P's manufacturing plants supplied a large volume of the stores' products. Why were these plants a liability in recent years?
7. Vast numbers of stores were closed in 1974 and 1981. What other areas of the company would this affect?
8. Now that A & P's costs have been controlled, suggest a strategy for increasing A & P's sales.

NOTES

1. Godfrey M. Lebhar, *Chain Stores in America, 1859-1962,* 3rd ed. (New York: Chain Store Publishing Corporation, 1963), p. 31.
2. Peter W. Bernstein, "Jonathan Scott's Surprising Failure at A & P," *Fortune,* November 6, 1978, p. 35.
3. Ibid.
4. Gwen Kinkead "The Executive Suite Struggle behind A & P's Profits," *Fortune,* November 1, 1982, p. 104.

12

INTERNATIONAL HARVESTER

INTRODUCTION

International Harvester (IH), one of America's pioneer industrial organizations, dates back to 1831 when Cyrus McCormick invented the reaper, a mechanical machine used to harvest grain.

The reaper significantly increased productivity on the farm by allowing one man to do the work of six. It created an agricultural revolution that changed forever the farming practices of the United States.

This invention is ranked as a leading technological advancement of the nineteenth century, and Cyrus McCormick is held in the same category of high esteem as other famous early American inventors such as Eli Whitney, inventor of the cotton gin in 1793 and of interchangeable parts used in the manufacture of guns; and Robert Fulton, inventor of the steamboat in 1807.

Cyrus McCormick also made contributions in the field of factory layout and design. By 1860, the McCormick Harvesting Company was one of the largest factories of assembled equipment in the United States producing 4,000 reapers a year. It was one of the earliest companies to centralize management and to develop a national dealership organization and national sales organization. It was a precursor of the modern corporate structure.

International Harvester Company, a trust, was formed in 1902. It gradually diversified into several lines of business manufacturing a multiplicity of products (see Table 12-1). This capital-intensive enterprise's major lines of business were agricultural equipment and trucks.

Corporate headquarters were located in Chicago. Most manufactur-

TABLE 12-1   Partial List of Products Manufactured by Product Line by International Harvester

Agricultural Equipment
Plows
Tillage equipment
Planters
Hay balers
Combines
Tractors, all types
Cub cadet (very small tractor)
Manure spreader
Binders
Cornheads
Construction Equipment
Loaders
Forklifts
Backhoes
Bulldozers
Off highway trucks
Road rollers
Crawlers
Mowers
Earthmovers
Trucks (all types)
Light, medium, heavy
Refrigeration Equipment
Refrigerators
Freezers
Air conditioners
Coolers
Dehumidifiers
Miscellaneous
Steel
Cream separators
Milking machines
Engines (gas, turbine, diesel)

Source: Company records.

ing facilities were located in the industrial heartland of America, the midwest, with significant manufacturing facilities overseas (see Table 12-2).

By 1917, IH was a premier company, worldwide in scope, manufacturing and distributing its products in more than 100 countries. In sales, it ranked as the seventh largest company in the United States.

After World War II, IH dwarfed its major competitors, Caterpillar and John Deere, in sales and capital expenditures, but the gap in profits was much narrower.

During the 1960s and 1970s, IH began to slip. Its profit margins, return on assets, return on equity, research and development expendi-

TABLE 12-2 Number of International Harvester Plants, 1979–1985

Year	Worldwide	U.S.
1985	8	7
1984	22	12
1983	27	15
1982	41	21
1981	47	26
1980	50	29
1979	52	30

Source: Company records.

tures, and capital expenditures began to lag behind those of its major competitors. The company also diversified into new lines of business and failed to terminate those that were not doing well.

For the first time in its 150-year history, an outsider was brought in to straighten out the affairs of IH. Archie R. McCardell, the former president of Xerox Corporation, was named chief executive officer in 1977.

By 1979, it appeared that McCardell had reversed IH's fortunes. Sales reached an all-time high of $8.4 billion and profits of $370 million were the largest in the company's history (see Table 12-3). The company ranked twenty-seventh out of the *Fortune* 500 in sales. Employment peaked at nearly 100,000 workers worldwide in 52 plants (see Tables 12-2 and 12-4). The year 1979 was exceptional for the U.S. economy as a whole and especially for IH.

TABLE 12-3 International Harvester Selected Operating Statistics and Per Share Data, 1975–1985

Year Ended Oct. 31	Revenue (millions)	Net Income[a] (millions)	Dividends	Price Range Common Stock (rounded)
1985[a]	$3,508	$113	None	12–6
1984	4,802	(61)	None	14–5
1983	3,601	(533)	None	15–4
1982[a]	4,292	(1,266)	None	9–12
1981[a]	7,041	(636)	$0.30	27–6
1980[a]	6,312	(370)	2.50	40–22
1979	8,392	370	2.35	45–34
1978	6,664	187	2.10	45–26
1977[a]	5,975	201	1.85	38–26
1976	5,488	174	1.70	33–22
1975[a]	5,246	116	1.70	31–19

[a] Excludes discontinued operations.

Source: Standard & Poor's NYSE Stock Reports, Vol. 53, No. 49, Sec. 17, March 12, 1986, p. 1628.

TABLE 12-4 Number of International Harvester Employees, 1979–1985 (Rounded to Nearest Thousand)

Year	Worldwide	U.S.
1985	15,000	15,000
1984	31,000	18,000
1983	32,000	19,000
1982	43,000	24,000
1981	66,000	39,000
1980	87,000	57,000
1979	98,000	64,000

Source: Company records.

The banner year of 1979 was followed by the near total collapse of IH. During the next five years, the company experienced devasting losses (see Table 12-3). Before discontinued operations, losses were $1.7 billion in 1982. In 1984, the company announced the sale of the businesses on which the company was founded, agricultural equipment.

In 1985, IH only faintly resembled the company of its history. Sales of $3.7 billion gave it a ranking of 104 among the *Fortune 500*. Its 15,000 workers were employed in only four U.S. plants and its principal product was heavy-duty trucks.

HISTORY OF INTERNATIONAL HARVESTER

A summary of major events in the company's history is given in Table 12-5.

Acceptance of the Reaper. It took six weeks for Cyrus McCormick to invent the reaper in 1831 at the age of 22. The machine was demonstrated to a group of farmers near Steele's Tavern, Virginia. Four horses were hitched to the reaper and in half a day a six-acre oat field was harvested, work that would require six men using conventional farming methods.

Despite this highly successful demonstration, farmers did not rush to purchase a reaper. They were conservative by nature and leery of mechanical innovations. During the next nine years, Cyrus improved his invention and turned it into a viable commercial product. In 1840, two reapers were sold for $100. By 1845, 50 reapers a year were sold.

In 1846, Cyrus decided to relocate his business to the young frontier city of Chicago, which had 17,000 people and had been incorporated for only 13 years. In partnership with C. M. Gray and William Ogden, he opened the McCormick Harvester Machine Company in 1847.

TABLE 12-5 International Harvester Highlights, 1831–1986

Year	Highlights
1831	Reaper invented.
1840	Two reapers sold at $100 each.
1845	Fifty reapers sold a year.
1846	McCormick relocated to Chicago.
1850	Austria, first foreign sale.
1860	4,000 reapers sold.
1886	First major strike, Haymarket Square Riot.
1880–1890	Harvester Wars.
1902	International Harvester Co., a trust, formed.
1903	First factory outside U.S., Hamilton Works, Toronto.
1904	First European plant.
1906	First tractor.
1907	Cream separator.
1912	First piece of construction equipment.
1920	Company union, Industrial Work Council.
1922	Farmall tractor.
1923	Trucks.
1928	Crawler tractor.
1929	Milking machines.
1935	Farm milk coolers.
1937	Industrial Works Councils declared illegal by Supreme Court.
1940	Only 3 out of 23 plants unionized.
1946	Refrigerators.
1947	Construction equipment division created.
1952	Frank G. Hough Co. purchased, payloaders.
1954	Trucks became most important division.
1958	John Deere surpassed IH in farm equipment sales.
1959–1960	Solar Turbine purchased.
1975	Light-duty trucks dropped.
1978	Wisconsin Steel sold.
1979	Largest profits in IH history ($427 million).
1982	Construction equipment division sold.
1983	Fort Wayne, Indiana, truck plant closed.
1984	Agricultural division sold.
1985	Trucks, sole line of business.
1986	New name NAVISTAR International Corp.

Source: Company records.

By 1860, the factory was producing 4,000 reapers a year. Cyrus bought out Gray and Ogden and brought his two brothers into the business.

The McCormick reaper was a quality product that evolved and improved over a period of time. McCormick engineers kept abreast of competitive products and figured out ways of duplicating their strengths without violating patent rights. But the real success of the company rested on Cyrus McCormick's business acumen and its strong sales organization and dealership network, not just product advantages.

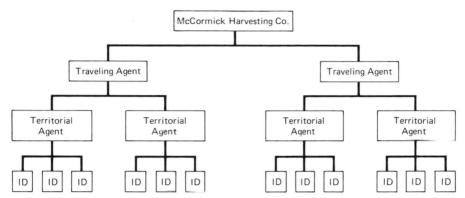

FIGURE 12-1 The Sales Organization of McCormick Harvesting Co., 1880–1885
Source: Company records.

IH's Early Sales Organizations. III was a pioneer in the development of a national sales organization. It was the first implement manufacturer to offer installment buying. The early contracts required one-third down the first fall after purchase and one-third after each of the next two harvests. Interest payments of 6 to 8 percent were charged on the second and third payments.

The original sales organization employed traveling agents, a concept rarely employed by competitors. The traveling agents supervised territorial agents whose task was to hire independent distributors who sold and serviced the machines. The territorial agents received a salary of $2 a week plus a commission of 5 to 10 percent of sales (see Figure 12-1).

Gradually the traveling agents evolved to regional sales managers, the territorial agents to district sales managers, and the independent distributors to dealers who had signed contracts. The IH dealers were one of the first franchised organizations in the United States, even preceding the early gasoline and automobile franchised dealerships. By 1900, there were 12,000 IH dealers.

By 1890, the sales organization became more centralized and took on the structure of a modern sales organization. A salaried general agent supervised 10 to 15 district sales managers. Although shown in Figure 12-2 as a line position, the regional sales managers functioned more as a service support to the dealers by providing them with specialists to solve their problems. Canvassers were added to assist dealers, make direct sales, and establish contact with customers. By 1900, there were 2,000 employed canvassers. Figure 12-2 depicts the McCormick sales organization of 1890.

FIGURE 12-2 The Sales Organization of McCormick Harvesting Co., 1890

Source: Company records.

THE MAJOR DIVISIONS of IH

Table 12-6 shows IH's major lines of business and competitors from 1931 to 1985.

Agricultural Equipment, 1831–1984. IH has always been known as a manufacturer of agricultural equipment and its reaper (harvester) remained its major product until the early 1900s.

In the 1880s and 1890s, fierce competition developed among the

TABLE 12-6 International Harvester's Major Lines of Business and Competitors, 1931–1985

Major Line of Business	Entry Date	Exit Date	Major Competitors
Agricultural equipment	1831	1984	John Deere, Kubota, J.I. Case, Fiat, Massey Ferguson, Allis-Chalmers, Oliver
Trucks (light, medium, heavy)	1923	Ongoing	Peterbilt, Mack, GM, Ford, European trucks
Construction equipment	1928	1982	Caterpillar
Refrigerators	1945	1955	Frigidaire, GE,
Home appliances			Amana, Kenmore,
Air conditioning line			Carrier, Westinghouse
Dehumidifers			
Solar turbines	1960	1981	Diesel engine manufacturers

Source: Company records.

various manufacturers of farm equipment. Price cutting became so severe that these years became known as the "Harvester Wars." Numerous attempts were made at consolidations and mergers, but all failed until 1902 when the McCormick Harvesting Company merged with William Deering to create the International Harvester Company. This trust controlled 90 percent of the domestic production of grain binders and 80 percent of all the domestic production of mowers, the two major types of harvesting machines.

In order to better serve its customers, IH diversified into other agricultural equipment (see Tables 12-1 and 12-5) by purchasing its competitors in related lines of business. For example, it rounded out its agricultural equipment by purchasing Parlin and Aendorff, a manufacturer of plows, in 1919. IH also developed new products.

In 1906, IH introduced its first tractor. This tractor had an internal combustion engine and offered farmers an alternative to the dangerous steam-driven tractors.

In 1915, The Ford Motor Company entered the tractor market and sold its Fordson tractor abroad in 1916 and 1917. In 1918, the Fordson was marketed in the United States for $365, far below IH's comparable $670 Titan International model. Ford quickly became number one in tractor sales, followed by IH and J. I. Case.

Harvester fought back by stressing product quality and challenging Ford tractors to public contests, called "field days."

IH had fallen behind in low-cost production techniques. It quickly adopted Ford's assembly-line methods and differentiated its tractors from Ford's.

In 1922, IH introduced the second most important product in its history, the revolutionary Farmall tractor. The Farmall had rear wheel drive and narrow front wheels that would allow it to run between rows of crops. Designed for the small to medium-sized farm, it was an all-purpose tractor to which many types of implements and accessories could be attached. Previously many of these accessories were purchased as separate machines.

By 1927, IH was the undisputed leader in the tractor industry. Ford abandoned the business in 1928 and only Case and Deere, who introduced an all-purpose tractor in 1923, remained competitors.

As discussed earlier, IH had developed a strong sales and dealership organization. Most of its top executives had risen through the sales ranks and the company promoted exclusively from within.

In 1946, John L. McCaffery was elected president. He had joined IH in 1909 at age 17 as a warehouse clerk. In 1912, he had become a motor truck salesman and rose through the ranks to become head of domestic sales. McCaffery was the consummate salesman. The pervading philosophy at IH was that a good salesman could sell anything.

When McCaffery became president, IH was the undisputed leader in agricultural equipment. Its only major challenge was the Fordson tractor from 1918 to 1927.

During the 1920s, 1930s, and 1940s, the red agricultural equipment of IH dominated the farmland of America. Customer loyalty was very strong, with many customers purchasing only IH equipment. The 1940s and 1950s also saw farmers spending an increasing percentage of their income on equipment.

The IH dealership network was the largest in the industry. It was easy for IH to sign up dealers because of its solid reputation and strong demand for its products. IH signed up as many dealers as possible. John Deere also had many dealers. Eventually this proliferation of dealers resulted in a drastic reduction of the total number during the late 1950s.

During the 1950s with the emergence of large mechanized farms, IH began to loose sales to John Deere. These farms demanded a new type of product. John Deere recognized these changes and stressed its large equipment line. Their new plows, planters, harrows, and cultivators would work four to six rows of crops instead of two.

In the early 1950s, IH invested its money in plants that produced relatively small tractors. The Farmall plants were not expanded and the company continued to manufacture the Farmall through 1954, the longest-produced model of any tractor. In 1959, a new two-cylinder hotrod 560 tractor was introduced. It had numerous mechanical problems and was an unsuccessful product.

Deer countered with its 4010 model, a big powerful six-cylinder tractor. Designed to accommodate the new equipment and larger farms, it was an immediate success. IH had the revolutionary tractor of the 1920s, 1930s, and 1940s, but Deere had the tractor of the 1960s and 1970s.

IH could no longer sell anything that it produced. Its sales-oriented hierarchy had misread the market. In 1958, John Deere became the new leader in agricultural equipment and has retained that position to the present.

During the early 1980s, most divisions of IH lost money. The agricultural equipment division lost about $300 million annually for several years. In late 1984, IH announced the sale of its agricultural equipment division to Tenneco, Inc., for $430 million. Tenneco owned J. I. Case, a harvester competitor.

Tenneco planned to close IH's tractor plant in Racine, Wisconsin, which would eliminate 30 to 40 percent of the nation's capacity to make farm tractors. IH's other implement plants were to be integrated into Case's operations to broaden its product lines. IH's 1,700 dealers would triple Case's dealer network to a size rivaling Deere. Foreign operations

TABLE 12-7 Estimated Worldwide Farm Equipment Market Shares, 1984 (Percent)

Company	Market Share
Deere	32.4
International Harvester	15.2
Massey Ferguson	11.1
Kuboto	9.0
Fiat	8.7
Ford	8.6
Sperry–New Holland	6.4
J.I. Case (Tenneco)	4.6
Allis-Chalmers	4.6
Total	100.0

Source: Wertheim & Co.

in Germany, France, and Denmark were also to be acquired. Table 12-7 depicts estimated worldwide farm equipment market shares for 1984.

Donald Lennox, IH's chairman, said the sale was "the only decision possible. You have a degree of emotion when you see the passing of the facet of the business on which the company was founded, but you can only pay so much for tradition and history."[1]

Trucks, 1923–Present.   IH produced its first trucks in 1907. They were purchased primarily by farmers through the agricultural equipment dealers.

A major truck-producing facility was built in 1922 at Ft. Worth, Indiana. This facility, along with another plant in Springfield, Ohio, became the major truck-producing facility.

Gradually the company diversified towards larger trucks. Its trucks would be eventually classified as light, medium, heavy, and miscellaneous.

The larger trucks necessitated the development of a separate dealership system. In time, the 3,000 independent dealers set the company apart from its competition. The dealers were financially sound and very loyal to IH. The company also owned and operated 200 branches that provided service and parts for the cross-country trucker.

In 1954, the truck division became and remained the leading division in sales. Its profit margins, however, lagged behind those of the agricultural division.

By 1969, IH was the leader in the profitable market for heavy-duty, long-distance trucks with 25 percent of the market share. The company was a close second to Ford for medium-duty trucks, and it offered numerous light-duty trucks that included pickup trucks, its Travelall station wagons, and Scout utility vehicles. A miscellaneous category included specialized vehicles such as cattle, garbage, fire, iron ore, and other types of trucks. The numerous models, adaptations, and proliferations that resulted from IH's attempt to fill every niche in the market affected production efficiency and cost.

IH's main problem was with its small trucks that lost their profitability during the 1950s and 1960s. Small trucks are produced in the same manner as cars. Their parts are produced in-house, which gave companies like General Motors economies of scale. In contrast, many of the components for heavy and medium-duty trucks are purchased from outside vendors at similar prices. This practice allowed IH to remain competitive with the industry.

Another problem for IH was the shift in the marketplace. Families were now buying trucks as a second or third vehicle. The car manufacturers had a distinct advantage because they distributed their small trucks through their automotive dealers. IH had no such outlets; they had to rely on their truck dealers.

Attempts to tie in with auto dealers who did not carry truck lines proved to be unsuccessful. As the transportation industry changed in the 1960s more towards heavy and medium trucks, the IH dealers gave less emphasis to the lower-margin light trucks. Between 1961 and 1969, IH's market share in light trucks shrank from 9 to 4 percent.[2]

The energy crisis of 1974 affected sales of the Travelall station wagon because it was viewed as a gas guzzler. In 1975, the recession adversely affected sales and IH discontinued its line of light trucks.

IH did attempt to penetrate the European market and become a worldwide presence in the trucking business as it was in agricultural equipment. However, the company entered the European market too late. Shortly after World War II, the European countries erected trade barriers that made it virtually impossible to export trucks to Europe. An attempt made in 1965 to produce trucks at an IH tractor plant in England failed due to labor and manufacturing problems. Other attempts were made at mergers which proved unsatisfactory.

As a result, IH never became a worldwide force in trucks as it had in agricultural equipment. However, domestic truck sales rose from 57 percent of total business in 1979 to 78 percent in 1984 (see Table 12-8).

Construction Equipment, 1928–1982. The pioneer in construction equipment was the Caterpillar Tractor Company. Its beginnings were in 1906 when Benjamin Holt invented a new machine that could be used on the boggy soil of the Stockton, California, delta. A pair of tracks were substituted for the steel wheels on a steam engine tractor. The tracks distributed the weight of the tractor and provided the maneuverability, stability, and traction necessary for those farming conditions. Shortly thereafter, the gasoline engine was substituted for steam and the Caterpillar tractor was modified into various types of construction equipment.

TABLE 12-8 Comparison of International Harvester's Agricultural Equipment Sales and Truck Sales, 1979–1985
(Sales in Billions)

Year	Total Combined Agricultural Equipment and Truck Sales	Agricultural Equipment Sales		Truck Sales	
		Amount	Percent of Total	Amount	Percent of Total
1985	$3.5	—	—	$3.5	100
1984	4.1	$0.9	22	3.2	78
1983	3.6	1.3	36	2.25	64
1982	4.3	1.8	42	2.5	58
1981	6.3	2.9	46	3.4	54
1980	5.2	2.5	48	2.7	52
1979	7	3	43	4	57

Source: Annual Reports.

IH entered the construction business in the early 1920s by modifying its basic tractors for its first moves into construction equipment.

After World War II, IH created a construction division to counter the effort of Caterpillar. It poured millions of dollars into new products to seize the opportunities created by the postwar construction boom and the new interstate highway network. Table 12-1 lists some of the many types of construction equipment produced by IH.

But Caterpillar emerged from World War II in a unique position. It had established itself as a key supplier for the military around the world. Returning army engineers and construction workers were familiar and favorably impressed with Caterpillar's equipment. Caterpillar had established an image of quality and reliability.

At the end of World War II, Caterpillar had two plants, but outspent IH's construction division by adding 12 new plants: 6 domestically and 6 internationally.

Caterpillar also highly centralized its operations and products. The machinery manufactured abroad was identical to the domestic equipment. Parts and equipment were interchangeable on a worldwide basis.

A summary of how Caterpillar strengthened its position in the decade following World War II follows:

1. Effective use of a favorable worldwide image to increase sales.
2. Massive capital investment in new plants at home and abroad.
3. Highly standardized lines of equipment and parts on a worldwide basis.
4. Development of the strongest dealership network in the industry.

In 1952, IH purchased the Frank G. Hough Company, a manufacturer of payloaders (earth-moving equipment). Frank Hough had developed a new concept with his payloaders. Instead of putting them on tracks, he went back to wheels. Up until 1960, this business was IH's single most profitable unit, but it was never fully integrated into the construction equipment division. IH executives wanted the Hough unit isolated because of its success. Gradually Caterpillar and Clark Equipment Company cut into the payloader's sales and affected profit margins.

During the 1960s, IH produced a number of products that performed poorly in the marketplace. This affected their overall image and the sale of the related product lines.

In 1960, Caterpillar's sales were three times those of IH; by 1971, the gap had increased to five times.[3] Caterpillar was clearly the dominant firm in the industry.

By the 1970s, the possibilities of selling the construction equipment division were discussed. Profit margins were low and the division was never highly profitable. This decision was complicated by the fact that the engine division's capacity was tied to sales in agricultural equipment, construction equipment, and trucks. If the construction equipment division were sold, it would significantly reduce the output of engines.

Although IH's sales peaked in 1979 at $1 billion, profits continued to lag. Caterpillar's sales increased to $7.6 billion with a return of sales of 6.5 percent.

In November 1982, hard-pressed for cash, IH sold the construction equipment division to Dresser Industries for $70 million.

Refrigeration, 1945–1955. IH's refrigeration division lasted ten years. The history of related products that preceded this division included the cream separator in 1907, milking machines in 1929, and farm milk coolers in 1935.

In 1945, the company expanded into refrigerators and home freezers to be shortly followed by air conditioning and dehumidifiers. By 1951, the company ranked number one in home freezers and ninth in refrigerators.[4]

Distribution was primarily through the farm dealers. In the early years, this was an effective method of distribution because IH had many farm dealers. By 1951, IH completely dominated the rural market but was very weak in the urban market. The problem with this strategy was that most of the customers were in the urban market and the growing suburban market.

As farms became larger and rural towns more urbanized, the appliance dealers on Main Street acquired a wider assortment of merchandise. IH was affected by these changing conditions because it offered a limited assortment of consumer appliances.

IH was at an even greater disadvantage in the growing suburbs and big cities because of the unrelated diversity of stores carrying its products.

By 1955, refrigeration accounted for less than 5 percent of $1 billion of sales. A heavy investment was needed to broaden the refrigeration and air conditioning lines. Independent appliance dealers in rural America had to be brought into the distribution network and offered a broader assortment of merchandise. In the urban areas the company had to decide who would be their dealers.

IH executives realized that building a more efficient dealership network and diversifying its product lines would entail a major capital expenditure. This, coupled with low profit margins, lead to the decision to sell the division.

In 1955, the refrigeration division was sold to Whirlpool Seeger Corporation. It was IH's first major divestiture.

Solar Turbine, 1960–1981.   The purchase of Solar Turbine in 1960 for $13 million was the second major diversification effort of IH. Solar was a supplier of parts to the aerospace industry. It had also developed expertise in metals and gas turbine technology—a field that IH was interested in. IH believed that gas turbine engines could be used in its trucks, farm, and construction equipment. Solar perfected the gas turbine engine but the diesel engine proved to be a better product for those markets.

Solar made a significant contribution to earnings. Its 1975 sales of $250 million constituted 20 percent of IH's earnings. However, because it was never a part of IH's major businesses, it was sold to Caterpillar Tractor in 1981 for $500 million.

CONCLUSION

Recent *Fortune* surveys of America's 250 most-admired industrial corporations ranked IH as follows:

1984	245 out of 250
1983	250 out of 250
1982	200 out of 200

Clearly IH in recent years has been one of America's least-admired corporations. Experts agree that the company has been poorly managed for years. The collapse that began in 1980 after the historic profits and sales in 1979 had roots dating back to the 1940s.

IH diversified into too many lines of unrelated businesses. When these businesses began to slip, millions were spent trying to revive them.

Although these businesses rarely became profitable, they were allowed to languish for years. This resulted in IH becoming a behemoth in sales with low profit margins.

Competitors initiated more aggressive capital expenditure and research and development programs. IH eventually became the high-cost producer. Its plants became outdated and competitors gained a cost advantage in manufacturing.

IH executives misread the market. In the 1950s, they wrongly predicted a boom in small tractors just as sales of the bigger 100-horsepower tractor exploded. Deere recognized—far ahead of its competitors—that the trend in agriculture was towards bigger and bigger farms relying on the increasingly larger and more powerful machines. Deere recognized the partial demise of the small farmer and the rise of the corporate farm.

When Archie McCardell was hired to revive IH in 1977, the company had been run almost continuously for nearly 150 years by descendants of founder Cyrus McCormick. A strong corporate culture had evolved. An early history of innovation followed by a strong sales orientation and eventual world leadership fostered a belief of invincibility.

There is no one single reason why IH failed. The fact is that many poor decisions led to its demise.

Effective February 20, 1986, International Harvester Co. changed its name to Navistar International Corp., a little more than a year after it sold its unprofitable agricultural equipment division along with the International Harvester name and the IH symbol to Tenneco Inc.

QUESTIONS

1. Did Cyrus McCormick make a wise choice in relocating in Chicago?
2. Why were farmers slow in adopting a revolutionary new product, the reaper?
3. IH had three dealership networks: agricultural, truck, and construction equipment. Would one network have been sufficient?
4. Why did the refrigeration division fail?
5. The farm equipment market remained depressed during the period from 1981 to 1985. Why?
6. IH produced heavy-duty, medium, and light trucks. Why did the light truck division fail?
7. Why was IH able to hold its own in heavy-duty and light-duty trucks?
8. Discuss the marketing implications of the Farmall tractor, 1922–1954.
9. What risk does IH assume by selling its farm equipment division?

10. Should J. I. Case retain the IH name? What should Case do with the IH dealers?
11. Discuss the evolution of IH's sales organization as shown in Figures 12-1 and 12-2.
12. IH emphasized a sales philosophy. Was this a good decision?
13. What were the strengths and weaknesses of IH's extensive diversification?
14. React to the new name Navistar International Corp.

NOTES

1. "International Harvester Sells AG Division," *Sacramento Bee,* November 27, 1984, p. AA7.
2. Barbara Marsh and Sally Saville, "International Harvester's Story: How a Great Company Lost Its Way," *Crain's Chicago Business,* Part II, November 15, 1982, p. 21.
3. Ibid., Part I, November 8, 1982, p. 41.
4. Ibid., Part I, November 8, 1982, p. 30.

13

CHRYSLER

INTRODUCTION

Between 1978 and 1982, Chrysler Corporation came to the brink of bankruptcy. The company lost more than $3.5 billion, the biggest financial loss of any American company in history. Despite the bailout by Congress in December of 1979 under the Chrysler Corporation Loan Guarantee Act, the company almost collapsed.

The turnaround began in 1982 with a much reduced loss. By January 1985, Chrysler had reversed its financial losses. Its recovery has been spectacular. In 1983, a check for $813,487,500 paid off the balance of the $1.2 billion debt owed to the U.S. government, seven years ahead of schedule. Chrysler's pretax earning of $2.4 billion in 1984 was more than it had earned in all the previous 58 years of its existence combined.

The architect behind this renascence was Lee Iacocca. Under his leadership Chrysler Corporation was cut almost in half. Sixteen of its 52 plants were closed, overseas operations and unrelated businesses were auctioned off to raise cash, and the number of employees was reduced from 157,000 to 80,000. The management team was completely restructured. Of the 28 highest ranking executives, only four remain from the old Chrysler.

The smaller, slimmer Chrysler can make a profit selling only 1.2 million vehicles instead of the 2.3 million required in 1980. During 1984, the company built 19.9 vehicles per employee, versus 10.2 in 1980. Production increased from 1.0 million vehicles in 1981 to almost 2 million in 1984.

Chrysler has modernized its plants, controlled its costs, and become a much more efficient producer. Technologically, its plants are among the most automated in the world. Its marketing has been superb. Iacocca has a keen instinct for hot new products and not one of Chrysler's new products has failed.

In short, Chrysler has been resurrected. The company is innovative and reacts rapidly to changes in the marketplace.

In 1980, experts gave the company odds of one in a hundred of surviving.

This case illustrates that under the right set of circumstances a company that is in the most dire conditions can stage a dramatic turnaround.

HISTORY OF CHRYSLER CORPORATION

The Chrysler Corporation was incorporated in 1925, 22 years after Ford, and 17 years after General Motors. It was founded by a brilliant entrepreneur named Walter P. Chrysler who stressed engineering.

Chrysler is the third largest U.S. motor vehicle producer operating principally in one business segment, automobile operations, which con-

TABLE 13-1 Chrysler Highlights, 1924–1984

Year	Highlights
1924	First cars introduced at New York City Auto Show.
1925	Chrysler Corporation incorporated.
1928	Purchased Dodge Brothers which created Plymouth and DeSoto divisions.
1930	Produced industry's first eight-cylinder engines.
1937	First national United Auto Workers (UAW) contract.
1942	Auto production stopped because of World War II.
1945	Auto production resumed.
1946	Market share high of 26 percent.
1960	DeSoto line discontinued because of poor sales.
1978	Omni and Horizon introduced as America's first front-wheel drive cars on September 1, 1978.
1978	Lido Anthony Iacocca hired as president on November 21, 1978.
1979	Iacocca named chairman of the board on September 20, 1979.
1979	Chrysler Loan Guarantee Act ($1.5 billion) passed by Congress on December 21, 1979.
1980	New Chrysler Corporation campaign began in January 1980.
1980	Deficit of $1.7 billion. Market share low of 8.77 percent.
1981	K Cars introduced: Dodge Aries and Plymouth Reliant.
1982	Five-year/50,000-mile warranty.
	Convertible Chrysler Le Baron and Dodge 400 Convertible introduced.
1983	Balance of $1.2 billion loan to U.S. government paid off.
1984	Successful new product introductions: minivans—Plymouth Voyager and Dodge Caravan; sports cars—Dodge Daytona and Chrysler Laser.
1984	Earnings of $2.4 billion. Net profit after taxes of $1.9 billion.

Sources: Annual Reports; Company records.

sist of the manufacture, assembly, and sale in North America of passenger cars, trucks, and related automotive parts and accessories.

The company's 1980 revenues placed it tenth among the world's automakers. Its 1984 revenues placed it fifth after General Motors, Ford, Toyota, and Nissan. Ranked by the number of cars and trucks produced, Chrysler placed twelfth in 1981 and fifth in 1984.

Table 13-1 illustrates the highlights of Chrysler's major decisions.

LIDO ANTHONY IACOCCA

Lee Iacocca was elected a director and president of Chrysler on November 2, 1978, and became chairman of the board on September 20, 1979. Previously his entire 32-year career from 1946 to 1978 was with the Ford Motor Company.

Both of Iacocca's parents were immigrants from Italy. His father arrived in 1902 and built a small auto rental business in Allentown, Pennsylvania. Most of the cars were Model A Fords, and Lee always wanted to work for Ford.

After graduating from Lehigh University and receiving a master's degree in engineering at Princeton, he joined Ford as an engineer but quickly switched to a district sales job. After serving in various fields, he was elected a director in 1965 and became president in 1970.

Iacocca had a keen sense of what consumers wanted. He was responsible for the Mustang that in 1964 set a record for automobile sales by a first-year model (418,000). He was also involved with the Continental Mark III.

Iacocca played a key role in the success of the Ford Motor Company in the 1960s and 1970s. He had built a strong power base and many of the key executives were loyal to him, but Iacocca was never completely his own man since he had to answer to Henry Ford II who seemed to resent his popularity, accomplishments, and growing power base.

On July 13, 1978, Henry Ford II fired Lee Iacocca. The reason given at the time was "Let's just say I don't like you."

Iacocca served four remaining months until October 30 in order to collect his retirement benefits. On November 2, 1978, he became Chrysler's president.

He chaired the committee to raise funds for the restoration of the Statue of Liberty and makes about 30 speeches a year. Typical topics are, "An Industrial Policy for America," and "Restoring the National Economy: An Action Plan for America."

His book, *Iacocca: An Autobiography* was published in September 1984. On November 4, 1984, it made the *New York Times* best-seller list for nonfiction—ranked number one. It is the best-selling autobiography ever published.

Rumors persisted throughout 1983 that Iacocca would soon retire from Chrysler. Others were trying to persuade him to run for president of the United States. Late in 1983, he made a decision to stay with Chrysler for three and possibly four more years as chairman and chief executive officer. He had accepted a generous stock grant and stock option offer from the Board of Directors in return for his services.

THE MANAGEMENT STRATEGY

Iacocca is a supersalesman. He exudes confidence, wears well-tailored clothes, smokes a big cigar, and has a self-satisfied smile. He is also an exceptional manager and leader who knows how to motivate people and get the best out of them.

In November 1984, a pep rally was staged for the introduction of the new H cars. The usual politicians, industry bigwigs, and journalists, as well as 2,300 recently laid off and retrained hourly workers were invited. Iacocca drove a silver Dodge Lance into the spotlight, stepped out, and declared, "At Chrysler we have one and only one ambition. To be the best. What else is there?" A tremendous roar that lasted five minutes came from the workers. There is no ambiguity who they work for. This behavior and loyalty by workers towards management is very unusual in America's heavily unionized industries. As John Burkart, a St. Louis plant manager said, "All of us at Chrysler believe in the man. I worship the guy."[1]

When Iacocca arrived at Chrysler, he found management in disarray. The fastest way to straighten things out was to bring in some of his former top executives from Ford who understood his management style and way of doing things. He persuaded many executives to leave Ford and join a nearly bankrupt company.

In order to raise cash, many divisions were sold. The profitable defense division (tanks) was sold to General Dynamics for $348.5 million. The earnings from the sale of this discontinued operation resulted in a net profit in 1982 of $170 million (see footnote, Table 13-2).

Another example of Iacocca's sales ability was convincing Congress to grant federal guarantees on $1.5 billion of Chrysler Corporation loans in December 1979. The loans made survival possible and allowed Chrysler to launch its new Chrysler Corporation campaign in January 1980. The guarantee on the loan was not a complete giveaway. Chrysler had to obtain $2 billion of concessions on its own—from the United Auto Workers, suppliers, state and local governments, and 446 lenders. The United Auto Workers took a pay cut that left them earning approximately $2 less than their counterparts at General Motors and Ford. The total of their relinquished benefits (pay and fringe) amounted to $1 billion.

TABLE 13-2   Chrysler Corporation Selected Operating Statistics and Per Share
Data, 1974–1985

Year	Net Sales (millions)	Net Income (millions)	Earnings per Share	Dividends	Common Stock Price Range (rounded)
1985	$21,260	$1,731	$9.38	$0.66	32–19
1984	19,573	1,496	7.83	0.56	22–13
1983	13,240	302	1.57	nil	24–9
1982[a]	10,045	(69)	(.85)	nil	13–3
1981	10,822	(476)	(4.79)	nil	5–2
1980	9,225	(1,710)	(17.33)	nil	8–3
1979	12,002	(1,097)	(11.45)	0.13	8–4
1978	13,618	(205)	(2.36)	0.56	9–5
1977	16,708	125	1.38	0.60	15–8
1976	15,538	328	3.63	0.20	15–6
1975	11,598	(207)	(3.46)	nil	12–5
1974	10,971	(52)	(0.92)	1.40	15–5

[a] Excludes discontinued operations.
Source: Standard & Poor's NYSE Stock Reports, Vol. 53, No. 51, Sec. 5, March 14, 1986, p. 532.

The following facts illustrate the effectiveness of the Chrysler management team:

1. Production of automobiles and trucks rose from 1.0 million in 1981 to 2.0 million in 1984.
2. Cars built per employee rose from 10.2 million in 1980 to 19.9 million in 1984.
3. Average number of employees was cut from 157,000 in 1978 to 80,000 in 1984.
4. Break-even point in number of cars to produce a profit dropped from 2.4 million in 1979 to 1.1 million in 1983.
5. Fixed costs (in constant 1983 dollars) were cut from $4.7 billion in 1979 to $3.54 billion in 1983.
6. Inventory was cut from $2.1 billion in 1979 to $1.3 billion in 1983.
7. Debt/equity ratio dropped from 6:1 in 1980 to 1:1 in 1983.
8. Warranty cost was reduced 45 percent from 1978 to 1983.

THE MARKETING STRATEGY

Image.   Lee Iacocca reversed the image of Chrysler Corporation from that of a loser to that of a winner. He injected a sense of style and pizazz that had been noticeably lacking and brought sales and marketing to the fore. In the early days of the turnaround, he convinced skeptical car buyers that underdog Chrysler deserved their business.

Lately the themes of quality and reliability have influenced Chrysler's image.

FIGURE 13-1 Brand Position Map of 21 U.S. and Foreign Automobiles

Source: Principles of Marketing Class, 1985, California State University, Sacramento.

In recent years Chrysler has improved the quality of its cars by 36 percent and its trucks by 40 percent. This has enhanced their reputation in the marketplace and cut their warranty cost by 45 percent. Sustained high quality is the foundation of their unique 5-year/50,000-mile warranty, the best on the market today.[2]

The theme, "To be the Best," conveys an image of excellence and reflects quality and reliability.

One of the tools that the U.S. automobile industry uses to develop an image and position its current and proposed products is called a product or brand positioning map. The map shown in Figure 13-1 was created by students in an introductory marketing course at California State University, Sacramento.

These maps can be used to position major divisions of auto companies or individual automobiles. A major advantage of maps done by the

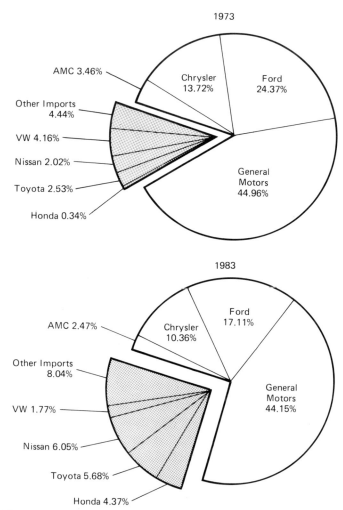

FIGURE 13-2 U.S. Car Sales for Major Manufacturers

Note: Reprinted from *1984 Ward's Automotive Yearbook,* p. 101. *AMC includes Renault imports and domestic makes in 1983; Chrysler includes Mitsubishi units sold with a Chrysler nameplate, both years; Ford includes captive imports sold in 1973; General Motors includes captive imports in 1973; Volkswagen includes both import and domestic sales in 1983; Honda includes domestic and import in 1983, just import in 1973. Source: Ward's Research Dept.*

auto companies is that they look at cars from a consumer perspective while also retaining some sort of tangible product orientation.

Target Market and Market Share. Chrysler is not producing a separate and distinct automobile for every price category and market segment. Instead, it is concentrating its effort on the middle 80 percent of the

TABLE 13-3 U.S. Car Production by Manufacturer, Selected Years, 1972–1983 (Percent of Total)

	1983	1982	1981	1980	1979	1978	1973	1972
General Motors	59.22	62.52	62.48	63.51	59.18	58.03	54.40	53.66
Ford	22.95	22.60	20.91	20.21	26.38	27.74	25.93	27.50
Chrysler	12.98	11.49	11.86	10.04	11.16	12.68	16.42	15.84
American Motors	2.97	1.37	2.06	2.94	1.84	1.55	3.25	3.00
Volkswagen Am.	1.29	2.02	2.69	3.30	1.44	—	—	—
Honda Am.	0.59	—	—	—	—	—	—	—
Total	100.00	100.00	100.00	100.00	100.00	100.00	100.00	100.00

Source: 1984 Ward's Automotive Yearbook, pp. 70–73.

North American car market. Chrysler is also developing vehicles for special market segments known as "niche" cars. These cars will reach a small but profitable market where other cars are not competing and their attractiveness is expected to flow over to the rest of the product line.

Chrysler's all-time high for market share was 26 percent in 1946. Its low for cars was 8.77 percent in 1980. Figure 13-2 shows U.S. market shares for domestic and foreign automakers in 1973 and 1983. Table 13-3 shows the percentage of cars produced by U.S. manufacturers in selected years, 1972–1983.

MARKETING MIX

Product. The purpose of this section is to provide insights on how management thinks about products, not to describe all of Chrysler's products or product lines.

Chrysler was the first to introduce American-made front-wheel drive cars in the Omni and Horizon in 1978. Today its fleet has the highest miles-per-gallon rating of the Big Three.

Management tries to find "niches" or unfilled needs in the market, and to fill those needs. Because the company is not encumbered with a bureaucracy, it can react rapidly to changing market conditions.

The minivans (Plymouth Voyager and Dodge Caravan) are a good example of filling a "niche." In 1984, 148,000 were sold with no television and little print advertising. General Motors and Ford were not in the market, and Toyota, restrained by import quotas, sold only 46,593 minivans. Critics felt that Chrysler's garageable van was superior to Toyota's. Demand has been very strong for the vans, and the average profit per van is $2,000 to $4,000.

Another "niche" that Chrysler filled was the convertible. No American automaker had built a convertible since 1976. The Chrysler LeBaron

"The New Chrysler Corporation gives the American car buyer guarantees no other car company has ever given before."

LEE A. IACOCCA
Chairman
The New Chrysler Corporation

The New Chrysler Corporation announces The Chrysler Guarantees.

1. The first 30-day/1000 mile money-back guarantee.

Buy one of our new 1980 passenger cars. Drive it up to 30 days or 1,000 miles, whichever comes first. If you're not completely satisfied, you'll get your money back. But not the finance and insurance charges you have accrued. All you do is bring your car back to your dealer in good condition. When he receives clear title, he returns your money. Nobody else does that. Not Ford. Not GM. Not the Imports. Only The New Chrysler Corporation.

2. The first guarantee of no-cost scheduled maintenance.

When you buy or lease a new 1980 car or truck, you'll receive oil changes, oil filters and other scheduled maintenance specified for each vehicle. For 2 years or 24,000 miles, whichever comes first. For 1 year or 12,000 miles on our imports. At no charge.
Nobody else does that. Not Ford. Not GM. Not the Imports. Only The New Chrysler Corporation.

FIGURE 13-3
Source: Reprinted by permission of Chrysler Corporation.

3. The first guarantee of no-cost motor club membership with emergency road service.

The New Chrysler Corporation provides a two year membership in the Amoco Motor Club when you buy or lease a new 1980 car or truck. Benefits include emergency road service, emergency towing, car theft reward. And a lot more. At no cost to you—subject to the conditions of membership. Nobody else does that. Not Ford. Not GM. Not the Imports. Only The New Chrysler Corporation.

And a $50 test drive offer to prove our confidence in Chrysler Engineering.

Test drive one of our new 1980 cars or trucks. Buy one of ours. Or buy any qualifying new car or truck from one of our competitors within thirty days. Then return the test drive certificate with proof of purchase. And the fifty dollars is yours. Nobody else does that. Not Ford. Not GM. Not the Imports. Only The New Chrysler Corporation.

These New Chrysler Corporation commitments apply to new 1980 vehicles for personal use only. Your participating Dodge, Chrysler or Plymouth dealer will provide all the details.

The New Chrysler Corporation
We're doing business like Detroit never did it before.

FIGURE 3 (cont.)

and Dodge 400 were an instant success when introduced in 1982. General Motors and Ford followed with their own convertibles in 1983.

The majority of Chrysler's cars are directed to the middle market. Chrysler describes its 1984 models as, "Technically advanced, high-quality products offering what the public wants: front-wheel drive, fuel efficiency, good looks, high technology, and the best warranty protection on the market."[3]

Promotion. Kenyon and Eckhardt became the sole advertising agency to represent Chrysler. It was placed in charge of a $230 million budget worth $34.5 million in commissions. Previously, three agencies had served Chrysler. Kenyon and Eckhardt had represented Ford and many believed the agency was insane to switch accounts.

The initial program in 1979 was called the "confidence series." The underlying message was that Chrysler was worth saving.

> Nine different publics were identified: consumers, Congress, news media, the financial community, the Chrysler dealer organization, its employees, the United Auto Workers union, Chrysler suppliers, and U.S. communities where Chrysler-related businesses sustained the local economy.[4]

One ad that became a classic from this series posed the question, "Would America be better off without Chrysler?"

In the early stages of the confidence series, the employees of Chrysler were considered vital because of the emphasis placed on improving the quality of the company's products. It is believed that the ads were successful in gaining government support for the loan guarantees.

It became increasingly clear that Lee Iacocca was the perfect corporate spokesman. He had a 79-percent public awareness before he began appearing in ads.

Research was then conducted to explore if Iacocca should be the spokesperson for the Chrysler advertising. His appropriateness was rated at 82 percent; his sincerity, 76 percent; and his believability, 70 percent.

A second series of ads on "The New Chrysler Corporation" began on December 26, 1979, immediately following passage of the loan guarantees. Lee Iacocca was the spokesperson but remained in the background, especially in the print ads. The main theme was that Chrysler was in business to stay.

In February 1980, a third series of ads began promoting the theme, "The New Chrysler Corporation announces the Chrysler Guarantees." Again, Lee Iacocca was the spokesperson, but played a more dominant role. His picture appeared at the top of the ad (see Figure 13-3). The earlier New Chrysler Corporation ads were merely signed by Iacocca with his title.

By 1982, Lee Iacocca emerged as a dominant part of the message.

The New Chrysler Corporation theme no longer played a major role. The television ads presented a confident Iacocca giving us a brief message. The same message appears in the print media.

During 1982–1983 the message was, "You can go with us or you can go with someone else—and take your chances."

During 1984–1985 the message was, "At Chrysler we have one and only one ambition. To be the best. What else is there? . . . Nobody backs their cars the way we do. And now nobody backs their trucks the way we do."

Leo-Arthur Kelmenson, the president of Kenyon and Eckhardt, said, "No other man could have brought the company this far. Lee Iacocca is absolutely unique."[5]

Distribution.   Chrysler's two major foreign partners are Peugeot, the big French automaker, and Mitsubishi Motors of Japan. Chrysler has a 15-percent interest in both of these companies. It imports engines and various parts from Peugeot. From Mitsubishi it imports parts, engines, and the subcompact Colts and Ram 50 minipickups.

The relationship with Mitsubishi goes back to 1971 when an agreement was reached for Chrysler to become the sole distributor of Mitsubishi cars in the United States. These fuel-efficient vehicles have helped the dealers to maintain sales and profit levels. They have also given Chrysler an entree into the small car market.

During the financial crisis of 1979–1980, this relationship began to break down. The Japanese banks no longer wanted to finance the sale of Mitsubishi cars to Chrysler. Mitsubishi, unsure of Chrysler's future, wanted to set up its own independent distribution system. Finally, Mitsubishi agreed to finance the cars itself and Mitsubishi Motors of America, an independent network of dealers, was established to sell Mitsubishi cars not handled by the Chrysler dealers.

In June 1984 the Chrysler agreement with Mitsubishi to distribute cars was extended to 1995. Mitsubishi currently has a dual distribution channel in the U.S.—Chrysler and Mitsubishi Motors of America.

In 1985 Chrysler and Mitsubishi Motors Corp. announced a joint venture to produce 180,000 subcompact cars a year near Bloomington, Illinois, by 1988. The engines and transmissions for the cars would be imported from Japan. Initially the Japanese content would be 60 percent but may drop to 40 percent.

Chrysler and Mitsubishi will split the output. For Chrysler, the additional 90,000 cars would represent about a 9 percent increase to the 986,998 cars it sold in the U.S. in 1984. For Mitsubishi, which sold 39,104 cars in the U.S., the 90,000 additional cars would substantially increase its presence in this country. Mitsubishi plans to increase its number of dealers from 88 in 1985 to 300 by 1989.

TABLE 13-4   Number of Chrysler Dealers, 1969–1984

Year	Dealers	Year	Dealers
1984	3,870	1976	4,842
1983	3,872	1975	4,874
1982	3,645	1974	5,193
1981	3,693	1973	5,373
1980	3,834	1972	5,466
1979	4,800	1971	5,539
1978	4,806	1970	5,744
1977	4,846	1969	6,092

Source: Annual Reports.

Currently the following foreign-based firms have manufacturing facilities in the United States and began production as follows:

Volkswagen in 1978,

Honda in 1983,

Nissan (trucks) in 1983,

Toyota and General Motors in 1984,

Mazda in 1987, and

Mitsubishi-Chrysler in 1988.

Table 13-4 shows the reduction of Chrysler dealers. From a high of 6,092 in 1969 to a low of 3,645 in 1982, a net loss of 2,447 dealers or 36.9 percent occurred. From 1979 to 1982, the net loss was 1,155 dealers or 31.7 percent.

In 1980, only 52 percent of the dealers were making a profit, compared to 80 percent in 1982. Three hundred new dealers were added in 1982 and confidence has been restored to the distribution system.

Price.   Chrysler's prices are competitive and special deals and rebates are available from time to time. It is not company policy to engage in severe price competition or price wars.

IMPORTS

Table 13-5 reveals the increasing significance of imports as a percentage of total sales. In 1973, imports accounted for 14.91 percent of total car sales. By 1980, this had risen to 26.66 percent. The table also shows the rapid increase in the total number of imports.

Table 13-6 shows the shifts that have occurred among the three major import categories. Japan has dramatically increased its share of the market and by 1980 had captured 78 percent of all imports.

Because of this trend, a rapidly growing protectionist sentiment developed in the United States, and Japan's Ministry of Trade and

TABLE 13-5 U.S. Domestic and Import Car Sales, 1973–1983 (Millions of Cars)

Year	Domestic	Import	Total	Imports as Percent of Total
1983	6.8	2.4	9.2	26.08
1982	5.8	2.2	8.0	27.50
1981	6.2	2.3	8.5	27.05
1980	6.6	2.4	9.0	26.66
1979	8.3	2.3	10.6	21.69
1978	9.3	2.0	11.3	17.70
1977	9.1	2.1	11.2	18.75
1976	8.6	1.5	10.1	14.85
1975	7.0	1.6	8.6	18.60
1974	7.4	1.4	8.8	15.91
1973	9.7	1.7	11.4	14.91

Source: 1984 Ward's Automotive Yearbook, p. 10.

Industry announced voluntary export restrictions on Japanese auto producers shipping to the U.S. market. For 1981, only 1.68 million cars were allowed in. The restraint of 1.68 million cars was renewed for 1982 and 1983, but in 1984 it was increased 10 percent to 1.85 million cars because of increased domestic sales.

In November 1983, a United Auto Workers–backed "domestic content" bill nearly became law. The purpose of this bill was to restrict Detroit's Big Three from importing more parts from abroad. It was also aimed at forcing Japan's big automakers to make cars in this country.

Currently four foreign-based firms have manufacturing facilities in the United States. Volkswagen began U.S. car production in 1978, Honda in 1983, Nissan (trucks) in 1983, and the controversial Toyota and General Motors joint venture began in 1984.

TABLE 13-6 Shares of Import Sales in U.S. Selected Years, 1970–1984 (Percent)

Year	Japan	Germany	Others	Total
1984	79	13	8	100
1983	78	13	9	100
1982	78	13	9	100
1981	78	13	9	100
1980	78	13	9	100
1978	70	18	12	100
1976	60	24	16	100
1974	42	38	20	100
1972	40	41	19	100
1970	24	57	19	100

Sources: 1984 Ward's Automotive Yearbook, p. 110; 1982 Ward's Automotive Yearbook, p. 145; 1981 Ward's Automotive Yearbook, p. 24; Business Week, March 18, 1985, p. 117.

CHRYSLER'S FUTURE

Chrysler has directed its efforts to the middle of the market and attempts to fill market "niches" as they occur. Its penetration of the luxury car market is weak with little effort to compete against the European luxury imports. In the small-car market, Chrysler has filled the gap with its Mitsubishi imports, namely Colt and Ram 50 minipickups. The problems concerning what kind of car Mitsubishi will produce for Chrysler are severe since Chrysler seeks a mini-economy car. Mitsubishi feels that its profits will be limited with a minicar and continues to emphasize and expand its independent dealer network.

Chrysler has brought its costs under control, lowered its break-even point, and implemented new technologies in its factories. The company is lean and reacts rapidly to changing market conditions.

Its current image is well defined. Although its debt has been greatly reduced, Chrysler is still the most leveraged of the Big Three.

Chrysler is no longer a factor in international markets, having shed its foreign subsidiaries during its financial crisis. Its export sales are nonexistent and there is no foreign production.

If the economy remains strong, with interest rates and inflation under control, and if the Japanese extend their self-imposed export restraints, Chrysler will continue to be successful.

The strong dollar in 1986 has made Japanese automobiles so expensive that they no longer have a price advantage. In fact in many cases Japanese cars are more expensive than comparable American automobiles.

Another key issue is Lee Iacocca's tenure with Chrysler. He has vowed to stay on until 1988 and says he is not interested in running for the presidency of the United States. Still he is a key decision maker and leader who has shored up Chrysler's bottom line. His departure from Chrysler could create some serious leadership problems.

QUESTIONS

1. Identify and discuss the factors that lead to Chrysler's decline during the 1970s and early 1980s.
2. Discuss how Lee Iacocca turned Chrysler around.
3. Identify and discuss the environmental factors that favored Chrysler in 1983 and 1984.
4. Lee Iacocca is a supersalesman. What arguments do you suppose he used to convince Congress to back Chrysler's loans? Discuss them.
5. Who has the best image today—Chrysler, Ford, or General Motors? Identify the image of each of the Big Three.

6. Lee Iacocca appears in many of Chrysler's advertisements. Is this good or bad? Why?

7. Why have the imports increased their share of the market? How do the markets differ between Japanese and European imports?

8. Chrysler operates exclusively in the North American market. Is this good or bad?

9. Lee Iacocca believes that the ideal American auto company would be a top Japanese producer at the low end, a high-tech European company for the luxury segment, and an American company for the middle of the market. Should Chrysler form Global Motors?

10. Is Mitsubishi going to make a viable partner for Chrysler in the long run? What channel of distribution problems do Chrysler and Mitsubishi have?

NOTES

1. Alexander L. Taylor, "Iacocca's Tightrope Act," *Time,* March 21, 1983, p. 53.
2. 1983 Chrysler Annual Report, p. 7.
3. Ibid., p. 4.
4. Leo-Arthur Kelmenson, "Teamwork Spurs Resurgence of Chrysler," *Marketing News,* June 24, 1983, p. 16.
5. Ibid., p. 16.

14

USA TODAY

INTRODUCTION

The first-day issue of *USA Today* was September 15, 1982. No large general interest daily has been launched successfully in this country since Long Island's *Newsday,* which debuted in 1940. Initial reaction by many journalists and business analysts was that the paper would not make it. Not all agreed. R. Joseph Fuchs of Kidder Peabody rated its chances as "better than even" in September 1982. In a special research report on the Gannett Company in September 1984, Fuchs said, "If our assumed breakeven objective for 1987 is to be attained or exceeded, management must cause the effort to continue to jump across a series of critical hurdles. If this can be accomplished, as we think it can, the cumulative operating losses until breakeven will approximate $350 million to $375 million."[1]

John Morton of Lynch, Jones and Ryan noted in 1982 that Gannett was at worst taking a gamble in which potential rewards greatly exceed risks. He said, "This is not an enormous investment, it is like buying a moderate-size newspaper, and it promises an enormous return."[2] However, almost two years later he said, "There is some question who the readers are. It has achieved an impressive circulation volume, but I am unconvinced the paper will find an economically rewarding niche."[3]

The introduction of this national newspaper, a truly new product, was an ambitious task. Management's goal from the beginning was to reach a circulation of 2.35 million by 1987. (By comparison, the *Wall Street Journal*'s current circulation is 2.1 million.) This would make *USA Today* the number one newspaper in the country in daily circulation.

On September 13, 1985, Allen H. Neuharth, the chairman and

founder of *USA Today,* said, "We think the risk-reward ratio looks even better now than it looked at the beginning. If *USA Today* continues toward a successful, profitable venture, the investment in it will have been much, much less than it would take to acquire an existing publication like it, if there were one."[4]

Gannett planned to substain substantial losses until 1987, their break-even year. Losses to date have been estimated as follows: $25 million in 1982, $130 million in 1983, $115 million in 1984, and $85 million in 1985, for a total loss of $355 million. Estimated losses for 1986 are $50 million. Projected profits for 1987 are $25 to $30 million.

THE GANNETT COMPANY, INC.

USA Today is published by the Gannett Company. The company was founded by Frank E. Gannett and associates in 1906. It is the nation's largest newspaper company and one of the nation's largest diversified information companies. It has been listed on the New York Stock Exchange since 1967. The company employs 27,000 employees and has 80 million shares of stock outstanding.

This leading publisher is primarily engaged in newspaper publishing, television and radio broadcasting, and outdoor advertising. Contributions to net profit by the business segment in 1985 were as follows: newspaper publishing, 75 percent; broadcasting, 16 percent; and outdoor advertising, 9 percent.

As of December 31, 1985, the company owned 91 daily newspapers and 40 nondaily newspapers. Most of these newspapers are published in small cities and monopolize the local market. The company owns 15 radio and 8 television stations. The outdoor advertising group is the largest in North America. It also owns Louis Harris and Associates, a public opinion research firm. With the exception of *USA Today,* the company has grown primarily by acquisition. In March 1985, Gannett acquired *Family Weekly* from CBS for $42.5 million; in July 1985, it purchased four newspapers, including the *Des Moines Register* from Des Moines Register and Tribune Company for $200 million; and in October 1985, in the largest acquisition in Gannett's history, the company purchased the Detroit Evening News Association which included the *Detroit News*—the nation's sixth largest daily—plus nine smaller newspapers, two radio stations, and five television stations for $717 million.

Table 14-1 reveals that Gannett had revenues of approximately $2.2 billion in 1985. It is a growth company that is financially sound. Other key statistics in recent years are as follows: return on equity, 20 percent; percentage long-term debt to capitalization, 20 percent; and an improving current ratio of 1.4 percent. Gannett has comfortably absorbed *USA Today's* losses since September 1982.

TABLE 14-1 Gannett Company, Inc., Selected Operating Statistics and Per Share Data, 1974–1985

Year	Revenue (millions)	Net Income (millions)	Earnings per Share	Dividends per Share
1985	$2,209	$253	3.16	$1.53
1984	1,960	224	2.80	1.33
1983	1,704	192	2.40	1.22
1982	1,520	181	2.26	1.16
1981	1,367	173	2.11	1.04
1980	1,215	152	1.87	0.92
1979	1,065	134	1.67	0.80
1978	690	83	1.38	0.62
1977	558	69	1.15	0.51
1976	413	48	0.99	0.38
1975	355	39	0.81	0.24
1974	327	33	0.70	0.17

Source: Standard & Poor's NYSE Stock Reports, Vol. 53, No. 76, Sec. 6, April 21, 1986, p. 936.

KEY PERSONNEL OF *USA TODAY*

Allen H. Neuharth, chairman and chief executive officer of Gannett, is the founder of *USA Today*. With the exception of his four years in the army during World War II, Neuharth's entire career has been in the newspaper industry. He began at age 11 as a newspaper carrier for the *Minneapolis Tribune*. He became editor of both his high school and college newspapers. In 1963, he joined Gannett as a general manager of two Rochester newspapers. After serving in a number of positions, he became chairman, president, and chief executive in 1979. He has received many awards, and in 1980 Gannett was named by *Dun's Review* as one of America's five best-managed companies. Before the birth of *USA Today*, none of Gannett's 120 newspapers were prestigious or national in scope. *USA Today* is the idea of Neuharth who wanted a national, general interest newspaper.

Thomas Curley was named president of *USA Today* on March 18, 1986. He was one of the four original researchers on the project that led to its creation, and formerly the executive vice president and general manager.

Cathleen Black joined *USA Today* as president in 1983. She was promoted to publisher on June 15, 1984. Her major responsibility is to increase advertising revenue. For the 12 years prior to joining *USA Today*, Black made a career of rescuing magazines in advertising trouble. She is the former publisher of *New York* and had previously served as advertising manager and then as associate publisher of *Ms*. Black has a history of working for a publication in its formative stages, convincing skeptical advertisers to sign up, and then moving on to a larger publication.

Besides these top three, there are four other top management people directing the business and editorial aspects of the paper. The total work force consists of 1,900 employees, including an editorial staff of 375.

HISTORY OF *USA TODAY*

In 1981, Gannett conducted extensive market research studies on the feasibility of a national newspaper. The results were positive and the project was approved by the Gannett Board of Directors in December 1981.

The first day of issue was September 15, 1982, with distribution then limited to Washington, D.C., and Baltimore. All 200,000 copies were sold. A rapid market-by-market and coast-to-coast phase-in followed. Circulation grew very rapidly (see Table 14-2).

A breakdown of the average daily net circulation for the first quarter of 1984 is shown in Table 14-3. The majority of sales were derived from vending machines and newsstands.

Losses in 1983 and 1984 were partially offset by a rapid increase in paid circulation. In 1985, however, the increased growth in circulation had slowed considerably, increasing slightly more than 100,000 from September 1984 to September 1985.

Advertising revenue, which was rather dismal in 1983, has risen rapidly since then. The averge number of paid advertising pages was:

    6.2 pages in 1983
    9.0 pages in 1984
    13.0 pages in 1985

TABLE 14-2   *USA Today*, Average Daily Net Paid Circulation, September 1982–September 1985

Date	Circulation
September 1985[a]	1,350,000
September 1984[a]	1,247,324
April 1984[b]	1,332,974
December 1983	1,328,781
November 1983	1,239,887
October 1983	1,151,416
March 1983	859,180
January 1983	531,438
November 1982	362,879
October 1982	221,978
September 1982	200,000

[a] Average daily paid circulation for the six-month periods ending September 30, 1984, and 1985.

[b] Average daily paid circulation for the first quarter of 1984.

Source: "An Advertisement," *USA Today*, January 23, 1984, p. 5A.

TABLE 14-3 *USA Today* Average Daily Net Paid Circulation by Distribution Category, First Quarter of 1984

Category	Circulation	Percent of Total
Single-copy sales at vending machines and newsstands	887,673	66.6
Home and office delivery	333,152	25.0
Mail subscription	63,788	4.8
"Blue chip" sales (hotels, motels, airlines, etc.)	48,361	3.6
Total	1,332,974	100.0

Source: USA Today Fact Sheet.

16.0 pages in the fourth quarter of 1985
21.0 pages in the week of December 16, 1985

On July 19, 1984, test distribution and sale of an international edition throughout Europe and parts of the Middle East began.

In October 1985 *USA Today* began printing via satellite in Singapore as its first print site outside the United States. In May 1986 distribution in Europe switched from air express to printing via satellite.

The international edition, although condensed, emphasizes the same news and features as *USA Today's* domestic edition with the exception of having the first daily world weather map in full color published anywhere.

The September 1982 page capacity of *USA Today* was 40 pages. This was expanded to 48 pages in July 1984 and 56 pages in November 1985. Full color available for news and advertising was originally eight pages. Full color was expanded to 16 pages in July 1984 and 22 pages in November 1985.

It is the author's opinion that if *USA Today* is to break even, its projected paid circulation must reach management's goal of 2.35 million by December 1987 and advertising must increase from an average of 13 pages an issue in 1985 to 17 pages an issue by December 1987. If this occurs, the projected profit plateau of $45 million will be reached.

USA Today is the fastest growing new newspaper ever. During its second year (1984), it became the third largest newspaper in circulation in the United States. In its third year (1985), it became the second largest newspaper in circulation in the United States.

MARKET RESEARCH

The research behind *USA Today* was one of the most exhaustive newspaper market research studies ever done. Researchers asked potential readers of *USA Today* questions about what they would read, what form the material should take, and how it should be displayed. This information was fed back to the editors, who created several prototypes of the paper that were pretested on potential readers in numerous markets.

The research was conducted by two independent firms: Simmons Market Research Bureau of New York, the leading media market research firm; and Louis Harris and Associates, a major public opinion pollster. Additionally, about 4,500 prototypes were distributed to opinion leaders in government, business, and the media across the country. Based on this information, the final product was produced.

Magazines have long created products to capture a market share but this approach was something relatively new for newspapers. In the 1970s, a national readership project engaged in extensive research to determine the causes of declining newspaper circulation. It was found that lifestyles and information tastes had changed. Newspapers were encouraged to redesign and reflect these new conditions. New sections focusing on lifestyles, weekend entertainment, and the social scene were added. Other characteristics of the redesigned newspapers were short capsule reports, bolder graphics, and more color. Most newspapers made only slight modifications. The editors continued their old ways of giving the public the news the editors wanted them to read and displayed the way editors wanted to display it.

USA Today used a completely different approach. It focused on the needs of its potential readers and produced a product to satisfy those needs.

The product caused a storm of criticism. Editors called it "junk food journalism," "newspaper from nowhere," "written radio," and "Al Neuharth's technicolor baby."[5]

DEMAND FORECASTING AND COMPETITION

The research findings of Simmons Market Research Bureau found the market had room for one to two national daily newspapers. This research indicated an eventual circulation of some 3 million—between 4 and 5 percent of the country's regular 61 million daily newspaper buyers.

Neuharth believes that *USA Today* is not in competition with the daily local papers. He said, "*Today* will be different from what you are publishing . . . and it will not be published at the expense of what you're doing."[6] He referred to the paper as a "second read." After one has read the local paper, one would purchase *USA Today*. The market for the newspaper was also different. The target audience was not city residents. *USA Today* was aimed at visitors, especially businessmen; people who have moved into a new region yet remain interested in news and sports from their local homes; and suburbanites whose local dailies are just too local.

USA Today's major distribution strategy in entering new markets was to push their ubiquitous vending machine and newsstand sales. Local newspapers did not like USA Today entering their local markets and viewed them as a threat. Some used legal methods in an attempt to keep Today's vending machines off the street. Others matched USA Today vending machine for vending machine. Pressure was also applied to newsstand operators to promote the local paper and give USA Today poor visibility.

Edward Estlow, president of the Scripps-Howard chain, said, "Everywhere they have appeared, it's forced local papers to reevaluate."[7] Home delivery campaigns were intensified and earlier morning deliveries stressed. In some cases, minor format changes occurred. The editorial and especially the sports section were improved. More color was used. More charts and graphs were used to illustrate stories.

MARKETING STRATEGIES OF USA TODAY

Target Market. An analysis of 15 markets by Simmons Market Research Bureau in 1981 revealed a target audience of some 23.6 million Americans with the following characteristics: heavy newspaper readers, frequent sports participants, frequent travelers, and/or heavy sports TV viewers.[8] Of this total, 13.6 million (57%) were male and 10 million (43%) were female. Based on the Simmons analysis, the following audience profile was projected:

Characteristic	Percent of Target Audience
Age 25–54	59.5
College graduates	28.6
Professionals & managers	31.8
Household income $40,000+	25.5
Household income $25,000+	59.6

The research (demand forecasting) indicated a circulation of 2 to 3 million or 4 to 5 percent of the 61 million daily newspaper buyers. USA Today would be their second-buy newspaper in addition to one local newspaper. Circulation was projected to be 85 percent single-copy sales and 15 percent subscription and home delivery.

Market Positioning. USA Today is the only national general interest newspaper. An interesting question can now be raised. Is USA Today in competition with newspapers or weekly magazines? Al Neuharth said the paper would not be in head-to-head competition with other newspapers. It

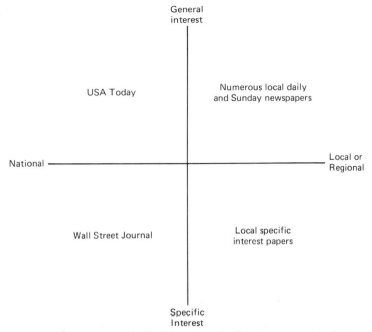

FIGURE 14-1 *USA Today* Product Position Map in the Newspaper Industry

Note: Reprinted from a *USA Today* term paper summer 1984 with permission of Shuk Yee Tam.

was to contain general interest, financial, and national sports news, and lifestyle features that are generally not available in local newspapers. The advertising and much of the news content was similar to magazines. Only one ad was to be printed on a page because the newspaper had promised no clutter. The ads were to be national or global in scope. There would be no regional editions or regional ads. Figure 14-1 shows how *USA Today* can be positioned in the newspaper industry, and Figure 14-2 shows how *USA Today* is positioned in the printing and publication industry.

PHILOSOPHY OF *USA TODAY*

Allen H. Neuharth stated the philosophy of *USA Today* in the first issue (September 15, 1982) on the editorial page when he said, "*USA Today* hopes to serve as a forum for better understanding and unity to help make the USA truly one nation."[9] This statement still appears on the editorial page of every issue.

FIGURE 14-2 *USA Today* Product Position Map in the Printing and Publishing Industry

Note: Reprinted from a *USA Today* term paper summer 1984 with permission of Shuk Yee Tam.

MARKETING MIX OF *USA TODAY*

The market mix was based on the target market and positioning of the paper.

Product. The core product of *USA Today* is to provide timely national information in concise short stories. The tangible product is the newspaper per se. It has five characteristics: quality level, features, styling, brand name, and packaging.

Quality Level. The paper quality of *USA Today* is above average, and in terms of printing quality it rates as one of the best-printed newspapers in the industry. The color printing is exceptional for a newspaper and on a par with most magazines. Rarely will any ink remain on your hands after you are finished reading the paper.

There is a divergence of opinion on the quality of newspaper contents. Many editors feel that stories are too concise and brief and lacking in depth and explanation. The editorial page has been described as wishy-washy. However, the overall performance is above average compared to most newspapers.

Features. The paper is divided into four sections: A, news; B, money; C, sports; and D, life. An indexed newsline on the front page gives a quick read on the news in outline form. A unique weather map and temperature chart appear on the back page of Section A. Other features include many colorful graphics, tables, charts, and a wide variety of stories.

Styling. A soft makeup is used in reporting the news. The paper has been named the "happy talk" newspaper. Some have called it the "TV paper" or the picture paper. Others have called it "McPaper," the newspaper equivalent of a fast-food meal. Articles are brief and precise, most of them fewer than 500 words. Readers receive their information quickly.

Brand Name. The name *USA Today* suggests the content of the paper. The line immediately above the logo says, "The Nation's Newspaper." The news coverage is national in scope. The paper also tries to project a unifying force. It attempts to bring the nation together on issues.

Packaging. *USA Today's* vending machines have been called ubiquitous TV sets. The exclusive design stands out from other newsracks. The machines look like a 21-inch television set on a pedestal. The *USA Today* logotype, in blue, appears on all sides. The machine allows a full view of the paper above the fold through a slanted window. The vending machines can be spotted from a considerable distance.

The augmented product is the newspaper with delivery to home and office. Original circulation was projected to be 85 percent single-copy sales and 15 percent subscription and home delivery. Table 14-3 reveals that by early 1984 home and office delivery and mail subscriptions already accounted for 30 percent of total circulation. By September 1985, this category had increased to 40 percent. Delivery and mail subscriptions increase the cost of the paper but add value to the product. Advertising agencies prefer a high percentage of subscription rather than single-copy buying. This gives them a clearer profile of who the consistent readers are.

Place. *USA Today* did not go national immediately. It expanded on a market-by-market basis. Vending machines and newsstands were used initially to open new markets. Locations were computerized to determine the best location mix between the two. The circulation emphasis has changed. The current emphasis is to increase home and office delivery and especially mail subscriptions, in anticipation that this will make the paper more attractive to advertisers.

The paper is truly national. It is sold in all 50 states and is available on the day of publication to about 80 percent of the U.S. population as of June 1986.

TABLE 14-4 Published Subscription Rates for Selected Newspapers and Magazines as of November 1985

		Rate		
Publication	Type of Delivery	52 Weeks	26 Weeks	13 Weeks
USA Today	Home	$130.00	$65.00	$32.50
	Mail	130.00	65.00	32.50
Wall Street Journal	Home	107.00	56.00	28.00
	Mail	107.00	56.00	28.00
Sacramento Bee	Home (daily & Sunday $7.50 per month)	90.00	45.00	22.50
	Mail	114.00	57.00	28.50
Time	Mail	58.24	—	—
Business Week	Mail	39.95	—	—
Fortune	Mail	42.00	—	—

Price. The structure of the newspaper industry is monopolistic competition. Newspapers are differentiated and as a result are able to charge different prices. In the introductory stage, *USA Today* used a penetration pricing strategy. From September 15, 1982, to August 26, 1984, the single-copy price was 25 cents and its delivered price was $1.50 a week. These prices were competitive with most other daily newspapers. On August 27, 1984, its single-copy price was increased to 35 cents and its delivered price to $1.75 a week.

On August 26, 1985, its single-copy price was increased to 50 cents and its delivered price to $2.50 a week. *USA Today* was designed to be worth 50 cents from the beginning. The 25-cent and 35-cent prices were introductory offers. The readers seem to believe the value is there since nearly all of those who were buying at 35 cents continued to buy at 50 cents.

Single-copy prices for comparable media are as follows: *Sacramento Bee* (local newspaper), 25 cents; *Wall Street Journal*, 50 cents; *Business Week*, $2.00; *Time*, $1.95; and *Fortune*, $3.50.

Table 14-4 shows the published subscription rates for these media.

Promotion. A multimillion dollar effort was used to promote *USA Today*. All four elements of the promotional mix—advertising, sales promotion, personal selling, and publicity—were used.

The promotional task of a newspaper is twofold. First, newspapers try to build circulation. Second, they try to obtain clients to advertise in their newspaper. Therefore, newspapers direct their promotional effort towards two different target markets—their subscribers and their advertisers. In 1982, 1983, and 1984, as *USA Today* entered new markets, circulation substantially increased, but advertising revenues lagged. In

1985, however, as its circulation stabilized, advertising revenues increased 85 percent over 1984.

ADVERTISING AND CIRCULATION

The typical newspaper in the United States obtains 60 to 70 percent of its revenue from advertising. The remaining 30 to 40 percent comes from circulation. Publishers attempt to increase circulation because their advertising rates are tied to circulation figures. As circulation increases, they are able to increase their advertising rates.

USA Today as initially planned was to run full-page ads in order to avoid clutter. The paper was to contain 30 percent advertising, which is equivalent to 10 to 12 pages of the 36-to-40-page paper. This figure is considerably below the 55-to-60-percent advertising figure for most metropolitan issues. A 40-percent advertising figure for *USA Today* would translate to 18 pages for a typical 45-page paper and would lead to profitability.

In February 1985 a new classified section was launched and since has averaged more than two pages daily. Individuals and companies who use these columns exclaim about their results.

USA Today must compete against both newspapers and magazines for advertising. In 1983, 57 percent of newspaper advertising came from local retailers. The remaining 43 percent came from national advertisers who typically advertise in saturated key local markets. *USA Today* does not accept local advertising. It has broad national distribution but lacks the market penetration of hometown papers. Thus, it is at a disadvantage in competing for advertising against local newspapers.

Since *USA Today* sells only national ads, its primary competition is magazines. The newsweeklies offer a large well-defined audience with over 90 percent of their circulation based on subscription. For example, about 95 percent of *Time*'s 4.6 million copies go to subscribers identified by income, education, and occupation. By contrast, as of September 1985, only 40 percent of *USA Today*'s copies were sold through home and office delivery and mail subscriptions. Although research shows that *USA Today* has an affluent, educated audience, space buyers remain skeptical. They question who the readers are and believe that many of them may be only occasional readers.

With a press capacity of 56 pages and a dramatic increase in the amount of full color pages available for news and advertising, *USA Today* may become profitable. In the first quarter of 1986, *USA Today* was ahead 9 percent in ad pages and 40 percent in revenue over the corresponding quarter of 1985.

The advertising rates are considered attractively priced. As of October 1, 1985, they were as follows:

Type of Ad	Cost
Four-color spread	$56,659
Full-page, four-color	$31,163
Full-page, spot-color	$28,671
Full-page, black-and-white	$24,931

USA WEEKEND

On September 8, 1985, Gannett launched *USA Weekend,* its revamped version of *Family Weekly,* the Sunday supplement it bought from CBS in March 1985. *Family Weekly,* which had 362 newspaper clients, began losing customers to *Parade,* its main competitor, within three weeks of the announcement. *Family Weekly* lost 130 newspapers while picking up 52, most of which were owned by Gannett. *Parade,* which had 135 clients before the announced revision, picked up 145 new subscribers. Newspaper executives who made the switch believed *USA Weekend*'s affinity with *USA Today* was too apparent. They felt uncomfortable carrying what amounts to a weekly advertisement for a competitor.

Currently, both *Parade* and *USA Weekend* are jousting for clients. The situation for Sunday supplements is not all that favorable. In 1984, advertising revenue at *Family Weekly* declined 10 percent while *Parade* declined 8.6 percent, according to the Publishers Information Bureau.

FLORIDA TODAY

In another development, in September 1985 Gannett began testing a new paper called *Florida Today,* a *USA Today* clone that covers local news. Gannett removed most national and foreign news and transformed their locally owned paper *(Today)* into an entirely new local product. It covers Brevard County like *USA Today* covers the nation: with snappy stories, snazzy graphics, lots of color, and seas of trivial information. Its format is revolutionary for a local newspaper.

This strategy was designed to motivate readers to subscribe to both the local papers *Florida Today* and *USA Today.* While this change hurt the local paper's sales, it helped *USA Today* which gained about 15,000 subscribers.

Florida Today is designed for the two-newspaper reader. Mr.

Neuharth believes that people in the United States are ready for two newspapers—one local and one national.

Soon after launching *Florida Today*, the company gave away *USA Today* with it. As of February 1986 it offered two papers for a total of $3.25 a week—higher than the average cost of a paper in this country.

Gannett officials say they do not know where *Florida Today* will lead. It is referred to as an experiment and research project. Mr. Neuharth said he was investigating whether a synergy existed between *USA Today* and his company's 84 other newspapers.

If this reformulation succeeds, Gannett may use the same formula elsewhere. They currently have 19 *USA Today* print sites where they also produce a local paper.

CONCLUSION

This case illustrates the substantial losses that can occur in the introduction of a creative new product. Gannett had to be prepared to subsidize *USA Today* over a five-year period (1982–1987) until its projected break-even point can be obtained. Only a large financially secure firm such as Gannett would assume such a risk. Gannett's task of turning *USA Today* from a loss to a profit will be a formidable marketing task.

QUESTIONS

1. Examine a copy of *USA Today*. Will local papers be influenced by this new product?
2. Gannett usually grew through acquisitions. Is the risk of developing a new product worth the losses *USA Today* will incur?
3. Who is *USA Today*'s competition?
4. Discuss the segmentation variables used to segment the market for *USA Today*.
5. Using another set of variables, develop a product position map for *USA Today*.
6. Construct a demographic profile of *USA Today*'s readers. Use your imagination.
7. How has *USA Today*'s marketing mix changed over the product life cycle thus far?
8. What do we mean when we say that the newspaper industry has the structure of monopolistic competition?
9. Did *USA Today* implement a good pricing strategy?
10. Is *USA Today*'s extensive usage of vending machines a good distribution strategy?

11. *USA Today*'s circulation was projected to be 85 percent single-copy sales and 15 percent subscription and home delivery. Discuss the distribution mix.
12. Has *USA Today* stayed with a one-page, no-clutter ad policy?
13. Describe the client that should advertise in *USA Today*.
14. Was the extension of the product line to *USA Weekend* a good idea?
15. What is the rationale for *Florida Today?*

NOTES

1. R. Joseph Fuchs, *Gannett Co., Inc., Research Report,* Kidder Peabody & Co., September 10, 1984, p. 1.
2. "Staking a Fortune on Gypsies," *Time,* September 20, 1982, p. 80.
3. "McPaper Stakes Its Claim," *Time,* July 9, 1984, p. 69.
4. Inquiry, "Topic: USA Today," an interview with Allen H. Neuharth, *USA Today,* September 13, 1985, p. 11A.
5. Everette E. Dennis, "Not Off The Satellite," *Northwest Orient Magazine,* June 1983, p. 57.
6. Celeste Huenergard, "Gannett to Pit National Daily against News Magazines," *Editor and Publisher,* May 16, 1984, p. 9.
7. "USA Today Unnerves Rivals Coast to Coast," *Business Week,* February 7, 1983, p. 71.
8. Bill Gloede, "Gannett Hoists USA Today to See if Admen Salute," *Editor and Publisher,* July 3, 1982, p. 10.
9. *USA Today,* September 16, 1985, p. 10A.

15

SEARS, ROEBUCK AND COMPANY

THE BUSINESS OF SEARS, ROEBUCK AND COMPANY

Sears, Roebuck and Company is a New York corporation headquartered in Sears Tower, Chicago. Its principal businesses were described in the company's 1983 Annual Report as follows:

> *Sears Merchandise Group,* which includes domestic and foreign merchandising and credit operations. Three segments comprise Sears Merchandise Group: domestic merchandising operations, the world's largest retailer, which distribute goods and services in the United States; domestic credit operations, which provide credit services to domestic merchandising customers; and foreign operations, which as of December 31, 1983, distributed goods and services on a continuing basis in Canada, Mexico, and Puerto Rico.
>
> *Allstate Insurance Group,* which includes property-liability insurance and life-health insurance. Allstate Insurance is the second largest property-liability insurer in the United States.
>
> *Coldwell Banker Real Estate Group,* which invests in, develops, and manages real estate, and performs commercial and residential real estate brokerage and related services.
>
> *Dean Witter Financial Services Group,* which includes securities-related operations and consumer deposit and lending operations. The securities-related businesses engage in securities brokerage, principal trading, domestic and foreign investment banking and related services. The consumer deposit and lending businesses engage in savings and loan, consumer finance, mortgage banking and related services.
>
> *Sears World Trade, Inc.,* which assists businesses and governments in the exporting and importing of products, technology, and management services and provides related counseling services.[1]

HISTORY OF SEARS, ROEBUCK AND COMPANY, 1886–1960

In 1886, Richard W. Sears founded the R. W. Sears Watch Company in Minneapolis. The company was moved to Chicago in 1887 where it was joined by Mr. Alvah C. Roebuck. The corporate name Sears, Roebuck and Company was established in 1893. This company became the largest mail order–retail chain in the world.

The first catalog of 1888 featured only watches and jewelry. In 1896, the first large general catalog of over 500 pages was published.

Sears did most of its catalog business in small towns and rural areas; however, Richard Sears was aware that opportunities did exist in the cities. In 1906 he wrote, "We do comparatively very little business in cities, and we assume the cities are not at all in our field—maybe they are not—but I think it is our duty to prove thay are not."[2]

In 1906, Sears opened a 40-acre, $5 million mail order plant and office building on Chicago's West Side. When opened, it was the largest business building in the world.

During this period, the company began insisting not only on accurate catalog descriptions but also on quality merchandise. The improvement in the quality of Sears' goods goes hand in hand with the story of Sears Laboratories.

The first laboratory opened in 1911 and became known as the "watchdog of the catalog." Its purpose was to improve the quality of Sears' products. Merchandise was tested and minimum standards were set. Comparisons were made between Sears' and competitors' products. The laboratory also helped to develop new products.

Also in 1911, credit was offered for the first time. Selling, advertising, and merchandising were Richard Sears' talents and the company rapidly became very large. Sears however was lacking in certain management skills which were adeptly filled by Julius Rosenwald, who purchased an interest in the firm in 1895. Rosenwald was president from 1908 to 1924 and chairman from 1924 to 1932.

Rosenwald established the formal company policy of "Satisfaction guaranteed or your money back" in the early 1920s. He also hired General Robert E. Wood who eventually became the single most dominant personality in the company's history. General Wood was president from 1928 to 1939 and chairman from 1939 to 1954.

Early in 1925, General Wood, then a senior vice-president, experimented with a retail store in Chicago. This store was so successful that Sears decided to open a chain of retail stores. General Wood made the critical decisions on what to sell in the new stores, where to locate the stores, how large the stores would be, and how to staff them.

TABLE 15-1 Sears Retail Stores, Selected Years, 1925–1985

Year	Number of Stores
1985	799
1984	806
1983	813
1979	864
1975	858
1970	827
1948	632
1943	596
1941	600
1933	400
1929	324
1928	192
1927	27
1925	1

Sources: Annual Reports; *Merchant to the Millions* (Sears, Roebuck and Company, 1978).

The early stores were located in the central business districts of large and medium-sized cities. They were so successful that Sears rapidly expanded its number of stores (see Table 15-1).

In 1931, Sears' retail store sales topped mail order sales for the first time. Stores accounted for 53.4 percent of total sales of more than $180 million.

General Wood also recognized the average family's need for an automobile and low-cost insurance. The Allstate Insurance Company was formed as a wholly owned Sears subsidiary in 1931. At first, Allstate operated only by mail. By 1933, however, management discovered that most sales were being made in smaller towns where the catalog business was big, while the large metropolitan markets were not responding. As a result, Allstate pioneered a bold merchandising idea—the installation of sales locations in Sears stores.

After World War II, General Wood made another major decision. The larger Sears stores would not be located in crowded downtown shopping districts. Wood understood the age of suburbia and the motorist-shopper. He insisted that large stores be located in outlying districts with plenty of free parking. He also made a vigorous commitment to opening many new stores.

Throughout most of Sears' history a philosophy of lower prices prevailed. Eventually the company adopted the motto, "Shop at Sears and save."

A summary of major events in Sears' history is given in Table 15-2.

TABLE 15-2 Sears Highlights, 1886–1986

Year	Highlights
1886	Richard W. Sears began selling watches to supplement his income as a station agent at North Redwood, Minnesota.
1887	Sears settled in the company's first Chicago location and hired a watchmaker named Alvan C. Roebuck.
1888	Date of the earliest catalog featuring only watches and jewelry.
1895	Roebuck sold his one-third interest in the company. Julius Rosenwald purchased an interest in the firm.
1896	First large general catalog issued.
1906	First catalog merchandise distribution center opened in Chicago.
1908	Richard Sears retired but continued as a company director.
1911	Sears testing laboratory established.
1911	Credit extended to customers.
1916	Savings and Profit Sharing Fund of Sears Employees established.
1924	General Robert E. Wood joined Sears.
1925	First Sears retail store opened in a catalog center on Chicago's West Side.
1931	Allstate Insurance Company formed.
1931	Retail store sales topped mail order sales.
1934	First catalog sales office opened in Grand Coulee, Washington.
1941	Pacific Coast Territory formed.
1942	Sears Latin American operations began with establishment of retail store in Havana, Cuba.
1945	Sales exceeded $1 billion.
1946	Eastern and Southern Territories formed.
1948	Midwestern and Southwestern Territories formed.
1953	Simpson-Sears Limited formed as Canadian retail and catalog order affiliate.
1954	First independent catalog merchant office opened in Mora, Minnesota.
1967	First retail store in Europe opened in Barcelona, Spain.
1973	National headquarters moved to Sears Tower.
1974	Sears merchandise furnished to Seibu's retail stores in Japan.
1976	Office of the Chairman created.
1981	Coldwell Banker, the nation's largest residential real estate broker, and Dean Witter Reynolds, the fifth biggest U.S. brokerage house, acquired for $809 million.
1981	The first five Sears Business Systems Centers began operations in Dallas, Chicago, and Boston.
1982	Sears World Trade, Inc., created as a world trading company.
1982	First "store of the future" opened.
1983	Sears increased its interest in Simpson-Sears from 50% to 75%.
1983	Paint and Hardware Specialty stores test marketed.
1984	New logo adopted.
1984	Mature Outlook—a club for those 55 and over—established.
1984	Greenwood Trust Co., Greenwood, Delaware, purchased.
1985	Discover, a national credit card, test marketed.
1985	Sears celebrated its 100th birthday on October 23, 1985.
1986	Discover credit card launched nationally in January.

Sources: Annual Reports; press releases; *Merchants to the Millions* (Sears, Roebuck and Company, 1978), p. 28.

TABLE 15-3   Sears Selected Operating Statistics and Per Share Data, 1975–1985

Year	Net Sales (millions)	Net Income (millions)	Earnings per Share	Dividends	Common Stock Price Range (rounded)
1985	$40,715	$1,303	$3.53	$1.76	41–30
1984	38,828	1,455	4.01	1.76	40–29
1983	35,883	1,342	3.80	1.52	45–27
1982	30,020	861	2.46	1.36	32–15
1981	27,357	650	2.06	1.36	21–14
1980	25,195	606	1.92	1.36	20–15
1979	24,549	810	2.54	1.28	22–18
1978	24,490	922	2.86	1.27	18–20
1977	22,906	838	2.62	1.08	35–27
1976	19,643	695	2.18	0.80	40–31
1975	17,771	523	1.65	0.92	37–24
1974	16,201	495	1.57	0.92	45–21
1973	15,306	675	2.15	0.87	58–39
1972	14,192	627	2.01	0.80	62–49
1971	12,457	557	1.80	0.75	52–38
1970	11,253	468	1.52	0.67	41–26

Source: Annual Reports.
Note: For the 1975–1979 period, figures reflect the contributions of the Allstate Group and other companies. For the 1980–1985 period, figures reflect contributions of all subsidiaries: Sears Merchandise Group, Allstate Insurance Group, Coldwell Banker Real Estate Group, Dean Witter Financial Services Group, and Sears World Trade.

SEARS, 1970–1979: A FAILURE?

The proper answer to this question depends on what division of the company one focuses on. Although the Sears Merchandise Group began to falter in the mid-1970s, the Allstate Group performed well during this decade.

During the 1950s and 1960s Sears' financial statistics were more impressive than they were in the 1970s. Table 15-3 shows that the price of Sears stock hit an all-time high of 62 in 1972. By 1981, the stock had fallen to a low of 14. A gradual decline in the price range of the stock occurred during the last half of the 1970s.

Tables 15-4, 15-5, and 15-6 illustrate the deterioration of the Sears Merchandise Group. Table 15-4 shows net sales leveling off at approximately $17 billion for 1977, 1978, and 1979. Net income as well as net profit margin declined. Table 15-5 shows that the contribution to income of the Sears Merchandise Group, which was 73 percent in 1970, declined to 35 percent in 1979. Table 15-6 shows the decline in earnings per share for the Sears Merchandise Group.

The story is very different in the 1970s for the Allstate Group. Table 15-5 shows that the Allstate Group and others contributed 57 percent of the income in 1977. This was the first time that the Sears Merchandise

TABLE 15-4 Net Sales, Net Income and Net Profit Margin for Sears Merchandise Group, 1970–1985

Year	Net Sales (millions)	Net Income (millions)	Net Profit Margin (%)
1985	$26,552	$766	2.88
1984	26,508	905	3.41
1983	25,089	781	3.11
1982	20,667	432	2.09
1981	20,202	285	1.41
1980	18,675	229	1.23
1979	17,514	281	1.60
1978	17,946	355	1.97
1977	17,224	364	2.11
1976	14,950	442	2.96
1975	13,640	394	2.89
1974	13,101	289	2.21
1973	12,306	425	3.45
1972	10,991	419	3.81
1971	10,006	392	3.92
1970	9,251	343	3.71

Source: Annual Reports.

Group had contributed less than 50 percent of the total income. Table 15-6 shows the dramatic increase in profitability for the Allstate Group. Earnings per share increased from $0.24 in 1975 to $1.45 in 1979.

In 1977 Sears' retailing operations experienced a particularly bad

TABLE 15-5 Contribution to Total Net Income of Allstate Group and Others and Sears Merchandise Group, 1977–1985 (Millions)

Year	Total Net Income	Allstate and Others Amount	%	Sears Merchandise Group Amount	%
1985	$1,303	$537	41	$766	59
1984	1,455	550	38	905	62
1983	1,342	561	42	781	58
1982	861	429	50	432	50
1981	650	365	56	285	44
1980	606	377	62	229	38
1979	810	529	65	281	35
1978	922	567	61	355	39
1977	838	474	57	364	43
1976	695	253	36	442	64
1975	523	129	25	394	75
1974	495	206	42	289	58
1973	675	250	37	425	63
1972	627	208	33	419	67
1971	557	165	30	392	70
1970	468	125	27	343	73

Source: Annual Reports.

TABLE 15-6 Earnings per Share for Allstate Group, Others, and Sears Merchandise Group, 1975–1979

	1979	*1978*	*1977*	*1976*	*1975*
Allstate Group	$1.45	$1.44	$1.30	$ .66	$ .24
Others	.21	.32	.19	.12	.17
Subtotal	$1.66	$1.76	$1.49	$ .78	$.41
Sears Merchandise Group	.88	1.10	1.13	1.40	1.24
Total	$2.54	$2.86	$2.62	$2.14	$1.65
Sears Merchandise Group as a Percent of Total	35%	39%	43%	64%	75%

Source: 1979 Annual Report.

year. Although Allstate's profits almost doubled, accounting for about half of the corporate net, profits from retailing declined by 13 percent. Sears' performance was particularly dismal when compared with its biggest retail competitors. Penney's net income rose by 28 percent, K Mart's by 13 percent, and Montgomery Ward's by 17 percent. These companies had record profits. Sears' merchandise profits were lower in 1977 than they were in 1971 when sales were $7 billion lower.

K MART VERSUS SEARS

A comparison of K Mart's key statistics for the 16-year period from 1970 to 1985 (Table 15-7) with those of Sears (Table 15-4) reveals the following:

	K Mart	*Sears*
Increase in sales	776%	187%
Increase in income	572%	123%
Average net profit margin	2.51%	2.67%

K Mart is growing in net sales and net income at a much faster rate than Sears. However, financial statistics do not explain the differences. An interesting comparison has been made between the operational policies of these two retailing giants:

> K Mart has no credit operations; Sears' credit system is one of the largest. K Mart leases its stores so that capital is not tied up in real estate and is available for merchandise; Sears owns its stores. K Mart stays out of shopping centers, because it likes to be able to open a store quickly and independently; Sears not only puts stores in shopping centers, it also develops the centers themselves. All K Mart stores are built from the same master plans; Sears tries to adjust its stores to local conditions. K Mart

TABLE 15-7 K Mart Selected Operating Statistics and Per Share Data, 1970—1985

Year	Net Sales (millions)	Net Income (millions)	Net Profit Margin (%)	Earnings per Share	Dividends	Common Stock Price Range (rounded)
1985	$22,420	$457	2.03	$3.63	$1.36	42–30
1984	21,303	499	2.34	3.84	1.20	38–26
1983	18,598	492	2.64	3.80	1.08	39–21
1982	16,772	262	1.56	2.06	1.00	27–15
1981	16,527	220	1.33	1.75	0.96	24–15
1980	14,204	261	1.84	1.07	0.92	27–15
1979	12,731	358	2.81	2.84	0.84	29–22
1978	11,696	344	2.94	2.74	0.72	30–22
1977	9,941	298	3.00	2.39	0.56	41–25
1976	8,382	262	3.13	2.11	0.32	44–31
1975	6,798	196	2.88	1.61	0.24	36–20
1974	5,536	102	1.84	0.85	0.22	39–18
1973	4,633	138	2.98	1.15	0.20	51–29
1972	3,837	117	3.05	1.00	0.17	50–32
1971	3,100	98	3.16	0.85	0.16	34–19
1970	2,559	68	2.66	0.62	0.14	20–11

Source: K Mart Annual Reports.

combines centralized control of both buying and selling operations; until recently, Sears favored centralized buying and decentralized selling.[3]

K Mart is the second largest retailer in the United States. If current growth trends continue, K Mart could surpass Sears' merchandising division by 1990.

THE MARKETING STRATEGIES OF 1967, 1977, AND 1978

In 1967, Sears began to upgrade its product lines by adding more expensive merchandise. This was a deliberate switch from lower-priced goods to higher-priced goods. It was believed that the higher priced items with their higher margins would bring the company more profit if volume was maintained.

This concept worked for a while but eventually ran into trouble. Throughout its history, Sears' fundamental appeal had been standard-quality goods at low prices. Its image as a merchandiser of low-priced products was gradually eroding and Sears was losing its traditional target market. This first attempt at a fashion-oriented store for more affluent customers failed.

In 1977, Sears slashed prices and engaged in lengthy and more frequent sales which lasted three to four weeks instead of three to nine days. Advertising expenditures were raised from $419 million in 1976 to $518 million in 1977. The ads were used to push sales. The result of this strategy was that sales went way up but profits went down (see Table 15-4), and 1977 became known as Sears' price-cutting and promotion year. This program was dropped in 1978.

The new quality improvement program began in 1978. This strategy proposed to attract customers by emphasizing quality and value. Sears improved the quality of its products while holding costs in line. The strategy—to pass value on to the customer—was based on the belief that the customer was more concerned with value than price. Inflation obscured some of the benefits of this program. By 1980, net income fell to $229 million, its lowest level in many years (see Table 15-4).

The following year, 1979, saw the beginning of a $2-billion five-year expansion and improvement program to open 239 retail stores. One hundred of the stores were planned for new market areas and 139 stores were planned to replace existing stores in the same market. This expansion and improvement program was considerably more aggressive than the previous five years (1975–1979), in which only 139 stores were opened. Moreover, the new plan emphasized building stores in the Sunbelt and growth section of the United States. Money was channeled away from the Snowbelt and the older cities into the Sunbelt and newer growth cities.

The mail order business was also expanded. Catalog merchandise distribution centers were expanded and more catalog outlets were opened in smaller towns and cities.

THE 1980s: A RETURN TO PROFITABILITY

Executives at Sears knew the company was faltering. A secret document known as the "Yellow Book" leaked out of Chicago headquarters in 1978. It admitted the company's shortcomings and warned that Sears had to get back to its roots. The study said, "We are not a fashion store; we are not a store for the whimsical nor the affluent. Sears is a family store for middle-class, homeowning Americans."[4]

The quality improvement program that began in 1978 was continued. In March 1980, Edward A. Brennan, the new president of Sears, said "We've adopted quality as our number one strategy for the years ahead. The customer has told us loud and clear that is what she wants. The customer also expects to go into a store and find that store in stock. The customer wants good service. Its the store that puts all those things together best that will get the best market share."[5] Brennan quickly added, but not market share at all costs.

Brennan also approved of Sears' recent trend to centralize major policy decisions in Chicago and the company's latest marketing target— the middle-class homeowner. He believed, however, that Sears is diversified enough to appeal to more than just one class of customer.

Brennan revolutionized Sears' stores and its merchandising policies. In 1982, the first "store of the future" opened in King of Prussia, Pennsylvania. This store was a complete departure from the traditional Sears store. It incorporated the store-within-a-store concept. It had a friendlier, more welcome look than the Sears stores of old, with more aisles, lower ceilings, and merchandise displays with flair and style at eye level. In 1983, 12 new or remodeled stores opened; in 1984, 100 new or remodeled stores opened. By 1989, all of Sears stores will fit the "store of the future" prototype.

Traditionally Sears has promoted its house brands such as Craftsman tools, Kenmore appliances, and Diehard batteries. The new Sears is emphasizing apparel, and national brands and signatures are being sold along side the company's private labels. Sears now sells Levis, Wrangler, Wilson, McGregor, Converse, Adidas, and many others.

In 1981, the first five Sears Business System Centers began operations in Dallas, Chicago, and Boston. These small, leased, retail stores have approximately 2,500 square feet. The professional salespeople employed in the centers are extensively trained by Sears. The centers specialize in selling business equipment and are more than just computer stores. Fifty additional stores were opened in 1983, and 100 new stores in 1984.

The Sears Merchandise Group has emerged from its period of drift and uncertainty. It has shed its old image of being staid and conservative. Its new image stresses fashion and reaches back to its basic formula: giving the consumer quality and value.

A quote from Sears' 1983 Annual Report summarizes top management's merchandise mission. "The historical strength of Sears—its position as America's largest merchandiser—will be just as important to the future of Sears. We are dedicated to extending our leadership in the merchandising industry."[6]

SEARS' FINANCIAL EMPIRE

In 1981, Sears continued its diversification into financial services by acquiring Coldwell Banker, the nation's largest residential real estate broker, and Dean Witter Reynolds, the nation's fifth biggest brokerage house for $809 million. Only a few of the offices of these businesses were closed.

Allstate has successfully operated out of Sears' retail stores since 1935 and management believed Sears could successfully offer its new financial services in its retail stores.

In 1982, Sears opened its first Sears Financial Network centers in eight stores in the following markets: Chicago, Atlanta, Dallas, Denver, Houston, Los Angeles, San Francisco, and Washington, D.C.

The centers offered insurance, real estate, and brokerage services and were staffed by salespersons from Sears' Allstate, Coldwell Banker, and Dean Witter Reynolds.

Sears hoped that the combination of financial services and merchandising would turn its stores into a new breed of financial supermarkets, but analysts were skeptical that the centers would have an immediate impact on Sears' financial results.

In 1984, the name of Allstate Savings and Loan was changed to Sears Savings Bank. The major reason for the change was to describe more accurately the focus and direction of the financial institution, which was evolving into a modern consumer savings bank while continuing to provide many of the services of a traditional savings and loan association.

Sears Savings Bank offers the following services: mortgage and auto loans, checking and savings accounts, and money market and term accounts. It has evolved to a full-service consumer bank.

In October 1984, Sears announced it would purchase Greenwood Trust, a small commercial Delaware bank, and sell the bank's commercial loan portfolio which would convert Greenwood to a consumer bank. Sears' intent is to use this bank as a step towards establishing a national consumer banking system.

In September and October 1985, Sears began to test market a new national credit card named Discover whose major competitors would be Visa, Mastercard, and American Express.

In March 1986, Sears began its national rollout of the Discover Card. For the first two years there will be no annual fee. Sears has preapproved 26 million Sears cardholders for Discover.

As of June 1986 more than 2,200 companies have agreed to honor Discover; even some major competitors such as: Montgomery Ward, Walgreen's, Toys "R" Us, most F. W. Woolworth specialty divisions, Dayton Hudson, and Radio Shack.

Sears expects to lose $115 million on Discover in 1986.

Table 15-8 depicts Sears' financial empire as of December 1984.

A quote from Sears' 1983 Annual Report summarizes top management's financial services mission. "It is a key business strategy at Sears to become as important a factor in financial services as we are in consumer sales."[7]

Table 15-9 shows the changes that have occurred in revenue and income for Sears' principal businesses over a five-year period.

CONCLUSION

In 1900, Sears was the largest general merchandise catalog retailer in the United States. In 1986, Sears was 100 years old. In total sales as well as in merchandise sales it is by far the largest diversified retailer in the

TABLE 15-8   Sears' Financial Empire, December 1984

Type of Service	Provided by	Size and Scope
Customer credit	Sears credit cards	40 million customers
Financial	Sears Financial Network Centers	300 centers
Brokerage	Dean Witter Reynolds	488 offices $2 billion revenue
Savings and loan	Sears Savings Banks	112 branch offices $6 billion assets
Insurance	Allstate Insurance Co.	1,170 offices $8 billion revenue
Real estate	Coldwell Banker	934 offices and branches $500 million commissions
Consumer banking	Greenwood Trust Co.	Acquisition announced

Source: 1984 Annual Report.

United States. In recent years economic conditions with inflation and recession have not been favorable to Sears' type of operation, and the surge in discount stores, catalog showrooms, and off-price retailers has cut into Sears' profits and sales.

In adjusting to these challenges, Sears has tried four different strategies. In the late 1960s, it emphasized stylish, high-priced merchandise. In 1977, it slashed prices and ran lots of promotions, an approach that increased market share but was disastrous for profits. In 1978, Sears returned to quality, value, and service in an attempt to recapture its lost image. In 1980, Sears both diversified into financial services and created a new image based on the new "store of the future" that featured fashion, quality, and value.

Sears has successfully repositioned itself and created a new image.

TABLE 15-9   Sears' Sources of Revenue (Sales) and Income, 1978 and 1983 (Rounded Percents)

Source	Revenue		Income	
	1983	1978	1983	1978
Sears Merchandise Group	69	73	58	39
Allstate	23	22	41	50
Others	0	5	0	11
Dean Witter	6	0	7.5	0
Coldwell Banker	2	0	3.6	0
World Trade	0.2	0	(1.0)	0
Corporate Intergroup Transfer	0	0	(9.1)	0
Total	100.2[a]	100	100.0	100

[a] Rounding error.

Source: Annual Reports.

Today it is a financial empire as well as a merchandising empire. All major components of the business are profitable.

QUESTIONS

1. Why did Chicago become the catalog mail order capital of the United States by 1900?
2. Is catalog retailing important today?
3. Why did Sears diversify to retail stores in 1925?
4. Why did Sears initially locate its retail stores in large cities?
5. State some reasons why Sears decided to locate the Sears Business Systems Centers in separate stores.
6. What are some of the reasons for the new "store of the future" concept?
7. Should Sears have located its Financial Network Centers in its retail stores?
8. Evaluate Sears' decision to use national brands and signatures.
9. Discuss Sears' involvement in services marketing.
10. Should Sears create a large interstate consumer banking system?
11. Will the Discover credit card be able to compete against Visa and MasterCard?
12. Sears sells just about everything from socks to stocks. Comment on this business strategy.
13. Does the concept of one-stop shopping apply to Sears?
14. Why did Sears keep changing its marketing strategy in 1967, 1977, 1978, and 1980?
15. As chairman of the board, would you favor Sears' financial division or its merchandising division?
16. The discount houses, catalog showrooms, and new off-price merchants are giving Sears some tough competition. Devise a strategy for handling these competitors.

NOTES

1. Sears 1983 Annual Report, p. 27.
2. *Merchant to the Millions* (Sears, Roebuck and Co., 1978), p. 9.
3. Gordon L. Weil, "Sears: Not So Lonely At the Top," *Chicago Magazine,* May 1978, pp. 203–4.
4. John S. Demott, "Sears' Sizzling New Vitality," *Time,* August 20, 1984, p. 84.
5. Joseph Winski, "New President Hopes to Strike Balance at Sears," *Chicago Tribune,* March 17, 1980, sec. 5, p. 10.
6. Sears 1983 Annual Report, p. 5.
7. Ibid., p. 11.

16

COCA-COLA

INTRODUCTION

The Coca-Cola Company is the world's largest soft drink company. It was founded in Atlanta, Georgia, in 1886 and celebrated its one-hundredth anniversary in May 1986. It also produces juices (including Minute Maid) and is involved in the entertainment industry through Columbia Pictures.

The percent contribution of various divisions to corporate sales and profits is shown in Table 16-1. For purposes of comparison, similar data for PepsiCo are given in Table 16-2.

Although this case will focus on domestic issues, it should be noted that foreign operations play a significant role in Coca-Cola's soft drink business. In 1984, they accounted for 38 percent of sales and 52 percent of operating income. They contributed two-thirds of Coke's earnings in 1980 and 60 percent in 1985. Roberto C. Goizueta, Coca-Cola's chief executive officer, would like a 50/50 split in earnings between domestic and international soft drink sales by 1990.[1]

Table 16-3 depicts the highlights in Coca-Cola's history from 1981 to 1986.

THE DECISION TO DELETE OLD COKE

This case concentrates on events that have transpired since 1981. In particular, it discusses the April 1985 decision to delete old Coke, the company's 99-year-old flagship brand, in favor of new Coke. This decision was heralded as the marketing blunder of the decade. By July 1985, management reversed itself and brought back old Coke as Coca-Cola Classic while still retaining new Coke.

TABLE 16-1   Coca-Cola Company Revenues and Profits by Division, 1980 and 1984 (Percent of Total)

Division	1984 Revenue	Profit	1980 Revenue	Profit
Soft drinks	68%	77%	88%	90%
Food	20	12	12	10
Entertainment	12	11	—	—
Total	100%	100%	100%	100%

Sources: 1980 Annual Report; *Standard & Poor's NYSE Stock Reports,* Vol. 52, No. 127, Sec. 10, July 2, 1985, p. 562.

The major factor influencing the deletion decision was the steady decline of Coke's market share against Pepsi-Cola (see Tables 16-7 and 16-8). The rival cola had been outselling Coke in U.S. food stores since 1977. Coke had been unable to refute the "Pepsi Challenge," which convinced Americans that Pepsi tasted better than Coke.

ROBERTO C. GOIZUETA

In 1980, Roberto C. Goizueta, a former Cuban, was named chairman and chief executive officer of Coca-Cola. After graduating from Yale, he had returned to Cuba to work in Coke's Cuban research labs. In 1959, he fled Cuba with his family just a month after Castro seized power and expropriated Coke's Cuban business.

He resettled in Miami and managed Coke's chemical research facilities in the Bahamas. He joined corporate headquarters in Atlanta in 1965. Coke was rapidly expanding its foreign operations and integrating more foreign nationals into its organization. Goizueta proved to be an exceptional manager and rose rapidly through the executive ranks.

During the 1970s, sales rose but earnings did not do as well. Coca-Cola's stock rose to a high of $73 a share in 1973 but by 1975 had fallen to a low of $26 a share (see Table 16-4). Coke had developed inertia.

TABLE 16-2   PepsiCo Revenues and Profits by Division, 1984 (Percent of Total)

Division	Revenue	Profit
Beverages	38%	31%
Food products	35	49
Food service	24	22
Sporting goods	3	(2)
Total	100%	100%

Source: Standard & Poor's NYSE Stock Reports, Vol. 52, No. 87, Sec. 15, May 6, 1985, p. 1802.

TABLE 16-3   Coca-Cola Company Highlights, 1981–1986

Date	Highlights
3/81	Roberto C. Goizueta named chairman and CEO.
11/81	Aqua Chem, Inc., a steam boiler maker, sold for $95 million.
1/82	Columbia Pictures Industries, Inc., purchased for $700 million in cash and stock.
2/82	"Coke is It" advertising campaign introduced.
7/82	Diet Coke introduced.
9/82	Ronco Enterprises, Inc., a pasta maker, purchased for $10 million. (Sold in 1984 for $20 million.)
11/82	Columbia put up $65 million to launch Tri-Star Pictures with CBA and HBO.
5/83	Three new products introduced: Caffeine-Free Coke, Caffeine-Free Tab, and Caffeine-Free Diet Coke.
11/83	Wine Spectrum and Taylor brand sold for $230 million.
4/85	Two new products introduced: New Coke and Cherry Coke. Old Coke, the 99-year flagship brand, deleted.
6/85	Embassy Communications and Tandem Productions, TV producers, purchased for $400 million.
7/85	Old Coke brought back as Coca-Cola Classic.
8/85	Announcement to purchase Nutri-Foods, a maker of frozen desserts, for $50 million.
2/86	Coca-Cola agrees to purchase Dr Pepper Co.
5/8/86	Coca-Cola is 100 years old.

Source: Coca-Cola fact sheets and press releases.

Goizueta has been a bold agent of change. Table 16-3 outlines the company's major diversifications and divestitures during his tenure. As can be seen from the table, a large number of new products were introduced in a relatively short time period.

A unique feature of Goizueta's top corporate staff was the large number of foreign-born executives. By 1982, many of the foreign managers who had been brought into the company during the 1960s and 1970s to expand foreign operations had risen to top executive positions. In fact, among American corporations, Coca-Cola's top management is one of the most internationalized. President Donald R. Keough, who is from Iowa, jokes that he is the company's "token American."[2]

Some of the top officials as of 1982 were:

Name	Position(s)	Nationality
Roberto C. Goizueta	Chairman and chief executive officer	Cuban
Donald R. Keough	President and chief operating officer	American
Sam Ayoub	Senior executive vice-president and chief financial officer	Egyptian
Claus M. Halle	Senior executive vice-president, currently in charge of international operations (1985)	German
Brian G. Dyson	Senior vice-president, currently head of Coca-Cola U.S.A. (1985)	Argentinian

TABLE 16-4 Coca-Cola Company Selected Operating Statistics and Per Share Data, 1975–1985

Year	Revenue (millions)	Net Income (millions)	Earnings per Share	Dividends per Share	Common Stock Price Range (rounded)
1985	$7,904	$678	$5.17	$2.96	88–59
1984	7,364	629	4.76	2.76	66–49
1983	6,829	558	4.10	2.68	58–45
1982	6,250	512	3.95	2.48	54–29
1981	5,889	447	3.62	2.32	40–30
1980	5,913	442	3.42	2.16	39–29
1979	4,961	420	3.40	1.96	46–31
1978	4,338	375	3.03	1.74	47–35
1977	3,560	326	2.67	1.54	41–35
1976	3,033	285	2.38	1.32	48–36
1975	2,873	239	2.00	1.15	47–26

Source: Standard & Poor's NYSE Stock Reports, Vol. 53, No. 48, Sec. 5, March 11, 1986, p. 562.

Because the company obtains more than half its earnings from international sales, some officials believe that the new Coke was conceived with the idea of increasing consumption both within and outside the United States. According to Claus Halle, bringing out new Coke was a global decision from the beginning.[3]

Others believe that the international executives who did a superb job managing Coke's global operations were out of touch with the domestic market. They never fully understood the American consumer's relationship with old Coke. They misjudged the emotional attachment and involvement with this product. In short, they missed the mystique of Coca-Cola.

PEPSI VERSUS COKE

Financial Data. A comparison of Coca-Cola's financial statistics (Table 16-4) with those of PepsiCo (Table 16-5) shows that both companies earned $2 billion in revenue in 1975 and had grown to $8 billion in revenue by 1985. For the period 1975–1984, however, Coca-Cola had a more impressive net income. Its average net income as a percentage of revenue for this period was 8.36 percent versus 4.42 percent for Pepsi. Coke also had greater earnings per share and dividends per share, and the market price of its common stock generally outperformed that of Pepsi.

A comparison of Tables 16-1 and 16-2 reveals that the two companies are structured differently. For example, Pepsi derives 38 percent of its revenues and 31 percent of its profits from beverages (soda) whereas

TABLE 16-5   PepsiCo Selected Operating Statistics and Per Share Data, 1975–1985

Year	Revenue (millions)	Net Income (millions)	Earnings per Share	Dividends per Share	Common Stock Price Range (rounded)
1985	$8,057	$420	$4.51	$1.75	76–40
1984	7,699	207	2.19	1.66	46–34
1983	7,896	284	3.01	1.62	40–32
1982	7,499	224	2.40	1.58	50–31
1981	7,027	333	3.61	1.42	39–27
1980	5,975	292	3.20	1.26	29–20
1979	5,091	265	2.85	1.10	29–21
1978	4,300	226	2.43	0.97	34–22
1977	3,546	187	2.15	0.82	29–22
1976	2,727	136	1.85	0.63	29–23
1975	2,321	105	1.47	0.50	25–13

Source: Standard & Poor's NYSE Stock Reports, Vol. 53, No. 63, Sec. 24, April 2, 1986, p. 1802.

Coke derives 68 percent of its revenues and 77 percent of its profits from soft drinks. Coke's soda profits as a percentage of its total profits are more than double those of Pepsi.

Pepsi began its diversification earlier than Coke. Its food products include Frito Lay, the largest maker of snack foods in the United States. Its food service includes Pizza Hut and Taco Bell. Its sporting goods company, Wilson Sporting Goods, was sold in October 1985.

Market Share Data.   The market for soda has expanded continuously in recent years. Table 16-6 shows retail sales expanding from $15 billion in 1975 to $23 billion in 1984 for a 54-percent increase in ten years or an average increase of 5.4 percent per year.

Both Coke and Pepsi have increased their market share in this expanding market. Table 16-7 shows the percentage of total soda sales (all brands) for both companies. Coke has increased its total market share by 2.3 percent, but Pepsi has outperformed Coke by increasing its market share by 4.6 percent.

TABLE 16-6   The U.S. Market for Soft Drinks, Selected Years, 1975–1986

Year	Retail Sales (billions)
1986	$30
1984	23
1980	19
1975	15

Note: Conflicting data exist on the size of the market.

Sources: Beverage Digest; Standard & Poor's Industry Surveys-Soft Drinks; Beverage Industry; Fortune, January 7, 1985, p. 67.

Table 16-7 Coca-Cola and PepsiCo Shares of the U.S. Soft Drink Market, 1970 and 1980 (Percent)

Company	1970	1980	Net Change
Coca-Cola	31.7	34.0	+2.3
PepsiCo	19.4	24.0	+4.6
All other brands	48.9	42.0	−6.9
Total	100.0	100.0	0.0

Source: "Coke Strikes Back," Fortune, June 1, 1981, p. 35.

Table 16-8 shows that the Pepsi-Cola brand has dramatically outperformed old Coke. In the 14-year period from 1971 to 1984, Pepsi has increased from 15 percent of the market to 19 percent for a net gain of 4 percentage points. Old Coke has declined from 25 percent of the market to 22 percent for a net loss of 3 percentage points. Pepsi narrowed Coke's 10-point lead in 1971 to 3 percentage points in 1984.

MARKETING RESEARCH AND CONSUMER RESEARCH

When Roberto C. Goizueta and Donald R. Keough were chosen for the top jobs at Coca-Cola, they were determined to reverse the Pepsi trend.

Pepsi in blind taste tests had discovered that Americans preferred its sweetness to the crisper taste of Coke. They decided to build a clever advertising campaign named the "Pepsi Challenge." Pepsi was becoming increasingly popular among younger drinkers and Pepsi named these new customers the "Pepsi Generation."

Coke was not able to refute the "Pepsi Challenge." It tried more marketing and more spending but never claimed product superiority. In fact, Coke's own taste test validated that consumers slightly preferred a sweeter Coke.

TABLE 16-8 Old Coke and Pepsi-Cola Brand Shares of the U.S. Soft Drink Market, Selected Years, 1971–1984 (Percent)

Year	Old Coke	Pepsi-Cola
1984	22.0	19.0
1983	21.1	16.9
1981	24.2	18.3
1979	23.9	17.9
1977	24.5	17.2
1975	24.2	17.4
1973	24.7	16.1
1971	25.0	15.0

Sources: Standard & Poor's Industry Surveys (Soft Drinks), April 11, 1985, pp. F21-F23, 1980, pp. B85; Fortune, June 1, 1981, pp. 32–35.

While developing Diet Coke, which was marketed in 1982, management came up with a new and sweeter formula. The decision was made to conduct taste tests on the sweeter product.

Coke embarked on the most extensive marketing research program in its history. Approximately 200,000 consumers were asked to participate over a three-year period.

The results of this research were rather close. When asked to compare unmarked beverages, 55 percent of the drinkers favored new Coke to 45 percent for old Coke, a 10-point spread. When both drinks were identified, 53 percent preferred new Coke to 47 percent for old Coke, a 6-point spread.

Based on this data, management decided to market a new product. One option was to market the new Coke under a different name, but this was rejected. In April 1985, the sweeter cola was marketed as "New Coke" and old Coke was terminated.

It was later revealed that a major flaw existed in Coke's test marketing. Consumers were not informed that choosing new Coke meant saying goodby to old Coke.

THE CONSUMER REVOLT

The consumer revolt against the switch began immediately. During May, June, and July, Coca-Cola's headquarters received approximately 1,500 phone calls daily plus a barrage of angry letters.

One letter began, "Dear Chief DoDo: What ignoramus decided to change the formula of Coke?"[4] In Seattle, a belligerent group of loyalists founded the Old Coke Drinkers of America. This Seattle group threatened to sue Coca-Cola if they did not bring back old Coke. Frank Olsen, a cofounder of the group, said, "They took a great American tradition and turned it into just another soda pop."[5] In June, Karen Wilson led a rally to protest the new Coke in San Francisco's Union Square.

Coke's 500 U.S. bottlers bore the brunt of the consumer's wrath. Distributors were inundated with nasty calls. Their delivery personnel were stopped on the streets by angry and argumentative Coke drinkers.

It appears that Coke's research on brand loyalty was also flawed. Marketers were not aware of the excessive brand insistence by Coke's patrons. They failed to realize the deep emotional attachment that consumers had towards their product.

As the consumer rebellion snowballed, Coke closely monitored shifting public opinion. By June, only 49 percent said they preferred new Coke with 51 percent preferring old Coke. In early July, the weekly survey of 900 consumers showed that only 30 percent preferred the new Coke while 70 percent preferred the old Coke.

On July 11, Goizueta brought back old Coke. He said:

> We knew some people were going to be unhappy, but we could never have predicted the depth of their unhappiness. Just as I could not have predicted the emotional disruption that resulted from my leaving Cuba—you cannot quantify emotion.[6]

President Keough said:

> The passion for original Coke was something that just caught us by surprise. The simple fact is that all of the time and money and skill poured into consumer research on the new Coca-Cola could not measure or reveal the depth and emotional attachment to the original Coca-Cola felt by so many people.[7]

THE MARKETING MIX

Product. The expansion of the cola line began in 1982 with the introduction of Diet Coke. This product was successful and by 1983 ranked number five among all brands sold, capturing 3.2 percent of the market. By 1984, it advanced to number three with 5.4 percent of the market (see Table 16-9). In the early 1980s, the diet sodas constituted the fastest-growing segment of the market, making up as much as 20 percent of total new market share increase.

The continuation of product line expansion continued in 1983 with the introduction of three products in the caffeine line: Caffeine-Free Coke, Caffeine-Free Tab, and Caffeine-Free Diet Coke (see Tables 16-3 and 16-10).

Caffeine-free introductions, which have been numerous in recent years, were precipitated by Seven-Up's decision to promote its 7-Up line as caffeine-free. Seven-Up was appealing to consumers' health concerns.

TABLE 16-9 Sales of the Eight Leading U.S. Brands of Soda as a Percent of All Soda Sold, Selected Years, 1974–1984

	1984		*1983*		*1977*		*1974*	
Rank	*Brand*	*%*	*Brand*	*%*	*Brand*	*%*	*Brand*	*%*
1	Coke	22.0	Coke	22.1	Coke	24.5	Coke	24.4
2	Pepsi	19.0	Pepsi	16.9	Pepsi	17.2	Pepsi	17.5
3	Diet Coke	5.4	7-UP	5.4	7-UP	6.0	7-UP	7.0
4	7-UP	5.1	Dr Pepper	4.9	Dr Pepper	5.3	Dr Pepper	4.8
5	Dr Pepper	4.5	Diet Coke	3.2	Royal Crown	3.2	Royal Crown	3.4
6	Sprite	3.6	Sprite	3.1	Sprite	2.8	Sprite	2.2
7	Diet Pepsi	3.0	Mountain Dew	2.7	Tab	2.6	Tab	2.2
8	Mountain Dew	2.9	Diet Pepsi	2.4	Fanta	2.3	Fanta	2.2

Sources: Standard & Poor's Industry Surveys (Soft Drinks), April 11, 1985, p. F22, 1980, p. B65.

TABLE 16-10 Products of the Major Cola Companies

Coca-Cola		PepsiCo		Royal Crown		Seven-UP	
Colas							
1886	Classic Coke	1893	Pepsi	1915	Royal Crown Cola		Dixie Cola
1982	Diet Coke	1964	Diet Pepsi	1962	Diet-Rite Cola	1982	Like (no Caffeine)
1983	Caffeine-Free Coke	1977	Pepsi Light	1981	Sugar-Free Cola	1983	Sugar-Free Like
1983	Caffeine-Free Diet Coke	1982	Pepsi Free	1980	RC 100		
1985	New Coke	1982	Diet Pepsi Free	1982	RC 100 Regular		
1985	Cherry Coke						
Noncola Beverages							
1960	Fanta (Orange)		Teem		Nehi Flavors:	1929	7-UP
1961	Sprite		Patio		Orange	1970	Diet 7-UP
1982	Diet Sprite	1985	Slice		Grape		
1963	Tab	1985	Diet Slice		Peach		
1983	Caffeine-Free Tab	1964	Mountain Dew				
1963	Fresca						
1982	Sugar-Free Fresca						
1972	Mr. Pibb						
1986	Minute Maid Orange Soda						
1986	Minute Maid Lemon Lime Soda						

Sources: Annual reports of Coca-Cola, PepsiCo, Seven-UP, Philip Morris; company literature of Coca-Cola, PepsiCo, Seven-UP.

PepsiCo, Coca-Cola, and others introduced caffeine-free products to prevent their customers from defecting to competing products. Although caffeine-free soft drinks have served to increase the total market, they have not been as significant a factor as the new, reformulated diet soft drinks.

The product line expansion continued in April 1985 with the additions of new Coke and Cherry Coke, and the deletion of old Coke.

It was Coca-Cola's intention to reposition its major cola brand to appeal to those preferring a sweeter cola. The new product was given the name "New Coke." The word "New" was to be removed from the label in a few months.

During its introductory stage, Cherry Coke failed to receive significant recognition because of the ensuing dispute between old Coke and new Coke. Cherry Coke's main competitors in the flavor arena are Dr Pepper and Coca-Cola's Mr. Pibb.

Table 16-10 outlines the products of the major cola companies, their colas as well as noncola beverages.

The immediate problem in relaunching old Coke was to give it a name. Marketing research tested the following alternative names:

Original Coke
Coke 100
Coke 1886
Old Coke
Coke I
Coca-Cola Classic

The product was named Coca-Cola Classic using the original Spencerian script for Coca-Cola. Also, included under the name were the words "original formula." The goal of this labeling was to appeal to the company's more traditional customers. By mid-July the word "New" had been removed from new Coke cans, which were thereafter simply labeled Coke.

Promotion.   On May 15, 1980, Coca-Cola became the first consumer product ever to be featured on a cover of *Time*. This was in recognition of the fact that Coke had become the world's favorite soft drink.

The best-known brand names in the world are Coca-Cola and Coke, which are registered trademarks.

The early executives at Coke developed a distinct philosophy for promoting the product:

> They believed that the job of advertising for Coca-Cola was to make the product an inherent part of people's lives and habits—a means of contributing to their pleasure. They wanted to make it a thing apart—to sell it to all classes of society as one of the pleasant things of life, distinctive, acceptable, and affordable to people everywhere.[8]

Table 16-11 presents Coca-Cola's memorable advertising campaign themes and slogans from 1929 to 1986. The major thrust of the advertising was to keep the image of the product contemporary. It should be noted that the famous slogan, "the pause that refreshes," was one of the longest-running slogans ever produced for a consumer product. More recent campaigns, slogans, and themes have experienced a shorter life cycle.

With the return of old Coke, the company was presented with the advertising dilemma of how to promote both products. In mid-September 1985, Coca-Cola USA discontinued its "Coke is It" slogan. Two new themes were introduced—"Coke belongs to you" and "We've got a taste for you."

TABLE 16-11 Coca-Cola's Major Advertising Campaign Themes and Slogans, 1929–1986

Slogan	Years
The pause that refreshes	1929–1959
Things go better with Coke	1969–1969
It's the real thing	1970–1973
Look UP America	1974–1975
Coke adds life	1976–1978
Have a Coke and a smile	1979–1981
Coke is It	1982–Sept. 1985
Coke belongs to you	Oct. 1985–Jan. 1986
We've got a taste for you	Oct. 1985–Jan. 1986
Red, White and You (Coca-Cola Classic)	Feb. 1986–Present
Catch the Wave (Coke)	Feb. 1986–Present

Source: Coca-Cola information sheets.

Unlike the earlier ads that showed people drinking Coke during every part of their daily routine, the new ads leaned heavily on shots of bottles and cans. The new commercials, complete with new music, did not include Bill Cosby who had been a Coke spokesman since 1979 and had been closely identified with new Coke. Cosby had been used more for specific brand advertising rather than image advertising.

The new slogans promoted the "megabrand strategy." Instead of pushing one product, the commercials are directed at the company's line of sugared cola drinks: new Coke, Coca-Cola Classic, and Cherry Coke.

The new advertising shift sold the corporation and the megabrand line rather than a specific drink. This campaign ran from October 1985 through January 1986.

In February 1986 a new two-tier advertising campaign was launched. The slogans were "Red, White and You" for the old Coke and "Catch the Wave" for new Coke. Coke Classic has been chosen to carry on a successful theme: Coke as a piece of the American landscape. The campaign relies on patriotic vignettes featuring ordinary Americans as well as athletes and entertainers. It recalls themes of patriotism and also plays on Coke's colors—red and white. The ads for the new Coke closely resemble the promotion of PepsiCo and its "Pepsi Generation." They are directed at the young and have overtones of fun and fast-living. Old Coke as of August 1986 was outselling new Coke six to one. The "Catch the Wave" campaign may determine whether new Coke lives or dies.

Distribution. One of Coca-Cola's greatest strengths is its extensive distribution system. The syrups and concentrates are manufactured by the Coca-Cola Company and sold to over 500 U.S. bottlers, most of whom are independent businesspeople. The bottlers package, market, and distribute the product in specific territories.

TABLE 16-12 Soft Drink Sales by Retail Outlet, 1970–1980

Retail Outlet	Percent of Total Sales
U.S. food stores	40
Fountains	33
Vending machines	27
Total	100

Sources: *Fortune*, June 1, 1981, p. 32; *Wall Street Journal*, July 30, 1985, p. 37; *Sacramento Bee*, May 26, 1986, p. C1.

Coke provides its bottlers with ongoing assistance in management, production, marketing, promotion, and other areas related to an efficient bottling operation.

This franchise arrangement has worked well for Coca-Cola and its bottlers since the turn of the century.

Coke's strength has varied in geographic markets. Old Coke has traditionally been well received in the South and Southwest. When new Coke was introduced, it did poorly in those markets but was well received in the northern states, California, and among young people in general.

The retail market for all brands of soft drinks between 1970 and 1980 has been relatively stable. Table 16-12 shows that U.S. food stores have the largest market share.

Historically Coke has been the leader in all three retail outlets but from 1920 to 1950 had an almost impregnable penetration in the fountain market, which at that time consisted of drug stores, variety stores, department stores, and sundry restaurants. The development of the fast-food franchisers of the 1960s and 1970s altered the composition of the fountain market. Most of these outlets carry only five or six individual brands of soda because of their limited spicket capacity. Coke was able to maintain its market share by signing such big accounts as McDonald's and Kentucky Fried Chicken.

The decision to reintroduce Coca-Cola Classic complicated the big fountain clients' product mix since most had to choose between new Coke and Classic Coke. A July 1985 survey by the *Wall Street Journal* of ten of Coca-Cola Company's big fountain clients showed that only Kentucky Fried Chicken planned to offer Coca-Cola Classic. Coca-Cola's biggest customer, McDonald's Corporation, had not decided what to do. Most of the fountain operators said it was too cumbersome to offer both brands and planned to stay with new Coke. Coke did not plan to offer any special incentives to fountain operators who stayed with new Coke.

Restaurant owners reported that customers just requested a Coke without specifying new Coke or Coca-Cola Classic. Marriott Corporation, who owns the Roy Roger and Big Boy restaurant chains, as well as many other restaurants, planned to remain with new Coke.

TABLE 16-13 Coke and Pepsi Brands Market Share in U.S. Food Stores, 1975–1980 (Percent)

Year	Pepsi	Coke	Leader	Lead
1980	22.3	21.7	Pepsi	.6
1979	22.7	21.0	Pepsi	1.7
1978	22.5	21.7	Pepsi	.8
1977	22.0	21.5	Pepsi	.5
1976	21.7	22.0	Coke	.3
1975	21.5	22.0	Coke	.5

Source: Fortune, June 1, 1981, p. 35.

Coke also did well in the developing vending machine market and held its leadership position as this market developed.

It was in food stores where Coke faltered, especially the supermarkets. Pepsi has been outselling Coke in U.S. food stores since 1977 and Coke has been unsuccessful in its efforts to recapture the top position. Table 16-13 shows market share data in U.S. food stores for the two brands. Between 1975 and 1980 Coke marketed only old Coke. PepsiCo had three brands: Pepsi, Diet Pepsi, and Pepsi Light.

Price.   Price is not a major issue in this case. Price could play a role in special promotions that would have a short-term effect, but other marketing variables are more important than price in determining the outcome of the cola wars.

CONCLUSION

The Coca-Cola case is a turnaround situation. It illustrates the struggle of the leading brand of soda (Coke) in attempting to reverse its declining market share against its major competitor (Pepsi).

As of October 1985, Coca-Cola declined to break out separate volume figures for new Coke, Coca-Cola Classic, and Cherry Coke.

Coke may surrender first place to Pepsi, but the combined might of Coke's dual entries could surpass Pepsi's market share.

At this point, it is not clear if Coca-Cola Classic and Coke will both survive or which one will become the dominant brand. It may take until 1988 before the final verdict of Coke's megabrand strategy is in.

In January 1986 PepsiCo agreed to purchase Seven-Up and in February 1986 Coca-Cola agreed to purchase Dr Pepper Company. The effect of these two acquisitions will increase their combined market share from 67 percent to 80.9 percent in 1986 and the industry will never be the same.

QUESTIONS

1. Why have Coca-Cola and Pepsi been able to dominate the cola market?
2. Discuss why the deletion of old Coke was called the marketing blunder of the decade.
3. Is the single image of Pepsi preferable to the split personality of Coke (old Coke, new Coke, and Cherry Coke)?
4. Is Coca-Cola Classic the best name for old Coke?
5. Discuss Coca-Cola's new marketing strategy now that they have six cola products.
6. Should Coca-Cola differentiate its sugared cola products or use a megabrand strategy?
7. Assume that Coke differentiates its three sugared cola products. Identify their markets and develop an advertising theme for each market.
8. Should the fast-food outlets serve Coca-Cola Classic or new Coke?
9. Discuss the favorable and unfavorable aspects of Coca-Cola's marketing research.
10. Was the decision to introduce new Coke based primarily on international factors or domestic factors?
11. What product(s) should Coca-Cola offer in its foreign markets—both Coca-Cola Classic and new Coke, or only new Coke?
12. Should PepsiCo introduce "Pepsi Supreme," a new less-sweet drink to compete with Coca-Cola Classic?
13. Research who is doing better in the soda wars—Coca-Cola Company or PepsiCo.

NOTES

1. "In The News," *Fortune*, September 8, 1980, p. 15.
2. "Coke's Man on the Spot," *Business Week*, July 29, 1985, p. 58.
3. Ibid., p. 61.
4. Anne B. Fisher, "Coke's Brand Loyalty Lesson," *Fortune*, August 5, 1985, p. 44.
5. Ibid., p. 45.
6. "Coke's Man on the Spot," p. 60.
7. "Coca-Cola's Big Fizzle," *Time*, July 22, 1985, p. 49.
8. "A New Look for Coca-Cola," A Coca-Cola Consumer Information Sheet, July 1979, p. 2.

WHAT CAN BE LEARNED

SUCCESSES

When examining successful institutions, there are a number of points to consider. First, institutions are not successful only because they practice good marketing. All of the functions of business—management, production, finance, and marketing—must be properly implemented. Second, a firm that is successful today may be a failure tomorrow. Success is an ongoing process, and the marketing strategy that made the institution a winner may not work indefinitely. Third, an institution succeeds because it does a number of marketing activities well. While it is sometimes assumed that an institution succeeds because of a particular marketing activity, success usually encompasses the execution of several marketing and business activities. The cases we have studied indicate that the following elements are required for success:

1. Leadership. The individual who is identified as the organization's leader should understand marketing, be aggressive, inspire confidence and enthusiasm throughout the organization, and have a strong desire to be a winner.
2. The Marketing Concept. The firm should strive for satisfied customers and profitable sales volume. All the functions of the business should embrace the marketing concept.
3. Clearly Defined Goals and Objectives. An institution needs a sense of direction so that employees know what to accomplish and a standard is set against which performance can be measured.
4. A Well-Defined Marketing Strategy. The target market as well as all the elements of the marketing mix (product, place, price, and promotion) should be clearly thought through.
5. A Positioning Strategy. Products must be properly positioned in relation to new and existing products as well as competitive products.

6. A Marketing Information System. Information is necessary in order to make intelligent decisions. An ongoing system that collects appropriate information is vital. This system should also encompass market research.

7. Proper Preparation for Expansion. Development of new products and entry into new markets must be properly planned.

8. A Clearly Defined Image. An institution should project a clear positive image of itself and its products and services.

9. Awareness of Economic, Social, Legal, Technological, and Environmental Factors. These noncontrollable factors can affect a business. They must be monitored.

10. Planning, Organization, and Control. The marketing factors must be properly managed. This means that planning, organization, and control are necessary.

FAILURES

Two of the six institutions in the failure section ceased to exist, namely Woolco and DeLorean Motors. Two of the six institutions are in serious trouble, namely the USFL and the reorganized Braniff. The last two, A&P and International Harvester, are only skeletons of their former selves.

Following are some of the major reasons why the six institutions may be viewed as failures.

1. Failure to Adjust to Changing Times. Business was conducted as it always had been conducted. Nothing new or different was done to keep up with the changing needs of today's consumers. The strategy that worked successfully in the past was the strategy used for the future. The institution maintained a status-quo orientation.

2. Improper Handling of the Market. The market was already saturated or the company overproduced for a limited market. The company failed to develop itself on a market-by-market basis.

3. Failure to Introduce New Products. There was not a continual stream of new or innovative products. Existing products were not revised or repositioned in the market.

4. Failure to Terminate Products, Lines of Products, or Whole Divisions. When a product, line of products, or division becomes unprofitable or has a low profit margin, it must be revived or terminated. Over the long run, the unprofitable elements of an organization can erode total organizational effectiveness.

5. Lack of a Favorable or Distinct Image. The institution developed a poor or negative image.

6. A Sales Orientation. Too much emphasis was placed on selling and not enough attention was devoted to giving customers what they need.

7. Overdiversification. If not handled properly, diversification can be disastrous. If a company is spread too thin in too many types of businesses, it will not be able to concentrate its resources. Competitors who specialize and concentrate their efforts will be formidable.

8. **Lack of a Competitive Strategy.** The institution did not fully understand its strengths and weaknesses. Therefore, a strategy that would give it a competitive advantage in some area such as better quality, better product, better service, lower price, or nonprice competition, was not developed. The institution was merely drifting and ineffectively competing in the marketplace.
9. **Improper Implementation of the Functions of Business.** The institution was not run like a business. The functions of business, namely management, marketing, production, and finance, were either omitted or not practiced properly.

TURNAROUNDS

Chrysler and Sears have been turned around. Chrysler's recovery has been spectacular. Sears has repositioned its store and diversified into financial services. *USA Today* has solidified its newspaper format, steadily increased circulation, but must increase its advertising revenue to obtain a turnaround status.

Coca-Cola made a marketing blunder by deleting old Coke but turned itself around by reversing that decision. This blunder may turn out to be a blessing in disguise. Coke with its megabrand strategy has further segmented the market. By having many Coke products, it may outperform Pepsi.

Following are some of the principles employed in reversing an institution's position:

1. A new leader was placed in charge. The new leader was a dynamic individual who was not afraid to make things happen.
2. Costs were brought under control. Drastic cost cutting, layoffs, and closing of plants followed.
3. Marginally profitable divisions were either closed or sold.
4. New production processes and technologies were employed.
5. New products were developed.
6. The institution was given a new image.
7. The institution was able to raise enough capital to see itself through the difficult period.
8. Management recognized a poor decision and rectified the decision immediately.
9. Management listened to disenchanted consumers.

QUESTIONS

1. From a marketing point of view, what do we mean when we say that an organization is successful?
2. State other reasons besides marketing that make a company successful.

3. Is marketing success hard to come by?

4. From a marketing point of view, why do institutions fail?

5. Do companies learn from their mistakes?

6. Why can a company be successful today and a failure tomorrow? Answer from a marketing point of view.

7. How do you turn a company around?

ABOUT THE AUTHOR

John B. Clark is Professor of Marketing at California State University, Sacramento. He previously taught at Chicago State University for nine years. He received a B.A. in history from Hamilton College in 1957, an accounting degree from Bentley College in 1960, and an M.B.A. in business administration from Babson College in 1963. After working four years for Dow Jones and Company's Educational Service Bureau, publisher of the *Wall Street Journal* and *Barron's,* he entered the doctorate program in business administration at Texas Tech University, where he was awarded his Ph.d. in 1972. Professor Clark has taught at a number of educational institutions, including Texas Tech University, Rosary College, Joliet Junior College, and St. Xavier College. He is a member of the American Marketing Association and other professional organizations, and has served as a consultant in business education to many colleges and universities. His previous text, *Businesses Today: Successes & Failures,* was adopted by over 200 colleges and universities.